BIPOLAR REFUGEE

A SAGA OF SURVIVAL AND RESILIENCE

HOLOCAUST SURVIVOR TRUE STORIES

PETER WIESNER

ISBN 9789493276970 (ebook)

ISBN 9789493276956 (paperback)

ISBN 9789493276963 (hardcover)

Publisher: Amsterdam Publishers, The Netherlands

info@amsterdampublishers.com

Bipolar Refugee is part of the series Holocaust Survivor True Stories

CONTENTS

*In commemoration of Mary Krotoczynski Wiesner, her parents and family,
and those who understood and helped her*

1

MY MOTHER'S SUITCASE

My mother, Mary Wiesner née Krotoczynski, left her legacy behind in a well-traveled red suitcase packed with the documents of her lifetime, her school records, identity cards, notebooks, personal letters, drawings, and official correspondence. Of particular interest was her wartime correspondence with her Jewish parents and other relatives. There was a folder containing Red Cross messages traded between England where she was safe and Germany where her loved ones were not. The messages were limited to 25 words and restricted in subject matter, but they conveyed volumes.

The suitcase also held a separate binder I had seen before, containing Mary's own typed manuscript about her complex and unconventional life. I remember her telling me with an ironic smile, "You should do something with my crazy story, maybe even make a movie out of it." Despite all her mock self-deprecation in making this request, she hoped I would eventually fulfill my *mitzvah* to preserve her memory and honor her parents by telling her story and that of her family. It has taken me years in fits and starts to pull together my mother's complex saga in Germany, England, and the United States.

Now that I am older than she was when she died, I finally have committed to writing this memoir in earnest about the person my sister and I called "Mutti" all our lives. At the heart of Mary's story is the devastating loss of her parents. Persistent feelings of guilt gnawed at her for having left them behind in Nazi Germany while she lived on in better places. She loved her parents deeply, but also deep down was her desire to be freed from the pain of their influence and expectations.

In addition to conveying the devastating loss of Mary's loved ones in the Holocaust during World War II, I also sought to portray the consequences of another kind of war, her battle with bipolar disorder and the impact it had on her life and family. The hardest task has been to tell a story that is often sad about a headstrong woman who faced immense challenges without shortchanging her irresistible charisma and her joyful appreciation of life and living things.

I have had a lot of help in writing this memoir about a life with twists and turns. My sister, Monika, and others among family and friends have contributed directly and indirectly to the making and the telling of our Mutti's heady saga that began in Mecklenburg, Germany and ended in Santa Monica, California. What follows is my best try at telling Mary Krotoczynski's "crazy" story based on the writings in her red suitcase.

2

MECKLENBURG

Fritz Reuter, a 19th-century writer from Mecklenburg, wrote that everything always happened 100 years later in that sleepy German state where Mary Krotoczynski was born. She arrived in 1922 during a time of economic and political upheaval after World War I. Whereas Reuter focused on the provincialism of her place of birth, Mary often recalled the natural joys of rural life that surrounded her in the small town of Friedland as a little child. She spoke longingly of the morning sounds of farm animals and of the meadows and forests that nourished her soul.

Abutting the Baltic Sea, the modern-day state of Mecklenburg-Vorpommern is an agricultural area with vacation spots and natural areas. Its Baltic coastline is dotted by a chain of towns that were once part of the long-defunct Hanseatic League that promoted commerce in the region. There have never been many Jews in this sparsely populated state in northeastern Germany. As elsewhere in Germany, the few who lived there were alternately tolerated and persecuted. During the 14th century, the Black Death persecutions decimated Mecklenburg Jewry. Twenty-seven Jews were burned at the stake and the rest were expelled. During the more tolerant years afterwards, Mecklenburg's Jewish population gradually increased and peaked to about 3,000 during the mid-19th century, less than one percent of the total population. Afterwards, many moved to Hamburg and Berlin, and by the time Mary was born in 1922, there were only about 1,200 Jews in the state of Mecklenburg. During War World II, the Jewish population in Mecklenburg dwindled due to forced emigration and deportations to concentration camps.

Immediately after the war, one of the Nazi-era transit camps in Mecklenburg temporarily sheltered returning prisoners of war as well as refugees from Eastern bloc countries. Twenty-five years after Mecklenburg ceased to be part of the DDR, the same facility housed a few thousand Syrian refugees taken during the refugee crisis that rocked Europe in 2015. After German Reunification in 1990, the state of Mecklenburg was transformed through an expanded highway system and economic development in fields such as biotechnology. There is still a small Jewish community in the town of Rostock, but today few, if any, Jews live in Friedland and neighboring Strasburg, the two small rural towns where Mary's paternal family lived after they arrived there from Poland in the late-19th century.

Mary's destiny as a refugee was foreshadowed by the migration of her paternal and maternal relatives from parts of Russia and Poland. Both her paternal great grandparents were born in Kleczew, a small town in the Pale of Settlement dominated by Russia. Isaac Joseph Krotoczynski had four children with his first wife, Lena, who died in 1870. These four children eventually migrated to America and settled in Macon, Georgia. His second marriage to Ruda Buki (1840-1928) resulted in five additional children. From that group, two siblings, Stephan Krotoczynski (1875-1941), and his younger brother, Charlie (1877-1936), joined their older four half-siblings in America. Their other three full siblings – Malka, Rosa, and Sally – stayed behind with their parents in Kleczew and subsequently migrated with them to Germany where they settled in Strasburg, Mecklenburg.

Several years after they arrived in America, Charlie and Stephan returned from America to live in England where both were granted citizenship in 1907. Charlie met and married Rebecca Champagne and started a family. In 1912, two years before the outbreak of World War I, Stephan left his brother to live with his widowed mother and his three siblings in Strasburg, Germany where there was a small Jewish community engaged in textiles and retailing.

In Germany, Stephan and the others his family used the Germanized spelling, Krotoschinski, for their surname. Stephan was no stranger to name changes and variations. When he was a child, his name was Czapse, which appears to be a variant of Shapsei. When he immigrated to America and then to England, he assumed "Steven" and "Steve" as his first name. Later in Germany, he was called "Stephan."

After Germany and England declared war, the German government designated Stephan as an enemy alien because of his British citizenship. Mary said that her father was considered a prisoner of war, but she did not specify the nature of his internment. This was not altogether unusual since civilians as well as military personnel were counted among the more than two million prisoners of war held in Germany during World War I.[1] Since he chose to remain in Germany, his British citizenship was revoked by the British government after the war. There is no evidence that he was ever granted German citizenship.

When Mary talked about the hiatus of her father's years in England and his decision to live in Germany, she mentioned that Stephan was reluctant to marry after having witnessed his brother's contentious relationship with Rebecca Champagne. This changed when his friend, Leo, introduced him to Jenny Flash, a 29-year-old woman from a Jewish family from nearby Friedland. After Stephan and Jenny married in 1916, her parents provided the newlyweds with a two-story home in Friedland where he started his business as a furrier and tailor. He also became a cantor for a congregation in the vicinity.

In 1918, two years into the marriage, Jenny died after a long bout with stomach cancer. She was buried in a small Jewish cemetery that was relocated after World War II to a fenced-off spot adjacent to Friedland's main Christian cemetery. Next to Jenny's grave are memorials to several people who had once been part of the small Jewish community in Friedland. According to the inscription in German, Richard Moses and his wife Louise Moses were deported from Berlin to Terezín and then to Auschwitz and murdered there in 1943 despite Richard having been awarded an iron cross during World War I. Another recently erected memorial is dedicated to Simon, Lotte, and Lissy, three members of the Wagner family who were deported from Berlin to Auschwitz where they died.

A year after Jenny's death, Stephan's brother, Sally, encouraged him to marry again. Sally introduced him to Siegfried Silberstein (1870-1939), a businessman from Berlin whose youngest sister, Gertrud, had finally become eligible to marry in her middle age after the death of their elderly father who had been in her care. Siegfried raised a dowry with the help of other siblings from the Berlin-based Silberstein family. Gertrud, born in 1875, had six married sisters: Anna, Regina, Minna, Martha, Rosa, and Hedwig.

Unlike the Krotoczynski family, the Silbersteins were strongly rooted in German culture despite their Polish origins. Their patriarch and matriarch, Abraham Silberstein (1840-1915) and Marie Silberstein née Rosenbaum (1843-1906), were born in the prosperous town of Schönlanke which was located in the German-speaking state of Prussia from 1772 to 1945 and later renamed Trzcianka when it became part of Poland again after World War II. During the 19th century right up through World War I, many of Schönlanke's Jews were culturally German and served in the Kaiser's Army. That gradually changed with the ascendance of antisemitism. By 1940, the Jewish presence in Schönlanke was obliterated by the Nazis.

Abraham and Marie Silberstein left Schönlanke as young adults during the late 19th century. Their eight children were born in Berlin. All had German given names, a fact that reinforced the perception that the prosperous Silberstein family was culturally German. They lived with their children in the Mitte section of the city.

Mary wrote about the arranged marriage of her mother to the widower, Stefan Krotoczynski. Unlike the doweries of her six sisters, Gertrud's was relatively modest. This inequity was the first stitch of deprivation that Mary wove into the broadcloth of her life.

I was told that my mother was a 40-year-old virgin when she married my father. Since she was the youngest of seven girls, money for dowries was exhausted and so she was out of luck getting a husband. This had nothing to do with the fact that my mother was the prettiest of her sisters. As years went by, my mother's married sisters and her brother finally decided to find her a husband. They made a collection of 10,000 Deutschmarks, got together the necessary household goods, and found her a groom. I often wondered whether it was "love at first sight." What I do know is that there was deep devotion and respect between them. When my mother married my father, she did everything to please him, including keeping a kosher house, something she was not used to.

Gertrud and Stephan married in Berlin Lichtenberg on April 5, 1921, and afterwards established their household in Friedland where he had lived with his first wife. The following year, this middle-aged couple had their first and only child, who always claimed facetiously that her father, an unabashed Anglophile, named her after Queen Mary. Most likely, the name was also chosen to honor Gertrud's mother, Marie Rosenbaum. For most of her adult life, she was known as Mary, but was also called Marie by her relatives in Germany and later Maria by her friends in California.

Mary often talked about her own birth and her mother's labor. "Three days and three nights. My mother was as strong as an ox," she said to celebrate Gertrud's victory over her biological clock, but she did not describe her childhood in glowing terms. As an only child who needed a lot of attention and supervision, she pictured herself as an unlikely presence alone in a strange world where her older parents, especially her deeply religious father, moved in the shadows. The only remaining photo of her early childhood depicts a little girl standing on a chair in a crocheted dress with a hairdo that makes her look like a boy. The photo always reminded her that her father had wished for a son.

Mary liked to reminisce about the long-lost simplicity of her early years in Friedland and the sounds of cows, goats, and roosters that contributed to the earthiness of rural living. She described in vivid terms how Gertrud killed chickens destined for the dinner table. Killing was also part of her father's work as tailor and furrier, who transformed rabbits and other furry animals into apparel.

I enjoyed playing in this large room with a cement floor. There were neat piles of old reading glasses, sunglasses with blue lenses, little dead rabbits with their insides missing, bones, piles of paper, old nails and more. I was not allowed to play in this large room, but I managed to slip in to steal some blue sunglasses as well as two of his little rabbits. I put them in my doll carriage and took them for a ride until my father discovered that they were missing.

Gertrud gave her daughter an occasional slap when she misbehaved and joked that she was a gypsy child whom her parents took in out of the goodness of their hearts. She became acutely aware of her dark Jewish looks that set her apart from the fair-skinned neighborhood children who ridiculed her for being different.

All the children in this little village had blond hair and my hair was dark brown. Their eyes were blue and mine were not. These blond, blue-eyed children used to stare at me, asking if there were others "like that" at home. I withdrew. But I did have one blond, blue-eyed friend, Hans-Joachim, who lived next door to us. He was about four years old, a year younger than I. Our favorite game, of course, was father and mother. My teddy bear served as our child. One day I got tired playing mother and gave the teddy bear to Hans-Joachim and took off to work. One day our happy little friendship came to a sad halt, for we were discovered in the outhouse while studying the difference of our sexes. We were scolded, and, in deep disgrace, our bare bottoms spanked. What hurt most of all was that we were not allowed to play together anymore. I don't know what impact this had on Hans-Joachim. For me, this experience was carried into adult life. Many years passed before I was able to look at male genitals without a strange feeling of guilt.

Mary made a lifelong quest of seeking liberation from the Victorian attitudes about sexuality imposed by her parents. Later in life, with Freudian terminology in tow, she parsed the emotional and clinical aspects of sexual intercourse, aligning herself in spirit, albeit reluctantly, with sexual freedom while at the same time retaining fatalistic romantic illusions and occasional prudery. The idea of subjugating herself completely to the demands of marriage, as her own mother had done, was out of the question. No matter how much she admired her mother's chaste moral fortitude and her father's religious devotion, she wanted something else.

Although Stephan was described as kind and loving, he was removed from the daily routines of family life and left it up to Gertrud to raise their lively and often difficult young daughter. A cheerful woman, she sang traditional German songs and told fairy tales at bedtime but also imposed parental discipline. Many years later when Mary became a mother, she gleefully demonstrated the *Backpfeife* [a slap across the face] that was used to keep misbehaving children in line. She also told stories of how her mother indulged her daughter by violating kosher laws. On one birthday morning, Gertrud surprised her daughter by decorating her chair with a ring of non-kosher sausages ready to be cooked for breakfast, the kind served in the homes of other children in the neighborhood.

Her mother's common sense and sense of humor mingled with her father's deep religious convictions to provide their child with measures of love, discipline, and stability to channel her adventurous and rebellious spirit, but Mary was out of her element. She claimed that she had more in common with her two "crazy" musician cousins, Heinz and James, the sons of Uncle Sally, who lived in Strasburg.

When we learned about our grandparents, my sister and I wished we could have known them because they represented the kind of stable family life that was foreign to us. There are only a few surviving photos of our grandparents to guide our imagination. Long gone are the wedding photos and family pictures of the many cousins, aunts, and uncles that our mother talked about. Most photos did not survive the horrors encountered by the intrepid little soul who challenged and delighted her parents. The cherished few that Mary managed to keep included photos of Stephan and his younger brother as young men in England, a portrait of her mother in middle age, and another of her aging father, wearing a prayer shawl and cantorial hat. In contrast to the down-to-earth description of her mother, she depicted her father in loving but distant terms.

He was a fine-looking man, with great dignity, soft spoken, well-mannered, and well-dressed. I never saw him in his underwear, only in his night shirt in bed when he was ill. My father kept all the Jewish Orthodox traditions. Born in Poland during the pogroms, he never went to school, but was tutored by the rabbi of his village who taught all the little boys to read and write Hebrew. He spoke five languages and had a fine handwriting.

Stephan's refinement was of little practical use during the hardship years that followed World War I. He had no head for business and struggled to stay afloat during the economic crisis and political uncertainty of the times. An avid newspaper reader, he observed the political turmoil that led to the founding of the Nazi Party in Bavaria in 1919. Ominously, Walther Rathenau, the most prominent Jewish political figure in Germany, was murdered in June 1922, about a month before Mary was born.

Gustav Stresemann became chancellor of a coalition government in 1923 and later foreign minister until 1929. During this period, he stabilized Germany's currency and renegotiated Germany's reparation payments. He also restored order in Bavaria after the failure of Hitler's Putsch. Until the Great Depression of 1929, the power of right wing parties was restrained through elections. During this period, Stephan struggled to keep his business afloat and increasingly relied on help from Gertrud's relatives in Berlin.

Mary remembered the loneliness of growing up Jewish in Friedland. Playmates mocked her and made her feel that there was something wrong with her. Her father's religious devotion accentuated the Jewishness that put her family at odds with their neighbors. Her alienation was symbolized by a slight indentation on her forehead, like the mark of Cain, which she attributed to the forceps that the doctor had used to facilitate her birth.

> I was never allowed to show this dent to the world. Ashamed of it, I covered it with the bangs of my hair. I thought I was the only child who was not perfect. Not knowing how it happened, I finally asked my mother who told me that I ran into the corner of a table. This didn't sound very convincing, but who else was there to ask? At that time, I must have been eight years old and had a vague notion that the stork had something to do with it. He couldn't have bitten me. Later in life I found out that Father wished for a boy who could recite the kaddish after his death. I felt hurt and ashamed for having been born a girl. But this didn't mean that my father didn't love me.

Mary's sense of isolation and marginalization, first as a child and later as an adult, was buffered by her teddy bear that became an emblem of her hopes and aspirations.

> My teddy bear remained the only toy I was ever attached to. It was given to me on my first birthday by an uncle who was a salesman at Wertheim, Berlin's largest department store. To me this bear was the brother I wanted and never had. He made up for all those little blond-headed and blue-eyed children who wouldn't play with me, who ridiculed me. Teddy was my comfort at bedtime when the dark of night frightened me. I never ill-treated him, and I believe, not a night passed without my having covered up Teddy with a little blanket, tenderly, as though he were my child. He was my comfort at bedtime. Teddy wore my baby jackets and first walking boots which were brown. Since he had no toes, the tips of the shoes were flat and wrinkled.

For Mary, the antisemitism she experienced on account of her dark looks was accentuated by the stigma associated with having Polish and Russian roots. Many assimilated German Jews, such as the Silberstein family on her mother's side, believed that antisemitism was fueled by the negative public image of Eastern European Jews. She felt that this stereotype was applied to her family just because the name Krotoczynski advertised their Polish origins.

After Stephan's business failed, his family left Friedland to live in Strasburg with his elderly mother, Ruda, and two sisters, Malka and Rosa. Sally and his sons lived nearby.

We left Friedland for Strasburg, another small village. I wasn't sad to leave because there were no friends to leave behind, but I felt insecure and ill at ease. I don't remember anything being packed or furniture being moved, nor do I remember the actual journey. Suddenly, I was among a lot of strangers who were supposed to be my relatives, two aunts on my father's side, two older cousins in their twenties, and one old grandmother (my father's mother) who was 89. We lived there for about a year. I don't remember where we lived or where I slept, or anything about the relatives who remained strangers. Nor do I have any pleasant memories of this place, except for a little garden behind the house which I considered my hide-out where I played among the weeds and dug up the soil.

Her older cousins paid scant attention to Mary. Heinz and James, the crazy musicians she enjoyed so much, were too busy to spend time with her. Her favorite memories were of her 89-year-old grandmother, Ruda, who like herself was inclined to defy conventional behavior.

> What I remember well is the old grandmother who sat outside the house on a little stool, dressed like a Polish peasant woman, which was not surprising since she was Polish. The children in the village made fun of her and poked their tongues out at her. Sometimes even I joined in. My aunts told me that she was senile and complained about her constantly. She was caught stealing goods from the household to bring to the poor people of the village. One day, my mother put a black apron on me. Everybody was crying because grandmother died after having fallen down an entire staircase. I remember seeing myself in a tall mirror in the kitchen, hating the black apron. With all the relatives running in and out of the kitchen crying, I felt it was my duty to cry, too. I tried very hard, but not a tear would fall. Rest in peace, dear old grandmother! I wish I had met you before you became senile.

3

NAZI BERLIN

In 1928, after an unhappy year of living with their Krotoschinski relatives in Strasburg, Stephan and Gertrud accepted an offer from her relations to help them start over again in Berlin. While still in Mecklenburg, Mary's parents had kept in touch with Gertrud's six sisters and Siegfried, the eldest sibling who had helped the family before.

Most of Mary's relatives were employed in the apparel industry, and through family connections, Stephan found work as a sales representative but still performed as a cantor for his congregation in Mecklenburg. The move from sleepy Mecklenburg to the big city of Berlin was disruptive.

> I don't remember packing anything, nor do I remember the train journey. I found myself in the center of a big city, Berlin, which made Strasburg seem like heaven when I saw long rows of tall identical houses surrounding me. There were no gardens behind these, just cement courtyards. How I longed for the cornfields back in my little village and the little garden where I could play and get away from my awful relatives. Now we lived in these huge walk-ups, four floors each with four apartments, about 20 families in one house, and across the cement courtyard there were more buildings like the one we now called home. We never had a house again.

Soon after her family arrived in Berlin, Mary became acutely aware of her family's status as the poor relations. Although she enjoyed seeing her aunts and uncles who treated her with warm affection, she felt out of place at large family gatherings where, as a seven-year-old, she was the youngest among her cousins. Since there were no family playmates her age, Mary felt isolated and on one occasion acted out.

> One day, I was brought home drunk from a Bar Mitzvah celebration. No one had noticed when I slipped into a room where there was a table with rows of glasses filled with red wine. I took several sips and fell asleep under the table. Carried home by my worried parents, I woke up in my bed when my mother slapped cold towels into my face. Sipping all this wine was fun; it surely didn't agree with me. I felt positively ill.

Mary came to be envious of the respectability, security, and confidence that came with the money to buy the alcohol that had made her sick. Mary would learn too soon about the fragility of Jewish prosperity during the Weimar era as it unraveled when the Nazis assumed power in 1933. By then, there were more than half a million Jews in Germany, accounting for one percent of the total population. The number of Jews in Berlin had grown to 176,000, including prominent businessmen, artists, writers, musicians, and scientists. Many assimilated Jews developed successful careers and businesses during the Weimar era and felt like true Berliners. Although successful Jews were highly visible during the prosperous years of the Weimar Republic, many who had recently come from Poland lived in poverty. Mary's immediate family had some trappings of the middle class, such as a piano, but nevertheless struggled to make ends meet with the help of more prosperous relatives.

For many Jews, assimilation appeared to be the key to success and prosperity. The increased secularization of Jewish life, especially in Berlin and other large cities, often resulted in intermarriage. Some Jews converted to Christianity. Aunt Martha was the only relative who married a non-Jew, a military man named Jeanil von Holn, who died while her children were young. Their daughter, Irene, never married but her sister, Elly, married Theodore Leib, a Jew who came from a wealthy family with holdings in Zoellnerwerke, a large paint and lacquer manufacturing company.

During these times, Mary's parents resisted assimilation. Her father was immersed in his religious duties as a cantor and her mother continued to keep a kosher home. They relied on their benefactor, Siegfried, who made a comfortable living in sales at Wertheim during the 1920s and afterwards started his own business that specialized in dressing gowns. Mary came to know his son, Freddie, a sophisticated adult with a taste for opera, who was 13 years older than she and who, like her other older cousins, was taken up with the social pursuits of his own set.

While her parents wrestled with financial problems and worried about their uncertain future, they struggled to cope with their difficult, high-strung little Mary. When their daughter had problems as a first grader in public school, they enrolled her in Pestalozzi Fröbel Haus, a pioneering progressive school founded in 1882 for training forward-thinking early childhood teachers. No doubt Uncle Siegfried helped to make that happen.

> My unhappiness in Berlin was expressed in unruly behavior. I became naughty and defiant, hard to control. My parents' finances must have worsened because my mother had to work, too, and I wound up in Pestalozzi Fröbel Haus, where I was constantly in trouble. Scolding me, they would shout, "*Die goldene Mittestrasse!*" This was the same phrase about finding the middle road that my mother used to shout at me, holding me up and shaking me by the shoulders. I prayed that my head wouldn't come off. Misbehaving during the day didn't stop me from being a frightened little girl at nighttime, afraid of grotesque moving shadows on the wall. When police cars and fire trucks made shrill noises, I would hide under my bed covers. When all this became too much, I fled into the bed of my mother.

Mary's difficulties in adjusting to big city life were taking place amidst the turmoil of the Nazi's rise to power. She remembers her father discussing newspaper reports of one political crisis after another as the Weimar Republic unraveled while the Nazis, communists, and socialists fought in the streets. He understood what the Nazi rise to power portended.

Her father feared for the worst when the social democrats and communists failed to form a government and when Hindenburg appointed Hitler as Chancellor to head a minority-led government in the belief that he could be controlled. After the Nazis torched the *Reichstag*, Hitler blamed the communists to give himself a pretext for eliminating his political opponents. The parliament passed the Enabling Act of 1933 on March 23 which enabled the Nazis to establish their dictatorship. Given his upbringing in Poland where the threat of pogroms was ever present, Stephan was keenly aware of growing antisemitism and the dangers posed by the Nazis, perhaps more so than his assimilated German-Jewish relatives. In desperation, he wrote to Albert Stanley, his nephew in California, concerning the possibility of his family emigrating to the United States as he had done as a young man.

Amidst the political turmoil as the Nazis seized power, Mary returned to Volksschule 156, a public school in her neighborhood.

> I started to come into my own. I went to the neighborhood elementary school for girls. Although my grades and conduct in school were poor, I was making many friends and was almost a gang leader. And then there came the first blow, the first of many more to follow. Hitler had come into power, and at first, I didn't know what that meant. My classmates started to avoid me, even my best friend Ruth Purtzel. I heard them whisper "*Jude.*" And when I confronted Ruth, she told me that she was not allowed to play with Jewish children, but she insisted that I wasn't Jewish. Perhaps as an oversight, my elementary school teacher recommended me at age 11 for admission to the lyceum, a local secondary school that prepared students for the university.

Mary spent several happy months as a student in the lyceum looking forward to a bright future, but her hopes and dreams for advanced learning were quickly shattered by decree.

> Each year of learning at the lyceum had a Latin name: Sexta, Quinta, etc. For an 11-year-old, the curriculum was heavy – French, Advanced

Math, English – but I was happy. Yes, even my conduct improved. I dreamed of becoming a doctor or a qualified nurse. But these weeks of dreams were instantly shattered by a notice I was given to take home to my parents. "We regret to inform you … on account of belonging to a Jewish father … your daughter can no longer attend this school." I don't remember how long I cried, or whether I cried at all.

On April 25, 1933, the Nazi government had passed a law limiting the number of Jewish students in high schools and universities, which effectively barred qualified children like Mary from continuing their education. Meanwhile, her family fell on hard times when her father stopped working because of poor health. Although their relatives continued to provide financial help, Gertrud had to find domestic work to make ends meet. When that happened, the Krotoczynski family moved three times within two years.

I remember our first apartment on the top floor where a lot of sunshine came through the front windows. We gave it up for what must have been financial reasons, moving into an apartment where my mother became the housekeeper for a Herr Hopp, a teacher with two grown-up sons in their twenties. I had a crush on the younger one, Alfred. Alfred always had time for me, and I could tell him everything that happened at school. One day, I showed him a gym exercise, lying on the floor, legs in the air, and I was scolded by my mother which I thought was unfair. Alfred even gave me his old bicycle. How happy I was! It took me no time to learn to ride it and later my parents allowed me to bike to school. I was very jealous of Alfred's girlfriend and used to tease him by singing heart-rending songs. Little did I know how sad this romance was because I realized later that his girlfriend was not Jewish. Something happened to Herr Hopp and his sons. They disappeared or moved away, and so we had to move. We found another place in East Berlin, a two-room apartment on Wallnertheaterstraße where we managed to stay until the bitter end. Unfortunately, my father's progressing heart condition limited his ability to climb the stairs to the second floor. But this time, we had nice furniture, which today would be considered antique – heavy oak, fancy designs, especially on the chairs. I oversaw all dusting. The front room was quite pleasant with two large double windows where mother kept little cactus plants. This front room was also my room where I slept on the couch. There was a writing desk which I shared with my father, and at one point we even had a piano (don't remember how it came into our possession) which I also shared with my father. To give me a feeling of privacy, my mother emptied the top drawer of a chest and handed me the key to this top drawer.

When the persecutions became widespread, her parents feared for Mary's safety and cautioned her to avoid crowds in public places.

All public life was verboten to us – movies, theaters, opera, visits to restaurants. My father was constantly worried that sadistic S.A. or S.S. men might abuse me. I was not afraid, as far as I can remember.

Since their daughter was barred from public school, Mary's parents enrolled her in the Jüdische Mädchenschule Berlin [Berlin Jewish Girls School], which was part of a network of educational institutions run by the Berlin Jewish Council.[1] This progressive school with an enrollment of about 400 was staffed by Jewish teachers who had been expelled from the lyceums. They taught Hebrew and Jewish culture along with the traditional subjects that would have been covered in public schools. Mary attended the Mädchenschule from 1933 to her graduation in 1937.

At first, I thought that the only good thing about this new school was that I was able to ride my bike there. This new Jewish school, not in my neighborhood, was in a poor district that was predominantly Jewish. In Berlin, Jews could live in neighborhoods of their choice, and that didn't change under the Nazis. The Nazis had no need for ghettos because they could rely on the old German system of police registration to keep track of Jews and everyone else. Anytime one moved, it was necessary to register with the police who paid special attention to place of birth and religion. By foot, it took 45 minutes each way to get to school, and after a lot of pleading, my parents agreed to let me take my bike. I promised to ride only the back streets, but promptly broke my promise the second day.

Her ride had all the exhilaration of Kurt Richter's 1927 documentary, *Berlin: Symphony of a Great City*, in which the people of Berlin – hordes of office workers, delivery drivers, tradesmen, and shoppers – filled the streets amidst sounds of taxis and trucks. She experienced the foul smell of rotten eggs fallen from delivery vans, shouts of street hawkers, and the occasional horse whinny that may have reminded her of rural life in Mecklenburg. After her wild ride, she had to settle down to her school routine.

> I showed absolutely no interest in my school. I always sat in back so that I could occupy myself with anything but school without being caught, playing cards on a shelf under the desk, reading and eating my lunch. One day, my Jewish history teacher, Fraulein Lewandowski, kept me after class. She didn't scold me for anything or try to make me feel ashamed. She just told me that she was convinced that I had the makings of a good student, obviously knowing more than I realized. Subsequently, I formed a strong attachment to Fraulein Lewandowski. I carried her books to school on my bicycle and on a few occasions, I was invited for tea at her apartment. I think I loved her and carried it as far as wishing she would be my mother. To my way of thinking, she knew everything. She carried herself with dignity and was kind and openly trusted me. My school was new, in contrast to the old dwellings next to it. Classrooms were bright with large windows, holding about 25 students. The gym was large and as well-equipped as one would find in any American high school. But the yard was small, barely enough space for a 50-yard dash. We had gymnastics every day, my favorite subject. There were no showers in school, and I didn't miss them because we didn't have a shower at home either. I had to wash myself in a basin which was a big nuisance. Looking back, the teachers were the best thing about this school. Most of them were fired from the German lyceums and were willing to give extra education after class to any student who showed promise. I took English, math, algebra, advanced history, geography, shorthand and typing with eagerness and pretended that life was all right, but I knew it wasn't.

During her years at the school from 1933 to 1937, Mary received a Jewish education with a breath of secularized fresh air. As much as she loved her parents, she resented being bridled and lectured and wanted to strike out on her own. Her school provided the opportunity to develop ideas and attitudes attuned to the progressive modernity outside the confines of her Victorian upbringing. Her excellent report cards were signed by her father, using the Germanized spelling of his last name.

There are only a few surviving photos of Mary as a young student. One pictures her on a day in the countryside with her best friend at school, Jenny Stanesco. They were "inseparable twins" during their time together as classmates, and after graduation they continued to see each other until Jenny and her mother went to Brussels to hide from persecution. In another photo taken in 1939, Mary posed with her dear friend, Thea-Margot Schindler, enjoying a musical moment playing flute and accordion. Thea was two years older than Mary. Since both of their families were neighbors on Wallnertheaterstrasse, the two teenage girls had the opportunity to form a close friendship that flourished until their lives were upended in 1939. The third surviving photo is a dramatic, studio-posed portrait of Mary in a peasant blouse taken on January 27, 1939. Years later when she showed this glamorous photo to friends, they said she must have been a movie star. By the time she enrolled in the Mädchenschule, Mary knew the dark beauty that had once troubled her could now turn heads. This happened around the time Rudi Sabor became a teacher at the Jüdische Mädchenschule in 1936 along with his future wife, Emmy Veit, whom he met during teachers training. Rudi recalled teaching at the Girls School.

> I taught a class of 14-year-old girls German and history and music. And the music soon took its main place. German lessons were music lessons, the history lessons became music lessons, and the music lessons remained music lessons. And we had a choir, and that was the choir of all choirs, die *Piepmätze* [the little songbirds]. And as far as I remember, although we had splendid choirs since then in this country in England, the Piepmätze were the finest. They were really excellent... I remember distinctly, in '36, '37 and part of '38, the school was calm; you could concentrate on your job; the girls were interested in anything you gave them. We did Kleist [Bernd Wilhelm von Kleist, 1777-1810] on the roof garden of the school.[2]

Mary was among Rudi's students more than one year before the Kristallnacht when there still was the occasion for young people to indulge in the vicissitudes of adolescence.

Before I became aware of our hopeless situation, I experienced, like all young girls, the first, most tender feelings of love. I had yet to sort out my story about the birds and bees, but that was not important. There was Rudi Sabor, our music teacher, who stood tall, could play the piano, flute, and guitar, and could also sing and compose music. He formed a choir for our class during my last year of school. I was going on 15, Rudi was 23, but he seemed so much older to me, for he knew so much. Rudi somehow responded to me. I was shy and remember blushing a lot. I blushed when he entered the classroom and when I had to answer a question. I was medium tall and slender, dark, and pale at the same time – a sensitive, soulful child with large brown eyes, a child who wished she were a woman. My love for Rudi was a painful romantic dream. On the level of a romantic escapade, we entered a relationship in secret, because it was considered unethical for a male teacher to entertain a young girl pupil at his home. I went to his home and lied to my parents about my whereabouts. They never found out. The hours spent with Rudi were happiness to me. He played his guitar and sang songs for me and gave me nice things to eat, especially the fruit salads he made that I liked best. My cheeks were constantly flushed, and on many occasions, I had trouble breathing, although he never touched me. My deepest wish was to have a baby from him, although I was not sure how to go about it. My hopes were crushed when I found out that Rudi was engaged to our fourth-grade teacher. I was filled with such sadness; I wanted to die. I showed no interest in boys or men for several years. I felt that no one could replace Rudi. Despite my sadness and crushed dream, I stayed in touch with Rudi throughout the years. Even now, after 40 years, we exchange tender notes. We even chose the same names for our children, knowingly or not.

Rudi befriended Mary beyond the normal student-teacher relationship but never took advantage of her at a time when solidarity at the Girls School provided a sanctuary from Nazi oppression. The school experience fostered the enthusiasm and innocent optimism of youth. It encouraged her to have expectations and to muster the will to rebel against the expectations of her upbringing that kept her lively spirit in check. Yet despite her exposure to a world of possibilities through her exposure to German secular culture, her future was elsewhere, perhaps Israel if not the United States as her parents had in mind.

> When I graduated from my school for Jewish girls in 1937, I was handed a book with beautiful pictures of Palestine with an inscription pronouncing me the best student of the graduating class. Of course, I was immensely proud and so were my parents. But what was I going to do with all this elementary learning? How was I to become a doctor or nurse?

The book, *Palestina by George Landauer,* was signed by her principal, Johanna Kaplan, and by her teacher, Frieda Levandt. The photos in this book depicted a future for Jews through the nation-building work by Jewish pioneers in agriculture, manufacturing, construction, education, and the arts. On page 64 was a photo of a factory with a huge sign, "The Only Jewish Cigarettes of Erez-Israel" that may have resonated with Mary who took up smoking with her friends as an act of defiance. Like many of her generation, Mary became a smoker for life.

Meanwhile, things turned for the worse. Not long after her graduation from the Mädchenschule, several Nazi paramilitary S.A. thugs attacked Mary while she walked home along Wallnertheaterstrasse. They pushed her to the ground and gave her a severe beating that injured her left eye and impaired her vision. Her parents were horrified and begged her to be careful. Very likely Mary kept in touch with Rudi and her other teachers when she learned of the deportation of several teachers and classmates. She found out that those deported included her favorite teacher, Fraulein Lewandowski. She never knew that another one of her teachers, Johanna Kaplan, would escape to Sweden in 1939 and then emigrate to Israel in 1951.

> One day she disappeared. She never said goodbye. Was she taken away like many other Jewish people who were born in Poland? I shall never know to this day. But I did know about the deportation of Jewish

Polish people. I had a classmate, who was the oldest of eight children, who was left behind with her little sisters and brothers when her parents were taken away. I believe she later went insane. Under the Nazi regime, we were only allowed to do domestic work or be an apprentice in a Jewish firm, of which there were but a few. I remember we received notices from the police advising us to leave the country. But where was one to go without money and backing and entrance visas? Countries had a quota for visas, including the United States.

When Mary graduated, there was no future for her in Germany. No relatives left in Berlin were in a position to help Mary and her family financially. Her benevolent Uncle Siegfried's business was expropriated by the Nazis in 1938 and liquidated in 1939, the same year he died at the age of 69.[3] Several of her younger relatives left Germany in whatever way possible, but it was difficult for the older generation of aunts and uncles to leave. Cousins on both sides of her family emigrated to the United States, Israel, South America, and South Africa. Sadly, most of the aunts and uncles were unable to obtain emigration visas and were forced to remain in Germany to face deportation and death. I don't know if Mary and Rudi were in touch during the war or how they finally reconnected afterwards. There are, however, letters from him dating from 1952.

Mary's parents could not get visas for the United States even after Stephan's nephew, Albert Stanley, agreed to sponsor the entire family. They were among the thousands of Jews who were denied entry by the US State Department. For Mary's parents, emigration to Shanghai was out of the question because of her father's poor health. Time was running out.

Every time the doorbell rang, we looked at each in horror. Jews and other people disappeared all the time. As fearful as my father was for my life, he didn't care for his own. I remember the last Passover celebration at home. Father sang the ritual melodies on top of his powerful tenor voice in defiance. Nothing happened. His lot had not been drawn.

Mary contrasted her father's dogged defiance and his increasingly frail condition with her mother's inner strength and self-discipline in coping with worsening conditions. She wanted to be more like her mother and later wrote that she was painfully aware of her own shortcomings.

> If you could see me, you would see my mother: we both have the same big brown sad eyes and full lips, but my mother held her head far higher than I was able to all my life. She was proud, yet humble. I have never seen her commit the slightest act of unkindness, no matter whom she dealt with. And how she could laugh! I feel close to her now, being of the approximate age (57) she was when I saw her last. At times, I say, I am my mother. And how she could sing! She sang without inhibitions. Her favorite songs were from German light opera.

As much as her mother sought to keep her family's spirits up, Mary felt trapped and unsettled. Since there were no options for further education, her mother urged Mary to work for her own good as well as to help her family, but Mary wanted to get out of Berlin like her friend, Jenny, who went into hiding in Belgium in 1938.

After Jenny left, Mary spent a good deal of time with her older friend, Thea Schindler and her fiancé, Edgar Steinmetz, as well as her parents' friend, Ernst Champanier, the son of a cantor from Breslau. Ernst sported nonsectarian ideas about religion that may have seemed irrelevant given the reality that Jews were persecuted by the Nazis no matter what their beliefs. I don't know the extent to which Mary and her parents were aware of Ernst's involvement in anthroposophy, a spiritualist movement that was reviled by the Nazis.[4] Clearly, Gertrud wanted her daughter to focus on practical matters instead of being diverted by Ernst's unconventional views.

> My mother thought it was bad for me, a 16-year-old girl, to stay home and she arranged for me to become a *Haustochter*. That sounded more pleasant than domestic servant, but the work did not differ. I truly hated it to the point that I have no recollection of the woman I worked for or where she lived. I don't remember how long I worked there or why I left. Again, no idle sitting at home, I found myself as an apprentice in a store making hats. There was an old stove which I had to clean out every morning. One day, I received a long, deep scratch inside my arm and still have the scar to prove it. As heartbreaking as it

was to leave my parents the following year, I thought at the time it was heaven to leave all this hopelessness behind, but was it really?

Mary paid increasing attention to her sick father's needs and joined her mother in supporting his struggle to carry out religious duties. Her recollection of her role in helping preside over services in Mecklenburg in her father's final days as a cantor may have mixed fact with fantasy, but it's clear that she was providing spiritual support as he tried to sustain his troubled congregations.

Father's health became progressively worse. He took nitroglycerin for his heart condition. I didn't know how serious it was, but I was frightened. My mother used to put towels on his abdomen to relieve pain. Father was a person who never wanted to be of trouble to anybody, who never complained. As a cantor, he served congregations in numerous small towns in the district where I was born, 50 kilometers north of Berlin. These dwindled after 1933-4 and finally, only the High Holy Days were observed. My father lived for this occasion, practicing all year round by the piano. His rich tenor voice must have been heard throughout the apartment house, but nobody ever complained. Father suffered several strokes, which resulted in the paralysis of his arm, leg, and mouth muscles. He used to sit at the piano practicing to get back the use of his fingers, struggling to keep his voice intact. And he made it in time for the High Holy Days. When the High Holy Days came, he insisted on going to Mecklenburg to give courage and hope to his congregation. My mother allowed this if I would go along and stay close by him. For me, traveling to Mecklenburg was a great novelty, and I was pleased that my mother trusted me to take care of him. Looking back, it's a mystery to me that Father did not have a single attack of angina pectoris during the high holidays. I was constantly petrified that this could happen, especially on Yom Kippur. On this Day of Atonement, my father fasted all day, wailed 45 minutes in the synagogue, and stood up singing all day with all his heart. He seemed a transformed person. Never did I see my father so tall, so steadfast and fulfilled. Before this last visit, the congregation had lost its rabbi who was deported, and my father told everybody that his daughter would hold the sermon. Somehow, I accepted this responsibility with ease, for I had a good knowledge of

Jewish history. I knew something of the Old Testament and some Hebrew. I told the story of Jonah and the whale, and that God, too, will save us from the jaws of our present enemy. Some people cried as I spoke and I thought they were touched by my presentation of the speech, but I must have been too young and too optimistic in failing to understand why these people were crying. They knew they were trapped.

4

KINDERTRANSPORT

In what was called "The Fateful Year" of 1938, the Nazis barred Jews from employment and expropriated Jewish businesses. They took away passports and only issued temporary ones for Jews who agreed to leave the country. On October 27, the SS expelled Polish Jews and forcibly drove them across the Polish border. On November 8, the Nazi government instigated *Kristallnacht* [Night of Broken Glass], a national pogrom that resulted in the destruction of Jewish-owned stores and homes, and many synagogues. More than 90 Jews were killed and over 30,000 were arrested and sent to concentration camps. The pretext for *Kristallnacht* was the assassination of the German diplomat, Ernst vom Rath, in Paris by a Jewish teenager, Herschel Grynszpan, who acted in protest to the persecution of his family and thousands of other Jews whom the Nazis deported to Poland.

On November 9, Nazi mobs smashed windows, and set synagogues on fire in the town of Alt-Strelitz, Prenzlau and the city of Neubrandenburg within the vicinity of the congregations where Mary's father served as a cantor. In Prenzlau, the Nazis forced the congregation to sell its property to pay for the removal of the ruins. After *Kristallnacht*, Mary was increasingly shut off from the outside world and felt more restricted by the expectations of her protective parents, who loved her very much but downplayed her longings and ambitions.

Amidst all fear, limitations, disappointments, I still had one constant friend, my diary. At least it was always there when I needed it because it could not hurt, misunderstand, or leave me. Unfortunately, it would soon be burned in the London Blitz. I wrote down my innermost secret thoughts, much of it about Rudi, which was, of course, very secret. But why didn't I think of my parents as my constant friends? They loved me dearly, more than their own lives. Was I too young to show my love? Or was I too old in my way of thinking and resentful to be treated as a child? I don't remember ever having a serious conversation or discussion with my parents. I even felt they wouldn't understand. But I realize now that my attitude was part of the pattern of growing up. On many occasions, I used to daydream about being an orphan and little did I know that my wish would soon be granted. I felt ashamed of my parents because they were much older than the parents of my classmates and friends. I didn't appreciate them until it was too late, this accounting for much unhappiness in my adult life, years spent in self-reproach. I felt unworthy having survived the Nazi years. My parents were planning for me to leave the country. They hoped that one country would provide me with a visa because I was a young person. They didn't have much hope for their own escape. Today I know they put their pride aside to beg for me, "Please save our child," but they wouldn't beg for themselves. Father had a lengthy correspondence with a nephew of his in America, and he always addressed him as "my dear sweet A." Finally, sweet Albert agreed to have me come over to America, but the good old USA closed its immigration quota. I was supposed to wait from 1938 to 1943.

There was little public support for admitting Jewish refugees to the United States that time. In 1939, Senator Robert Wagner (D-NY), who was born in Prussia, and Representative Edith Rogers the first woman elected to Congress from Massachusetts, sponsored a bill that would permit 20,000 German-Jewish children to come to America, but that bill never came up for a vote. Laura Delano Houghteling, a cousin of President Franklin Roosevelt and wife of the US Commissioner of Immigration, was heard complaining that "20,000 charming children would all too soon grow up into 20,000 ugly adults."[1]

When immigration to America was no longer an option for the entire family, Mary's desperate parents focused on saving their daughter.

The British government was willing to provide a visa if a family were willing to take full responsibility for me. But how soon? Every passing day seemed to us a day closer to doom. My parents also tried to get me into Palestine, but this seemed hopeless since entry was only possible by illegal means. At this time, I knew a boy, Manfred, two years older than I, who went to Holland into a camp preparing Jews to be pioneers in Palestine. He wanted me to come to Holland, get married and emigrate together to Palestine, legal or otherwise. But, of course, my parents wouldn't let me go. I cannot recall my true feelings about Manfred and a life with him on a Kibbutz, although I claimed to be a Zionist. I do know if Rudi had asked me to go with him anywhere, I would have gone, even against the wishes of my parents.

Then Mary's father found out about the *Kindertransport* through the *Jüdische Gemeinde zu Berlin* [Jewish Community in Berlin], a public corporation serving the needs of the Jewish community, which was established in 1847 and reestablished in 1946. The Kindertransport program came about after a delegation of British, Jewish, and Quaker leaders went to London to persuade the British Government to issue visas to unaccompanied children, 17 years or younger, whose parents had given up hope of being able to leave to leave Nazi-controlled areas. Close to the cut-off age, Mary barely qualified for the Kindertransport. Her acceptance into the program was expedited because there was a foster family in London willing to take her in.

Finally, a letter came with good news. I had been accepted to go to England on the Children's Transport and had to be at a railroad station in Berlin. My first reaction was joy, screams of happiness: London, England – a new life free from fear, new hope, a chance of going to school. My parents were overjoyed. I was moving on "cloud nine" until the day of my departure.

On May 4, 1939, Mary boarded the Kindertransport train at Berlin Friedrichstraße Station alongside frightened young children being cajoled to get on board.

I shall never forget this day so long as I live. I had never seen so many crying children and confused-looking adults, their parents. Mine were composed and we didn't exchange many words. When we had to say goodbye, my father started to cry, not just cry, but sob. But my mother stood there, tall, and strong, and kissed and smiled the smile of a Madonna. I didn't cry, but something died within me, and part of this is still dead to this present day. I was incapable of crying for many years to come. My dreams for a new life in England were washed away by my father's tears, and I must have realized that I didn't have my mother's smiling defiance of fate. Goodbye, sweet parents. You got me into safety, but what did I do with it? An endless journey out of Berlin, out of Germany! I was numbed. In Holland, we were greeted by ladies, who gave each of us a dish of home-cooked green beans. I don't remember much about the crossing of the Channel, but I had to take care of a lot of small children, many of them seasick and crying for their mothers.

For hours, her train clattered through the flat Dutch countryside on the way to London via Rotterdam from where she boarded a ferry to the British port of Harwich and then another train for London's Liverpool Station. The Kindertransport train arrived at Liverpool Station the next morning. With a nametag around her neck, she carried her suitcase to the waiting area where she was introduced to her new foster parents, Lilly and Louis Cohen. Had Mary known then that the Nazis would murder more than one million Jewish children, she would have counted herself lucky to be among the 10,000 or so Jewish children who were saved through the Kindertransport. Instead, the initial excitement and apprehension of leaving Berlin to start a new life was displaced by desolation by the time she met her new foster parents at Liverpool Station.

In London, still in a state of shock, I was brought into a large room filled with many people. Someone called out names and when mine was called, people came rushing towards me and a woman started hugging and kissing me. I didn't feel like being hugged and kissed and I hoped no one noticed it.

Her foster parents took Mary to their modest row home on 23 Balls Pond Road in North London. Mary unpacked her suitcase containing a change of clothing as well as a few keepsakes from her former life in

Berlin, including photos of her parents and her prized possession, the teddy bear from her Uncle Siegfried who died a day after Mary boarded the Kindertransport. There was also a packet containing official documents, including an inoculation certificate issued by Dr. Pistorius in Friedland, Mecklenburg, several swimming certificates as well as all her report cards. There was also the precious book of photographs about Israel given to her upon her graduation.

Her parents also packed a little hand-written booklet containing several prayers attesting to the protections granted by the Almighty, reminders to be grateful for being granted life on this earth, and the importance of honoring one's mother and father. One page was devoted to a saying by the wise rabbi Nahum Ish Gamzu, regarding his belief that, no matter how evil and unpleasant, what happens is for the good. Many years later, Mary often quoted this sage, *Gam zu l'tovah*, a Hebrew phrase translated as, "This, too, is for the best." On another page was the text of the *Maskir*, which is a prayer in memory of close relatives recited during the Jewish holidays of Yom Kippur, Passover, *Shavuot*, and *Shemini Atseret*. Below the *Maskir*, there was a hand-written blessing, the *Birkas Kohanim* [priestly blessing] Numbers 6, 24-26, inscribed by her father, "May G-d bless you and guard you. May G-d shine His countenance upon you and be gracious to you. May G-d turn His countenance toward you and grant you peace."

Armed with guidance from her parents, Mary confronted the realities of her situation. She had to share cramped quarters with her foster sister and brother, a girl her age and a ten-year-old boy. The Cohens expected her to tend the family's clothing store and to perform household duties, with the idea that someday soon she would marry a nice Jewish boy.

All of a sudden, I realized that I didn't want any of this. I also remember that I didn't know what I wanted. Whatever I was facing now had nothing to do with my dreams and hopes for safety and schooling. I never admitted it to myself, but all I wanted was to turn back, to go back to my parents, to be with parents. I wanted to erase the pain I had caused them by having them let me go. I realized this, but only subconsciously. I wanted to stay with them and share everything with them, to the end. But here I was in England, expected to smile and show gratitude, and there was no one I could tell how I really felt. The Cohens were good people and they obviously meant well. Otherwise, why would they have squeezed me into their small home? I even had to share a bed with my foster sister Stella. They lived in a typical two-story little house in North London and the ground floor was converted into a clothing store. All the rooms were small and so was the store. All houses seemed to look alike and stood at a tight squeeze.

Mary adapted quickly to her new situation. Her limited English became fluent, built on what she had learned in school and from her father, who attained fluency from his years in America and England. But her gratefulness for being taken in by the Cohens was tinged with resentment.

Stella went to school, I believe high school, but I didn't, which I considered an injustice. Instead, I was supposed to mind the store, which I despised. Cleaning the house was my other chore. One day I was trying to tell them that I needed a career for the future, but they laughed and said, "One day you will marry a nice Jewish boy."

On September 3, 1939, just four months after Mary arrived in England, England and France declared war on Germany. As the war with Germany intensified, the British government evacuated civilians living in cities to areas unlikely to be targeted for air attacks. In late 1939, she and the Cohen family relocated to Luton, a suburb about 30 miles north of London.

We spent close to a year in the country. I don't remember where, nor do I remember the house we lived in, or what I did during this one-year period. Just a few bed bugs and head lice. I was glad to get away from that horrible clothing store and the other Cinderella duties. On the day the war broke out, we sat in front of a radio listening to speeches by high officials. I didn't understand much of what was said but I surely knew how serious things were, and I froze when they played the national anthem. Up till now I still had hope that my parents might be able to leave Germany by some miracle. Nothing could save them now. I still couldn't cry.

Cut off from direct contact with her parents in Germany, Mary relied and counted on their relatives in America to receive and forward mail. She saved 20 letters from her parents that had been forwarded by American relatives over a two-year period from January 1940 to November 1941. Her parents usually wrote letters in German, penned by her mother with notes from her father. Some were addressed directly to Mary and others to relatives who could forward them to her. These contained news about her paternal and maternal relatives who had managed to leave Germany as well as those who remained.

Most of the letters to and from Germany were transmitted by Albert Stanley, her American cousin on her father's side who lived in Santa Monica, California. Since Albert Stanley didn't know German, he corresponded with Mary and her parents in English. None of his letters survived, nor did those from her Aunt Hedwig Unger and cousins Georg and Grete Unger, who had fled from Germany to Long Island, New York. Although Mary kept the letters from her parents, none of her outgoing correspondence was saved.

Aware of her daughter's emotional and rebellious nature, Gertrud encouraged her to heed the advice of her foster parents and to be grateful that Lilly was there to watch over her and to take care of her. Gertrud asked whether Stella was still in school and sent her regards to Louis. She also asked for the address of Louis's parents so that she could write to thank them, and added, "I hope with all my heart that the day will come that we will all see each other so that I can express my gratefulness in person. Often, I see Lilly's photo and it strikes me how kindhearted and diligent she looks."

Although she quickly mastered English and became used to living in England, Mary did not feel at home because of her uncertain status as an enemy alien. Lacking access to further education, she believed there would be a better future for her in America. She knew that this was what her father wanted for her based on his letters to Albert that were forwarded to her. Stephan wrote this final letter beseeching Albert in a humble, pleading way that would become galling to Mary when Albert was finally able to make good on his promise. Why should her father have had to beg for his daughter's right to survive?

Excuse me to trouble you once again. You have written to me to say that Mary's affidavit will take six months to a year. You see, Mary is a refugee, so they could possibly admit Mary sooner. My dear Albert, please see if this could be done. I know you will do your best to help my dear child. May the Lord in heaven pay you for all this that you are doing for my dear child, Mary. And may God in heaven give me that pleasure to see you once again and to thank you. I hope I will live to see you and your family in the very best of health, with love and my very best wishes to you and your family, and to my dear Mary, as I cannot write to her. Please tell her we are well. I am yours, with love, Uncle Steve.

During these desperate times, all the letters to Mary from her parents continued to exude normalcy and calm. They did not refer to the war and persecutions to avoid upsetting their daughter and to evade problems with the censors. One such letter from her mother was occasioned by her father's birthday.

Dear Mary,

We have received your birthday letter of Jan. 22, 1940. Father was pleased by it, and we spent this day happily. Aunt Regina came for lunch during a snowstorm, wrapped in furs, and brought Daddy some nursing care articles and warm stockings. I prepared some quick hot peppermint tea, which we drink often, and offered a homemade cake that turned out well. Also, joining us were Ernst and Aunt Rosa. Both brought our dear Father some refreshments. Ernst preferred having a vegetarian meal – beet soup and carrots with celery and potatoes. It tasted good and hearty. Later we talked over coffee and cake, and it was self-explanatory why we would have the picture of our sweet *Mulle* in the middle of the table, so that you would also be here and that you would be in our thoughts.[2] We understand that a more recent photo of you is on the way. Please ask Albert again if he had received our airmail letters. We haven't heard anything from him since you left. Oh yes, we received greetings from Dr. Orbach through Ernst. Albert wrote us that things are going well with you. We were wondering whether he would forward your picture to us. We wrote Albert that we have received nothing yet. For Albert, let's both keep our fingers crossed. Your dad's greatest wish is for you to travel to America. I have great faith that the time will come when we will all be together. Think of the Ungers [her aunt and uncle in America] and how things are going well with them. Have you received my initial letter from sister Helga? Please convey our heartfelt greetings to Edith and thank her for her efforts. We have also written to Louis' parents. As soon as we have news, we will convey it to Louis and Lilly right away. Be sure to give them and their children our love. It was nice of Louis that he sent you things in the early part of the year. How are things going with you? Are you paying more attention to your appearance, making yourself pretty, or are you still wearing sports clothing? If only I could be a little mouse and observe how things are going with you! Did you see *Carmen*? Do you play music? Among the newspapers we saw a notice for the concert musician, Emmy Leissner, Strauss, etc. Have you heard from Jenny? Are you well and are you keeping your spirits up? God will help us again! Many kisses, Mother.

Whereas Gertrud believed that her daughter's only option was to make the best of things in England, Stephan clung to the hope that Albert could still arrange his daughter's immigration to America, as was implied when he advised her to keep up correspondence with Albert.

We were happy to receive your birthday greetings and wishes and would like to have sent you a piece of the cake we had. But that won't work. I pray all day long to God that you are healthy and that we will see each other through Albert. It is good to hear from you and hope that all will be for the best. I am not disappointed with him, for he is a fine man. Please write him regularly and clearly. All our love, Father.

The letters from her parents made Mary think about a future separate from her parents and family, and the life in Berlin that she had left behind. All the aspirations nurtured through conversations with her aunts and cousins were nullified when she became a refugee. Until then, her family provided a comfort zone and words of caution at a time when a good marriage for a young woman without means was considered the only realistic option for a decent life that might include music, culture, and the chance to make a valuable contribution to society. When that prospect evaporated with the outbreak of war, she decided to take on nursing as her path despite the misgivings of her parents.

When Gertrud sent her daughter the letter, dated February 14, 1940, it took more than a month to reach her. By this time, Germany and England had been at war for nearly nine months. This letter urged caution with regards to Mary's plans to become a nurse.

> I can understand that you want to choose a profession. Your father and I certainly commend your eventual goal of becoming a nurse, but you are still very young and may lack the maturity to enter this demanding profession that involves a lot of suffering and hard work and has little to do with youthful enthusiasm. You should look to experienced people for guidance and good advice, such as the Cohen family and Albert Stanley. You should not act on pre-conceived ideas or on the advice of a single individual. If I am not mistaken, Ernst has influenced you very much in this matter. I know you listened to him a lot and that he is always trying to win you over, I mean for his ideas. You need to know, he is not necessarily correct in what he is telling you, and you must keep a clear head to evaluate what he has to say. There is no basis for his advising you to become a nurse. Just today he told me that he is quite sure that nursing is not a hard profession. Well, he's not in the strongest position to make that judgement. At a more mature age, you will make that choice yourself based on what is good for you. My advice is that you stay with the Cohen Family for the time being. You know that dear Lilly is very protective of you and has your interest at heart. I wish I could be like a mouse in a corner to see how my grown daughter decides her future. I cannot tell you, my dear girl, how proud I am of you for contributing to the Cohen household. Now I know you're Mutti's daughter. But Dad is just as pleased because of what you have learned in evening school, as advised by Albert. It will take a while for your affidavit to move forward, perhaps sooner than expected. You must always let people know that you are as free as a bird to immigrate to America. Albert Stanley writes nice letters, letting us know that presents are on the way. He is extremely interested in what you are doing and wants to know if you know steno and typing, which are skills that can be used everywhere. My advice to you is to improve your handwriting, perhaps work on a larger and clearer script. Beloved child! Please understand that because of our

physical separation, I can't help but give you all kinds of advice. We mean well and only want the best for you. Now it's now 11 clock. Time to sign off and to wish you a good night.

According to Jewish Refugee Committee records, the Cohen family spent a year in Bedfordshire after their evacuation from London when the war began. Committee records also indicate that the Cohens were informed that Mary had failed to register as an enemy alien with the police. After being properly registered, Mary returned to London with the Cohens shortly before Hitler targeted civilian areas in the London Blitz that began September 7, 1940. Mary wrote about surviving the bombing of the family home.

Since London had not been attacked by air yet as anticipated, we went back to London. Barely back a few days, Jerry let us have it. Air-raid alarms day and night. Bombs fell all around us. We were running in and out of air-raid shelters. I was not as afraid as I should have been. Could I have had a secret death wish? Today, I would say yes. I wanted to be united in death with my parents. Amidst the confusion and terror people displayed during the air raids (and there was more than enough reason for this), I was without emotion when I saw the bombed-out shambles of 23 Balls Pond Road. We were evacuated to the country for a second time. I was 18 years old and still with the Cohens. Away from the horrible bombings in London, I started to settle down a little and again the same question came up. What was to become of my future? The Cohens kept insisting on the Jewish boy who would come along, and I had little else on my mind but to run away.

5

NURSE MARY

This time the Cohens evacuated to Marlborough, a small city in Wiltshire about 80 miles from London. Mary decided then to leave her foster family at the first opportunity and strike out on her own to enter nurses training school. Now 18, she was old enough to be on her own. She knew that nurses were increasingly in demand because of the war. Since she could no longer help her parents, becoming a nurse was her way of doing some good that would make them proud despite her mother's misgivings.

When she wrote her parents about becoming a nurse, they responded with the expected encouragement and congratulations, but with some hesitation.

Dear Mary,

We have received your letters of December 12 and December 30. Daddy was particularly pleased, so this was an occasion for congratulation. We are happy that you are well and happy. I can tell you that thanks to God we are healthy. To whomever you have sent your picture, we are looking forward to having it forwarded. And now, my dear child, it comes to the part of the letter to talk about your choice of profession. We have discussed this extensively and hope that it will fulfill you. You are undoubtedly aware that nursing is a demanding profession that requires self-sacrifice. You will have to learn a lot of facts and pass exams. Your nerves must be steady to cope with the heartbreak and grief you will see. You must also be physically strong to do day and night shifts. Also, you must not faint when you are assisting doctors in operations. There comes a time when you will have to close a person's eyes after they die and prepare the body. Yes, my dear strong girl, I hope you understand why I want to make you aware of all these things. I worry about your health, and so does your dear father. But from the bottom of my heart, I wish to God that you will succeed in what you undertake, and that God will be there for you as you carry out the duties of this difficult profession. Today we visited Mr. and Mrs. Hirsch. I asked her what kind of profession she thought you would choose. She quickly replied, nursing. She thought you were suited for it and wished you luck. Mr. Hirsh had among his acquaintances a young woman who started out in nursing, and then went on to America to become a doctor, a gynecologist. He thought that this was a good goal for you and that it would be possible to achieve it in America. Please write Albert about your plans. As it will happen, there will always be someone to give good advice, and who will help you achieve your goals. It is fantastic that Albert has written you. Since you had gone, we have received nothing from him. I wonder if his letter was lost. We had written him twice by airmail. It is so nice of Lilly that she is watching out for you. Otherwise, there would be things that we would never learn about. What kind of illness did Heather have to overcome? Is she still going to school? Hopefully, things will go for the better. What is Stella doing? Is she going to school? Have you heard from Walters and Glassman? When you write, please give them our best. In anticipation of a thick letter from you, we send you our kisses. Your Mother and Father.

Although Mary informed her parents about her plans for nursing school, she did not convey to them the circumstances of her separation from the Cohens that she described years later.

I met a gentleman, Mr. Gross, who worked as a registrar. He knew the matron of the local cottage hospital, and he did not need a lot of persuasion to introduce me to her. I was interviewed and accepted. I secretly packed my two suitcases and Mr. Gross picked me up by car, and I was off to a new life. The Cohens did find out where I was. That wasn't too hard, but they couldn't take me back since I was of age at 18. At last, I was free of my foster parents who meant so well and helped to save my life. Yes, I was free and could pursue the nursing career I dreamed about for a long time.

In December 1940, Mary was accepted as a probationer in a training program at Savernake Hospital on the outskirts of Marlborough adjacent to the beautiful Savernake Forest. She would spend about four years in this cottage hospital from 1940 to 1944 as a nurse in training. For the first time in her life, she would no longer be tethered to the Jewish community. Mary wrote her parents often and kept them up to date with her nurses training, describing the routines that gave structure to her life.

"Twenty past six, nurse!" This was how the day started. We worked till 8:30 p.m. with two hours off, seven days a week, one day off a month. Everything was well organized. There was no confusion among the nurses. Everyone held a special title according to the rank and years served. The Matron, Miss Swale, was like a mother, but too strict. One could only talk to her by appointment. When she wanted to talk to you, you were usually in trouble. The sisters oversaw each ward, and under them worked the charge-nurses, and then came we, the little busy bees, first, second, and third-year probationers. We remained on probation until we passed the final examination and could be expelled at any time, the matron deciding who was fit for the profession of Florence Nightingale. During my time, six nurses were expelled for sleeping at the neighboring soldiers' barracks. We learned about thoroughness. First, we had to learn how to make a comfortable bed, this requiring the effort of two nurses. Gradually, I learned all the nursing skills: hypodermic injections, dressings, enemas, but most of all, the general care of the patient, not to mention the endless scrubbing of utensils and the utility room which was called the sluice. I did have the touch of our great Miss Nightingale and what I thought she stood for. All my patients were sacred to me. My smile for them was sincere and all I did for them was done with patience and loving care. I was called into the matron's office twice. Each time I thought I was going to be expelled. Yet, on the first occasion, she told me that

she had good reports from my patients about me and that she was
pleased. Still, my studies needed improvement, for I spent too much
time walking and dreaming about my beloved forest.

Savernake Hospital, like the Mädchenschule in Berlin, provided Mary
with a sanctuary that balanced order and discipline with a measure of
indulgence, even from her stern matron, Miss Swale.

The second time I was called into her office, I was reprimanded on a
nursing procedure. A patient had died and was put into the bathroom,
as always. A visitor had arrived with flowers for this patient. I took
these and put them in the patient's arms and folded them across his
chest. Matron pointed out to me that this was not done, but I think she
had a faint smile on her lips. Life at Savernake Hospital as a junior
probationer nurse was very pleasant. Each nurse had her own room
with the necessary comforts – bed, chair, dresser, and closet. Of
course, no private bath, but to me a bath just down the hall was a
luxury in comparison with the jug and bowl personal hygiene I was
used to for so many years. This was the first time I had a room to
myself. About 20 girls lived in the nurses' quarters, on the average 20
years old. Most of the girls were my friends, not on intimate terms, but
I can still remember their names. I was closest to Constance who
invited me to her home in Cardiff for vacation since I had nowhere
to go.

The time she spent with Constance's family in Cardiff opened her eyes
to a way of life embellished by privilege that she admired with a touch
of envy.

For all her talk about Constance, Mother didn't talk about her
background. While doing research, I found out that her friend had
been adopted by a German-born woman and her English husband.
She spoke both German and English and traveled frequently to
Germany with her parents before the war. Hers was a musical family
that first lived in Edinburg, then Birmingham, and finally in Cardiff
where she grew up. In 1946, after finishing nurses training, Constance
studied the cello at the Royal Academy of Music, and after a long
marriage, which produced three children, she obtained a divorce and
in 1989 married Klaus Dessecker after his wife, who happened to be

her cousin, died of cancer. She lived in Germany until the end of her life.

When Mother spoke about Constance, she did not emphasize the German connection, although the fact that they could speak German to each other might very well have been a key factor in their friendship. She was the grateful recipient of Constance's kindness and hospitality, but her feelings as a Jewish outsider still weighed on her.

> Today I know why I felt some reservations towards these girls, Constance included. I did not want any closeness. When I had left my parents, I had also left my two beloved girlfriends behind, not knowing what would become of them. I often wondered whether they, too, were sent into an unknown country on a children's transport, or whether they crossed the border out of Germany into Holland, like Werner Goldstein, my first little boyfriend, who gave me my first kiss on the cheek. Werner was shot to death trying to escape. My heart was not free to accept new friends, and yet I needed a friend very much. Life at Savernake Hospital was pleasant. No air raids, no foster parents. I had my own room, and I could pursue my career. And yet, I was unhappy.

Although she valued the opportunity to become a nurse and to be on her own, Mary missed her parents and worried about their safety. It took weeks for her parents' letters to reach her. She knew the situation was desperate because of the urgency of her father's solicitous letters to Cousin Albert that were forwarded to her from America. Meanwhile, she compartmentalized her fears to keep up with her nursing studies and duties.

> Nineteen forty-one, a black year. I did my nursing duties well, in general. Each probationer nurse had to stay a certain time on each ward. I started out at the women's ward, did my share of scrubbing and cleaning out bed pans, making beds twice a day. I even gave my first injection and almost passed out in fear of having hurt the patient. Then it was time to gain new experience and I was sent to the men's ward. The loving care I was able to give in the women's ward I was unable to apply here. The male patients made me feel self-conscious by the constant attention they gave me, and I responded by flirting

with them. Most were young soldiers. Of course, Matron found out about my conduct, and I was put into the nursery with the mothers and new-born babies, a safe place for a flirt. Matron did not consider that the nursery was located only a few doors down from the men's ward. They used to come by and visit me, and one day when I was kneeling in front of the bathtub full of dirty diapers, which we called napkins, I invited a couple of them to help me scrub them. Sure enough, Matron had to walk by, and you should have seen her face! I didn't get expelled but was sent back to the women's ward. After six months of training, I was put on night duty – three months of night duty. I hardly had any time to walk in my forest. Night duty didn't involve much active nursing, hardly any scrubbing. Most patients slept at night. I remember them waiting up for me to get tucked in. I also kissed them good night. The extremely sick needed constant attention, and I felt it was entirely up to me to get them well again. My heart was with those who had a chance to recover. I did manage to distance my emotions from the dying patients. I felt relief when death came, usually in the early morning, after days of inhuman suffering. The dimly lit ward made me feel afraid on more than one occasion. One time, Charley, an orderly, handed me a tall soldier, feet hanging way over the trolley (stretcher). He had died from a broken neck. About my age, he looked so peaceful, almost smiling, and it was my duty to lay him out. I kept thinking that he might wake up as I was undressing him and hit me.

Mary was aware that her father struggled with heart disease long before she left Berlin, but the letters she received from her mother didn't mention the deterioration of his health. After the United States and Germany declared war on December 11, 1941, the letters via America ceased and the only remaining option for reaching her mother and other relatives in Berlin was the International Red Cross messages that were limited to 25 words, restricted only to personal and family news. In England, these communications were brokered through the War Organization of the British Red Cross and Order of St. John, which forwarded messages to the International Committee of the Red Cross for distribution to its German counterpart. The responses from Germany were routed through this same circuitous path that took about 60 days.

The Red Cross communications had already started at the beginning of 1941. The first hand-written message from Mary's father, inquiring about her health, was signed on January 11 and sent on January 17, 1941, and for the first time included the middle name "Israel" in his signature as was mandated by the Nazis to indicate his Jewish identity. Before this message arrived, she had already sent a typed message to her parents at their Berlin address, 3 Wallnertheaterstraße. This message, dated February 12, 1941, arrived on May 10, 1941. Mary wrote, "Dear Parents. Everything is fine with me," and explained that she would begin nursing duties in a month. Her father hand-lettered his reply on the back, "Beloved child, we are also well. Greetings from Albert. We wish you good health and satisfaction in your profession. Love and kisses, Vati and Mutti." By the time this message reached England on June 5, 1941, her father had already died.

Mary did not learn about her father's death until early Fall 1941 when she received the fateful letter from her mother, one of the last forwarded by Albert Stanley, informing her that her father died on May 26, 1941; however, her mother did not mention that he had been severely beaten by the Gestapo. A subsequent Red Cross message from her mother, dated November 12, 1941, did not mention his death at all. All she wrote was, "I received your nice note and am happy that you are healthy. I am healthy and had satisfactory results from my doctor's visit. Don't worry about me. Love, Mutti."

When Mary talked about her history of mental illness, she pinpointed the onset of manic depression to when she learned about her father's death.

Back on day duty after three months, I sank into a deep depression. I felt limp, without energy, possessed by a growing death wish. For a couple of days, I pretended I was physically ill and stayed in my bed in the nurses' quarters. A few days later Matron had me transferred into a private room in the hospital. By then I refused to speak to anybody. I also refused food and wouldn't groom myself. I prayed that God should let me die. Nobody knew what happened to me. Some of the nurses thought I was pregnant, as I overheard in a conversation outside of my room. I had kept a letter under my pillow from my mother. This was when it was possible to correspond with my parents via the United States (until the bombing of Pearl Harbor), and the Matron, upon discovering it, had it translated by one of our German-born nurses. I don't recall whether this letter broke the news about the death of my father. Was I so attached to my father that I wanted to die? Didn't I love my mother enough to stay alive for her? Did my suppressed feelings of guilt for having deserted my parents two years earlier finally take hold in full force? All I remember is that I felt I didn't deserve to live and pursue a career while my parents were left alone to face death. I believe the matron understood and she didn't send me to a mental institution. She kept me in a private room for eight weeks. She brought in a psychiatrist who insisted I was hearing voices, which I didn't. In fact, I lived in a dead but painful silence. Despite being treated with much love and kindness, and patience, I prayed that God should let me die. Matron visited me every day and so did my fellow nurses. Our cook, a very capable young girl of 23, visited me every day and brought dishes prepared especially for me. I envied her because she was so capable. I simply had to recover. The staff at Savernake wanted me to get better, and I did. Matron arranged a vacation for me at a resort for nurses (long before I was entitled to it) with a chaperon, an older nurse, Nurse Faust, a German-speaking woman who came from Switzerland. I was the only nurse who was called by her first name, Nurse Mary, because my surname, Krotoczynski, was too hard to pronounce. I remember nothing of this vacation except that upon my return, my illness disappeared as suddenly as it had started. I continued to pursue my career and went from first year to third year probationer. Although I didn't have further breakdowns, I was not the same afterwards for years to come. At times, I showed great zest, and felt vibrant and radiant. On other occasions, I had periods of mild depression, lacked confidence, and had difficulty concentrating and remembering.

While continuing her nursing duties, Mary was on the lookout for news from her mother and relatives and friends who remained in Berlin. At the end of 1941, she still exchanged Red Cross messages with her mother. In 1942, there was a new return address, 33 Rankenstrasse, c/o Dr. Martin Salomonski instead of her family's old address on Wallnertheaterstrasse.[1] Her mother explained that she was taking care of Rabbi Salomonski's two children, 13-year-old Adolf Fritz and nine-year-old Ruth Miriam. The Rabbi's wife, Lotte née Norden, left their two children under his care when she divorced him under circumstances that were not explained in the public record. According to Yad Vashem, the Rabbi and his two children were deported to Theresienstadt and murdered in Poland during 1944. Indications are that Lotte may not have been Jewish.

On November 12, 1941, Mary replied to her mother c/o Rabbi Salomonski. For months, there was no reply. On February 9, 1942, she also wrote her best friend, Thea, who had announced her marriage to Edgar Steinmetz. On that same day, she had also sent a note to Ernst Champanier, the family friend who had encouraged her aspiration to become a nurse. She asked him to inquire about her mother. In the return message, dated February 27, 1942, Ernst informed Mary that there was no news about her mother and wrote a cryptic message that did not bode well. "I am healthy, same situation, changed address, alone but not lonely. I am happy to hear about your progress. Are there people who understand you?" Ernst mentioned that Cousin Irene and Aunt Rosa are still healthy and that he had responded to all inquiries immediately. There was also a reply from her friend, Thea, who thanked Mary for the note and announced her marriage to Edgar Steinmetz, but no news about her mother.

On the same day she picked up the message from Ernst, Mary sent a note to her aunt, Rosa Elias, expressing birthday and Hanukkah wishes for health, with assurances that everything was okay on her end. Using the phrase, *Sei oft mit Mutti* [keep in touch with Mummy] hoping to get more information from Rosa.

Several months passed and still Mary heard nothing about her mother. Ernst sent a message dated March 30, 1942, stating that he had not heard from her mother nor from her Aunt Regina and Uncle Salo Wellner. Ernst also informed her that another family friend, Richard Blinder, had no news either. Ernst's reply did not come until June, three months after it was sent.

Ernst's message was ominous in its obfuscation. He quoted a line, *"liebt das Böse gut"* from the poem "Brüder" by Christian Morgenstern, about the need to transform evil through love so that it becomes good. Referring to another poem by Rudolf Lavant (1893) about hope and the coming of Spring, he continued, "*Vertraue dem Pfingstgedanken. Bleib stark!*" that translates as, "Trust in the Pentecost. Be strong!"[2] Given the situation in Germany, Ernst's paradoxical message of hope and renewal gave away the sad truth with his final plea, "Remain strong!"

Despite receiving no replies from her mother, Mary wrote two more messages to her. In the first, she inquired about her health and assured her that, God willing, she would persevere in her job. Mary's second message, dated April 10, indicated that she was healthy and that she was a night shift nurse in charge of a ward of 23 patients. The next message she received was from Rosa, "Dear Mary, please remain healthy and strong, God willing. Mutti and the Wellners are no longer in Berlin, address unknown. Please be happy with your job. My best, Aunt Rosa."

On June 5, there was yet another outgoing message to Ernst Champanier sent on the same day she had received his message dated March 3, 1942. "How come there is no word from Mutti? What happened? Don't conceal anything. Mutti's birthday is August 1." Ernst's indirect reply, which reached her months later, did not mention her mother. Ernst wrote, "I am healthy, alone here. Trusted and thankful for true friendship. Only thing I know is the Wellner address. Always keep up your spirits. Best wishes for your exams from your Berlin friends. Your strong brother."

Desperate for news about her mother, Mary wrote a separate message on June 5, 1942, to her Aunt Rosa at the address of her Aunt Regina Wellner. She thanked Rosa for writing and wished her good health adding, "Is my mother doing well? Did she move? I am still doing all right." There was still no reply from Aunt Rosa. Months later, a message from her, dated June 23, indicated that there were no reports about her mother and urged her to be brave.

Finally, Mary's cousin, Irene, sent a message, dated August 8, 1942, with the devastating news, "My dear little Mary. Be strong. No more aunts in Germany. Your mother is in Riga since November. No sign of life. Keep healthy. With all my love, Cousin Irene." By the time she received this message, nine months had passed since her mother had been deported to Latvia. This was the last and final word about the deportation of her mother and aunts. Years later, she wrote about that period in her life with profound feelings of guilt.

> Where was I on November 27, 1941, on my mother's day of extermination? I had just recovered from my first mental illness, May to September 1941. By November I was well on the road to recovery. So what did I do on November 27? Did I go for a walk in the forest, or did I go dancing and laugh all night? I have tortured myself for over 20 years over the death of my mother, although I could not have helped her. I mourned my beautiful, innocent mother with every fiber of my heart, whom I loved so dearly, and I shall miss her to the end of my days.

After 1942, there were no more letters and messages of encouragement from family. After completing her training in early March, Mary failed her preliminary examination. Allowed to repeat the exam, she passed on the second try. On March 30, 1943, the Assistant Secretary of Region 7 of the Jewish Refugee Committee visited the hospital in Savernake and noted, "She is in full charge of a ward. Very nice girl indeed."

Records kept by the Jewish Refugee Council from this time indicate that Mary had been engaged to a man named Peter Barnes, a sergeant in the Army Intelligence Corp, a German Jew from Baden, who likely had an assumed name because of the nature of his work, On February 11, 1944, she wrote Dr. Van der Zyl at the Refugee Council about her marriage plans later that year in June, and on March 3, he sent his congratulations.[3] There was no further word about the marriage taking place. Mary never talked about this episode in her life, and it remains a mystery to this day. There is no publicly available military record of a Peter Barnes having served in British Army Intelligence.

On March 28, Mary informed the Jewish Refugee Council that she had been transferred from Savernake Hospital to the Radcliffe Infirmary.

> Our little cottage hospital was an accredited training school, but on account of its size, we had to transfer to the Radcliffe Infirmary, a large Oxford hospital for further training to graduate. In the beginning of 1944, I packed my two suitcases, waved a long farewell to Savernake Hospital and my beloved forest, and was off to Oxford

where I was to spend two more years in training to become a registered nurse. Oxford was a big town with many confusing streets, very different from Marlborough. It didn't have a High Street, so typical of little villages, with crooked pavements and cobble stone streets and small friendly shops. It didn't have a forest, but there was the Isis, a big river with green banks on each side. Oxford was a lively place, especially its many colleges, and this later became quite an attraction for me. The Radcliffe Infirmary was enormous. It even had medical students. I was separated from the nurses I knew at Savernake, and everything seemed impersonal. I don't remember any specific wards or duties I performed, or what I studied in class. I just remember running down to the river as fast as I could change clothes after coming off duty. There I felt free and happy. My studies suffered. Whatever happened to my dream of becoming another Miss Nightingale? I could have managed at Savernake, but the Radcliffe Infirmary had nothing to do with my idea of Miss Nightingale, who would tuck in her patients lovingly, and be patient, warm, and concerned at a moderate pace (except in case of fire and hemorrhage). I just wasn't suited for a big hospital, working like a machine. When I was called into the office of the Matron of the Radcliffe Infirmary and was told that I was not suited for finishing my training, I fell apart and blamed it all on the matron who, to my way of thinking at the time, must have been antisemitic. Only today do I remember that she also said I should go back to Savernake Hospital because I was best suited for a cottage hospital. There was no way to become a trained registered nurse that way. I felt angry, lost and disappointed. Where was I to go?

On July 25, 1944, Mary reported to the Jewish Refugee Council that she had been given a month notice to leave the Radcliffe Infirmary because her ward work was not considered up to standard. There may have been personality conflicts. On July 26, a representative from the Council talked to Nurse Williams of the Regional Nursing Offices, who confirmed that Mary ran afoul with her supervisor, stating, "In my opinion, Matron is anti-alien and the training school extremely strict." Nurse Williams wanted to see what could be done to help her and sought to have her placed as an assistant nurse in an orthopedic nursing facility where only two years of experience was required.

The Jewish Refugee Council also tried to help Mary deal with the emotional fallout from her forced change in career plans. It's not known whether she informed the Council about the broken engagement to Peter Barnes while she was at the Radcliffe. She kept the entire matter a secret for the rest of her life. Instead, she focused on how she got together with my father, Denis Horne, a student at Oxford.

> I met Denis swimming in my beautiful river Isis. He was in a punt, and we called out to each other. I was invited into the boat all dripping wet and he took me back to the place where I had my clothes. He was a student at one of the colleges, studying English literature. He was very tall, dark haired, hazel eyes – in other words, quite handsome, and my senior by about seven years. We became friends and I would say, good friends. I visited him in my free time, and he took me often with him to the Students Union, where a lot of debates took place, like in the House of Commons.

At some point during the halcyon days of their early romance, Denis became aware of Mary's difficulties in adjusting to the discipline and routines at the Radcliffe Infirmary and her forced departure. She gave a vague explanation for not wanting to accept help from the Jewish Council and explained what she expected from Denis from that point on.

> I packed my two suitcases again and tried to figure out where to go. I could have presented myself at a local Jewish committee asking for help, but I did not like organizations. They reminded me of being in a foster home. But I did have a friend, Denis, my only good friend. I arrived with suitcases at his doorstep and asked him if I could stay.

This turned out to be a big step since Mary and Denis became more than friends and he became my father.

6

OXFORD DAYS

More than two decades after Mary showed up at Denis's doorstep on Walton Street during his student days, I finally met my father in Rome where he had settled since leaving England for good a decade earlier. That was in 1967 shortly after I turned 22, about the same age Mary was when she first met him in Oxford. He hadn't seen me since I was a toddler, and knew very little about me, probably less than the little I knew about him based on what my mother had told me. Naturally, I wanted to see for myself and understand what this Englishman, Denis Faulkner Horne, might have had in common with Mary Krotoczynski when they first met.

My visit to Rome in 1967 revealed aspects of my father's personality, intellect, and interests that struck me as typically English until I realized how much his difficulties as an expat colored his outlook and perspective on England. Eventually, I came to understand that Italy served as a prism for his English past. It took much longer to get his account of his days with Mary in Oxford during the 1940s. It wasn't until 1980 when she sent my father a copy of her autobiography that he was prompted to write about how they met.

> I got a copy of the Krotoczynski Saga and have to say with you that I was disappointed; there is obviously a block somewhere in Mama's otherwise perfectly fictional subconscious. We must try to get it

51

published in "Mother's Own" or translated into Italian. I am sure it would be snapped up over here by "La Familia Cristiana" though there might be some difficulty about marriage rites. I have thought of writing in all the missing matters, which add little substantially to the story but at least would make it seem that it really happened and was not just invented. For example, why is there nothing about other characters at Oxford? I did not, by the way, pick Mary "all dripping wet" out of the Isis as she romantically "remembers." It was much more banal. An acquaintance, Lillie Price, introduced me to her and our first meeting was in the University Union Club.

I thought that my father's reaction was off the mark. He failed to acknowledge that she only set out to tell her story with a focus on her emotions and expectations, not to provide a chronicle of their Oxford circle. He sidestepped the emotional aspects of their relationship by focusing on their differences in temperament.

Omitting details, Mary presented a barebones account of events with a focus on her state of mind. I gave a nod to the romantic aspects of her telling and I didn't like it when my father proceeded to strip away whatever soft-focus possibilities their first encounter might have had. Her glossy account of their initial meeting made for a good story and made me feel lucky that he had fished her out of the water. There he was, the fisher of women, the appointed protector, the tall one with the gleam of my future in his eyes.

Even though he debunked how they met, Denis was taken by Mary's exotic good looks, notwithstanding her black, curly hair and dark complexion that would have marked her for immediate deportation and extermination had she stayed in Nazi Germany. Her bright eyes and winning smile counted for something with people willing to suspend their prejudices and celebrate what their eyes could plainly see, a beautiful young woman who managed to hide her insecurities, fears, and resentments with a sense of fun and gaiety that drew from her natural innocence.

In Mary's telling, it all started very innocently, which was hard to believe given that her training as a nurse included the facts of life. Her problem, as she described it later in life, was that she was a romantic at heart that fueled her sense of abandon.

I never dreamed of the complications we ran into. To begin with, we had to share the same bed. How long will a girl and a man share the same bed before being fully aware of the fact that this bed of friendship and accommodation would turn into a love bed? And it did. Unfortunately, we missed the happy and carefree times of courtship and the conventional time of being engaged. Most of all, there was no marriage ceremony which my mother used to dream for me quite often. But one thing we didn't miss: the planting of a seed for a baby. I was going to have a baby! This was the only thing in the world I cared for, I truly cherished, my baby. Nobody could take it away from me! Denis didn't leave me, and I continued to live with him in the small room on Walton Street. And there were times when we were happy together. I used to invite Denis when I took a bath to watch my big tummy change into all sorts of shapes, and we laughed. But a cloud of uncertainty hung over our heads.

Denis must have thought that beyond their attraction to each other, they had little in common and were not likely to transform infatuation into a constructive, mutually satisfying relationship. Of course, that didn't prevent nature from taking its course. He might have expected too much understanding from her concerning his capacity to fulfill the financial, practical, and emotional demands of marriage. Denis assumed that it would have been best for Mary to adapt to her situation after having escaped from Germany. On her part, she reported that "he didn't know what hit him," trying to explain my father's surprising naiveté about his own sexual and emotional response to her. He seemed to push matters of love aside. She took his aloofness as a form of ineptitude and an unwillingness to obey the forces of nature that bind men and women together. There is no indication that she fully understood Denis's mental struggles, many stemming from his troubled upbringing, nor that he fully understood hers as a refugee trying to complete nurses training while being wracked with guilt about the fate of her parents. According to him, she dropped out of the nursing program because she couldn't abide by its strict disciplinary code. There is no evidence that he ever knew about her mysterious broken engagement to Peter Barnes.

When her pregnancy came to light, Denis's failure to attend to her emotional needs cast him in an unsympathetic light with their mutual friends. Given his literary pursuits and involvement in the theater, she realized that he was not cut out for conventional family life and that convinced her to reject his pro forma marriage proposals before and after my birth. Neither my mother nor my father gave a full account of the financial and practical matters they faced during the pregnancy and after. The Jewish Refugee Council files contained notes by her caseworker, Miss Feldman, that provided some information.

Mary called because of various letters and requests for her to come in to discuss. She told us she was pregnant and expected a baby in May. Seemed very depressed and did not look at all well. Informed Nursing Office, who was most understanding and offered to keep girl's name on the register in case she wanted to start training again after the baby was born. She is living with friend, Miss McClaren, looking after the children while the mother works as masseuse at Loving Field Hospital. Father of child is invalidated out of Army, now works with ENSA (Entertainment National Services Association) and has grant from government to take degree in English with a view of teaching (Mary is not very explicit about this). Lived at one time at Southampton University – is not on good terms with his father, who sounds very unpleasant. Will pay for the baby, as far as he can but will not marry Mary.

Three months later, Miss Feldman observed: "It appears that she has been seeing a lot of the father, who is now asking to marry her. He has paid her quite a lot of money and kept in touch with her. She tells me that he has 'improved' a great deal. Feels that marriage will be a very good solution for both."

This optimistic social worker was not privy to the many aspects of the story that my father as well as my mother eventually revealed to me. Her own assessment raised more issues than it resolved.

Unfortunately, I later realized, I would not let Denis share my baby with me. He offered to marry. He offered to adopt my maiden name, Krotoczynski, but I wanted to stay alone. It didn't even bother me that there was the legal term of "illegitimacy" involved or being called an unwed mother. Even to this day I have no proper explanation for my attitude. Was I too young, too immature? Was I afraid of Denis's intellect? He seemed awfully learned compared to my limited education. Was he a poor provider? He was still a student, who held odd jobs. Didn't I love Denis enough? Or did I believe he didn't love me enough? We just didn't have the right start. We were both children, products of the war, which affected us in different ways. Denis had spent a year in prison for being a conscientious objector and I lived in a self-constructed prison.

When Denis read Mary's autobiography, he took a dim view of her account of their precarious relationship when they lived together on Walton Street. According to him, there was a chorus of judgmental bystanders who took a keen interest in their situation and muddied the waters.

Then again why the silence on the MacDonalds who lived on the floor above in the three-story corner house where Nicholson, a university lecturer in statistics, divided with me a three-room apartment, and on the ground floor was a greengrocer's shop. She lived with the MacDonalds for nearly the whole period of gestation. The omission is not so trivial as it sounds as MacDonald, another lecturer at the university, was, like Nicholson, a full member of the British Communist Party, and his girlfriend, daughter of an English Earl, and not then divorced, also had a baby "out of wedlock." As you can imagine, there was a great deal of social solidarity on the part of Nicholson and MacDonald and some rather typical "upper class" torch bearing for Mary on the part of the Lady who was convinced that it "would be better for the child to have a normal home." In the circumstances, a deliciously unconscious observation. I was not regarded with approval by MacDonald, a tough Glasgow Scot, who took the view that Mary deserved better than an anti-Stalinist Trotskyite with marked anarchist tendencies as I then was. The debate went on over my head (Nicholson remained coldly aloof in his typical albino way) for the whole of the time Mary was guested by the MacDonalds. At that time, I had no grant and lived on what I could earn by doing odd jobs which included carrying the dead out of Cowley Hospital into cold storage and tutoring candidates for pre-university exams.

In her writings, Mary only mentioned Joan MacDonald, but nothing about her except that she provided companionship and support during her pregnancy during Denis's long absences.

> In the flat upstairs was a young woman, Joan, who had a beautiful son, about four years old. His father was from India and the child was also born "illegitimately." I spent a lot of time with her because Denis was gone a lot, and I felt neglected. Joan introduced me to a home for unwed mothers in South Croydon where I could have my baby, and it was time to pack my suitcase again, but this time for a happy occasion!

The home for unwed mothers, Birdhurst Lodge, was in a London suburb about 15 miles from Oxford. It was established as a birthing center by the Mission of Hope. Mary made willing use of this organization but did not respond to their overtures to put her baby up for adoption.

> I was in labor about 36 hours, but this didn't really bother me. I was healthy and strong. The midwife in charge of me gave me a bucket with water and told me to scrub out the dining room, telling me that I had many hours of labor pains ahead of me. This didn't bother me either because I was too involved with the forthcoming event. I wanted a boy very much! Why a boy? Perhaps I felt that a boy might have an easier life, but that is not true. Perhaps I wanted a boy for my father so he could say kaddish for him, and to continue his name. No wonder the phrase "being in labor" is used to describe the act of giving birth. The powerful uterine contractions involved the entire body, every muscle, and finally the crescendo arrived, and I was able to push with all my strength, as though to move a mountain from one side to another, and suddenly my body opened, and all was calm. My baby had put his head into the world, and a few seconds later (and I don't remember the pain) his beautiful little body was simply sliding along my thighs to complete the journey of his birth. A healthy, beautiful, dark-headed baby boy! It is too simple to say that I was happy. I find it almost impossible to describe how I felt. This tiny creature who grew inside me, how complete a human being, equipped for life. I would give him all the love and tenderness and protection, and everything I was capable to

give him. I wonder how Denis felt. I never asked him. He brought me a bouquet of flowers, irises. Denis went with me to the registrar, signing his name on the baby's birth certificate with mine. I named my baby Peter.

After my birth, Mary returned to Oxford to stay with Denis, but because of quarrels and money problems she left him.

Nothing had changed between Denis and myself, and I kept insisting I didn't want to get married. I never understood my true reasons for refusal. Perhaps Denis did not match the Prince Charming I sometimes dreamed about, who would arrive on his magic carpet and fly us to a far land full of sunshine. Something had to be done about the unhappy situation between Denis and myself, and so I moved out with my baby into a domestic job.

The Jewish Committee helped Mary find housing and support herself through domestic work in Oxford where she wanted to remain. This brought a new set of challenges.

Now there was no one I could complain to about my domestic duties which lasted from morning to night. I didn't even have time to feel miserable. At night, I was so tired I simply fell into bed. Peter was such a good baby and fit right into my work schedule. When he needed a little entertainment, I used to put him in his carriage under a tree to watch the leaves. I was able to breastfeed Peter and we were a great team.

I didn't last too long on this domestic job. The people there acted unpleasant towards me. Besides, I didn't like being a domestic servant, but seemed to have no other choice. I wanted to provide for my baby. Denis showed up occasionally to see if I was treated well. I was treated as well as a domestic servant got treated. Besides all the endless duties, I had to eat alone in the kitchen. But there were the serene and rewarding hours I could spend with Peter in my room.

Due to the heavy work schedule and unfriendly working conditions, Mary left to find a similar situation, this time with a large family whose informality appealed to her.

I was taken into the family. There were other children, I think six, and I didn't feel the burden of the chores as before. I don't remember why I left this pleasant household. Then I kept house for a very old lady in a huge house on top of a hill outside Oxford. Denis visited often, but mostly to play chess with the old lady.

Although my financially strapped father visited my mother to make sure she was well treated, there was no path to reconciliation. She had already refused his marriage offer; and when her potential mother-in-law, Annie Elizabeth Horne, stopped by for what appeared to be little more than an inspection visit, it was clear to Mary that her future with Denis was not meant to be.

One day, I had a visit from Denis's mother who wanted to see her little grandson. When I tried to make excuses for not being married, she told me that I shouldn't feel guilty because Denis was very hard to get along with when he lived at home. As much as I didn't want to marry Denis, I did not like what his mother said about him. And so the months went by, with Peter getting bigger and more beautiful, as if that were possible. We seldom saw Denis.

Mary never met Denis's father, nor his brother, Jack; however, she met his sister, Monica, who served with distinction in the Royal Air Force in a unit attached to the Fighter Command, first as a wireless operator and then as a radar operator. The two women liked each other. Years later, Monica wrote me: "...I first met your mother, Mary, with Denis in London. She was very pretty and fun to be with and I became very fond of her." However, she said Denis and Mary had many roadblocks to their union. Monica echoed my father's account of the "risks" their marriage would face as Denis explained to me in a letter in which he blamed Mary for not taking the plunge.

My own view was that marriage would have been good for nobody except perhaps the lady on the floor above who would thus have justified, vicariously, her own situation. However, when it seemed that I was going to get a government bursary, I suggested to Mary that we might take the risk despite all the fundamental differences (of temperament, mental interests and so on). It was at this point that she dug her heels in, opted for the unmarried mother situation which on purely materialistic grounds was a real advantage for her at the time. She then had you in a private clinic and we celebrated the great event by going to York where I managed to make some much-needed money acting in the York Festival Company's production of "The Alchemist." After that we returned to Oxford and set up a ménage à trois with an ancient, titled lady who had taken a fancy to Mary. It was while we were there that M. met (I don't remember how) the POW Wiesner. The rest you know.

As for the rest of the story concerning POW Wiesner, there were a few things I didn't know until after my mother died when I obtained additional information from the archives of the Jewish Refugees Committee. These indicated that Dr. Van der Zyl counseled Mary during her pregnancy and also met with Denis to discuss her needs as an unwed mother. On one occasion, Mary contacted Dr. Van der Zyl to discuss the religious aspects of raising a child with a non-Jewish father. Apparently, he also forwarded a letter to her from Ernst Champanier, who wrote in 1945 that he was alive and well in Langfuhr, close to Danzig, Germany. To my knowledge, she never contacted him.

Perhaps most telling, from the Committee's perspective, are the notes from an interview with a social worker helping Mary to resolve the practical issues she faced as a single parent, including Denis's muddled role.

Mary came to discuss her immediate future. Has given notice at her present place as she cannot cope with the work. Cook for a family of four adults and six children. I will phone Miss Feldman who will try to fix Mary's child up at Bedford. Mary will then try to find a job near the child. Tried to impress upon her the importance of a solicitor's agreement for the father to sign. Mary had applied to the Home Office to be allowed a change of name. This was rejected. Her attitude towards the child's father is very protective; she describes him as generous and solicitous, but much against any interference from the Committee, etc., and "legal steps." Mary is of an appealing nature, but very weak, with rather vague ideas of how best to cope with life. Feels very inferior in every respect (education, experience, intelligence) to the father of her child. They do not intend to get married. Their relationship is, to quote Mary, "on an economic basis" which I am afraid has no solid foundation at all. Letter from Mary stating she is feeling better now and is more able to cope with things. Learning shorthand and typing and hopes to enter evening classes as soon as they open. The baby is doing well, and Mary sees him regularly.

Mary apparently did not tell her social worker that she had met Heinz Wiesner, a handsome red-haired German prisoner of war with blue eyes, three years her junior, perhaps a grown-up version of her childhood playmate, Hans-Joachim, the little blue-eyed, blond boy next door in Friedland, Mecklenburg.

Mary described the circumstances of how she met Heinz Wiesner while taking a walk in Oxford, away from her housekeeping duties for "the very old lady" who played chess with my father.

My duties with the old lady couldn't have been too demanding because I used to take Peter for long rides in his carriage and I was also walking alone at times. One day, outside Oxford, I walked by a big complex fenced in with barbed wire for POWs waiting for repatriation, most of them young, my age. I never made the connection that these men were soldiers of the *Vaterland* that persecuted the Jewish people, my people, and put them in death camps. Instead of remembering when I was torn away from my parents, I chatted with these soldiers of the Third Reich as if they were eligible boyfriends. I believed them when they told me that they had nothing to do with the war and they didn't even want to fight. We never touched the Jewish question. And I believed them and felt sorry for them for being so far away from home. One of the prisoners stood out, medium tall, reddish-blond wavy hair, bright blue eyes and athletic build. Heinz hailed from Berlin, my old or rather ex-hometown. He gave me more and more attention and I became starry-eyed. My handsome prince? I was so taken in that I didn't even notice that he spoke the worst Berlin dialect, like a thick Cockney, only worse. The prisoners received permission to leave the camp for a few hours a week which enabled me to meet Heinz in Oxford. I introduced him to Peterle. It was a great success. They really enjoyed each other. Usually, Peterle wasn't too happy about meeting men, but he had no objections to Heinz, and so the three of us went for many walks stopping occasionally for a glass of apple cider. Heinz focused his attention on Peterle, often remarking that he wished he were his son, something that pleased me. To this day, I believe Heinz loved Peterle with a sincere heart. We took walks alone, heading to the outskirts of Oxford into secluded parts of nature. He took me into his arms, and I knew then he didn't only love my baby, he also loved me. I wanted to give him a baby of his own and I was not afraid of the consequences. Meanwhile, Heinz had written his family about Peterle and me. He wanted us to go home with him, back to Berlin. I received mail from his mother expressing her anticipation and pleasure to greet us. When I told Heinz I was pregnant, he was not particularly surprised. He just told me that there was no time to get married, because his repatriation was due any time, and said that, no matter what happened, I was to plan immediately to return to Berlin with Peterle. I had mixed feeling about going back, but not strong enough to indulge any doubt, feelings of guilt, or hatred towards the old or even present-day enemy.

She was drawn to Heinz Wiesner whose declaration of love for her was unqualified. Meanwhile, she rejected Denis's final marriage offer to keep her in England. Miffed, she felt there was no reason for her to take up my father's empty-handed offer, too little and too late.

What did I have in England? Oh yes, I met Denis shortly before I left England and he offered to marry me with my unborn child, but I had committed us. We were about to leave for Berlin where we were anxiously awaited by Heinz, who had been repatriated a few months before, and his family. I did look forward to having a family again.

Mary put a fatalistic twist on her decision to leave Denis to marry Heinz. Since she was expecting a second child, there were no other desirable options but to leave England for a fresh start, no matter what. I can only speculate as to how her mind and emotions ricocheted between hope and despair, reality and fantasy, rejection and desire, as she lived through events in Oxford. As time went on, Denis became a somewhat idealized fixture in her thoughts as the realities of her troubled marriage to Heinz became obvious. Although Mary understood that there was no possibility of having a normal family in England, she was probably not aware of all the facts about

Denis's dysfunctional family, including the way his parents had flouted marriage norms themselves by living out of wedlock while his mother sought a dissolution of her previous marriage.

I found out about my father's family background when I first met him in Rome, 21 years after my mother and I had left for Germany. By that time, he had already spent ten years in Italy in a stable childless relationship with Fausta, a talented artist whom he would eventually marry. His professional and personal life had shifted to his new homeland, and he had mastered its language. He felt no incentive to return to England for either family or professional reasons.

He talked about his troubled childhood and early adult life to explain why he wasn't cut out for marriage. Perhaps his background may have accounted for his becoming an "angry young man" and a committed conscientious objector. After completing his heady but "impractical education" at Oxford, he had a promising career as a stage actor, playwright and filmmaker in London, interrupted by a short foray into politics in 1950 when he ran for Parliament as a Liberal. While he regaled me with the saga of his life, I could see that much of his animus was directed at those who prevented him from reaping the benefits of his award-winning film, *Together*, which had been shown at the Cannes Film Festival. It was co-directed with a former lover, Lorenza Mazzetti, during the early 1950s, under the auspices of the British Film Institute, but was completed in his absence by Lindsay Anderson. Lingering bitter disagreements with Anderson ensued. In his article, "The Free Cinema Hoax," Denis argues that Anderson wrongly lumped *Together*, an artistic experimental fiction film, with several BFI-funded point-of-view documentaries under the Free Cinema banner.[1]

I visited Denis again in 1970 and then not again until 2004, a year before his death. During the interim we corresponded sporadically. Although he mentioned his family in England, he was not inclined to put me in touch with them, nor did I press the issue. Denis was estranged from his younger brother, Jack, because of his fascist and racist outlook. Jack was married to a German woman with Nazi roots. This was in contrast with his younger sister, Monica Dewar, whose views were based on tolerance. Denis remained in touch with her and her children over the years because of their shared values and ideals.

My father's family background clearly indicated that he and my mother came from different worlds. Denis's father, John William Horne, descended from a well-to-do family in Northern Ireland, went to Cambridge and competed in the 1906 Olympics (1906 Intercalated Games) in Athens as a mid-distance runner.[2] He owned a preparatory school and taught his children to value education. He was said to have been an accomplished amateur pianist.

Years after my father's death in 2005, I learned more about his family from his two nieces, Naomi Boulding and Elizabeth Jones, based on what their mother, Monica Dewar, told them. J.W. Horne married Annie Elizabeth Temple in 1926 after her "scandalous" divorce from a man called Millington with whom she had one daughter, Peggy Millington.

Before they married, my grandparents had already formed a family that included 12-year-old Peggy as well as their own three children, who were born in the West Midlands.

Academically inclined but disinterested in athletics, Denis went to Bromsgrove School, one of the oldest public schools Britain, and then to University of London, and finally Oxford. His brother, Jack, went to Clayesmore, known for its rigorous athletic program. Jack was his father's favorite because of his athletic abilities. Like his father, he was a runner who trained for the Olympics, but unlike his father, he did not qualify. He served as an officer in the Royal Navy.

By 1929, at the onset of the Great Depression, Denis's father lost so much money that he could no longer afford private education for his third child, Monica, and out of snobbishness refused to send her to the village school. She spent one miserable year at a convent school in Northampton after which she ran away from home to join the RAF.[3]

Like his sister and brother, Denis followed the family tradition by serving in the military after the war started, but his pacifist leanings and leftist political views quickly put him at odds with the British government. After he had served in the Army for two years, he left the regiment and was court-martialed. His father came to his defense by attributing his son's dereliction to his being emotionally overwrought. Denis testified at the court martial proceedings that he was a conscientious objector based on political as well as moral grounds.

After being imprisoned for less than a year, he was assigned to alternative duty in Oxford in late 1942, where later on he applied to Oxford University and was accepted.

At age 27, Denis was older than the typical residential students affiliated with the established university colleges. He joined the university's Saint Catherine's Society which grew out of the Delegacy of Unattached Students that enabled students to gain an Oxford education without the costs of college membership. Unlike the other colleges at Oxford, today's "Catz" did not have its own campus at that time. Denis was well established at the university when he met Mary in early 1944.

Despite glaring differences in their backgrounds, Mary and Denis shared similar political views and spirited personalities. As a teenager, Mary had been exposed to the Communist Party through friends and could sing "The Internationale" in German with vigor and conviction. She would have applauded Denis's stand as a conscientious objector on political as well as moral grounds. They were kindred spirits in dissent. "All wars are criminal endeavors," Denis wrote to me one time. I heard echoes of my mother's voice in that statement and got a feeling for the flavor of the kind of opinions he might have shared with her. Once sympathetic to communism and then a Trotskyite, Denis had already rejected Stalinism. He certainly did not support any aspect of mainstream communism by the time he ran for parliament in the 1950 General election as a Liberal Party candidate for Brentford and Chiswick in West London. In that race, he came in third with 2086 votes behind the Tories and Labor, but ahead of the Communist candidate.

Several years ago, my Aunt Monica sent me a copy of a letter that Denis had sent to his father from jail to explain why he refused to fight for king and country on both political and moral grounds. The tone of this lengthy letter illustrates the aspects of his mindset that she did not fully understand. When Denis wrote this letter, he described himself as an anti-Stalinist Trotskyite. He never joined the Communist Party. In hindsight, I find it difficult to reconcile his pacifist political views, whatever they were at that time, with the moral imperative to defeat the Nazis. I find it intriguing that his sister, Monica, a decorated war veteran, acknowledged the sincerity of his moral and political outlook regarding Britain's involvement in World War II.

Mary never saw the convoluted letter that contained Denis's explanation of his anti-militarist pacifism. She preferred to think of him as an anarchist who was court martialed for driving a tank into a wall to rebel against military discipline. I believe she served up this fictitious tale, despite her own hatred for war, because she found it unthinkable not to stop Hitler. They clearly did share a distain of established authority but expressed it in different ways.

It is likely that Denis's political views were shaped during the time he spent at University of London before the war, several years before he was admitted to Oxford. He admired writers such as H.G. Wells, Bertrand Russel, and George Orwell. There is no evidence that he was ever a staunch ideologue despite the fleeting admiration for communism he described in this letter.

> My personal affection is Russia, and my hope is communism, and my belief is that the world will get communism just as soon as the people decide that communism is necessary. I decided this four years ago and so in a war like the present it is not surprising to those who know me that I have ended up in prison. My moral objection to war is of course implied in what I have said above. In a communist world, you would not have armies, you would have a police force, exactly as you do in sovereign states. (The idea of sovereignty might remain, dissociated from all class interests). The police use force to enforce law. An army uses violence to assert its will. The difference seems as plain to me as that between earning and stealing. I have a moral objection to the latter or why am I not here on a charge of petty larceny? (Nothing is easier in the army – most of my kit was stolen.) As far as I am concerned, the rightness of killing does not enter the question at all. It seems to me that if you really believe it is wrong to kill in all circumstances, then you must try to do away with all lethal weapons or instruments, including the motor car. This seems absurd. But as I say I am not concerned at present with that question. The real enemy is War, and I don't propose to be sidetracked by religious gentlemen with comfortable stipends who can preach "Christianity" and "justify" the war all in the same sermon.

Denis's letter went on further to describe his experience in jail, including work details and rules regarding contact with the outside world. He had no complaints about jail conditions, assuring his father that his basic needs were met. Matters related to education and intellectual pursuits served as a common ground in an otherwise fraught relationship between Denis and his father. Denis asked his father to contact publishers, such as *Poetry Review*, on his behalf regarding a review he had written about W.H. Auden. He also discussed his university education plans with his father in this concluding paragraph.

> I have not replied to a letter from London University asking me if I propose to register again. I should be able to make some plans perhaps if I had their syllabus for 1942-3. Perhaps you can get this and send. You can reassure Mother when you write – there were nearly 20 to inform, hence the 'so called letter.' I sent a similar one to her, so she knows. None of these Commissions are really urgent, except the note to Dr. Lister. If your headmaster asks about me, please let him know the facts. No medical excuses. Show him this letter if you like & ask his opinion whether I am "overwrought." That is all the news up to the present. All the best and a good term. Love, Denis.

After his stint in jail, the military authorities allowed him to do alternate service in a hospital morgue in Oxford. His conscientious objector status did not prevent him from seeking a degree at Oxford through a government grant. The authorities didn't treat him harshly, perhaps due to lobbying by his father, a military veteran, who believed that his son was the victim of a treatable psychological aberration that could be mitigated, if not through professional help, then through further education at Oxford. The letter Denis wrote to his father contains little of the simple intimacy and affection expressed in the wartime letters between Mary and her parents written during the war years. Instead, it was all about the class-bound negotiated expectations shared by the educated elite.

There is no indication that Mary fully understood Denis's mental struggles, or that he fully understood hers. Each saw the rebel in the other but didn't seem to forge a bond of understanding or common purpose. This wasn't the case when she met Heinz Wiesner, the POW who was smitten by her and wanted nothing more than to return to Germany with her. She believed him when he told her that he wasn't a Nazi and had surrendered willingly at the first opportunity. Since she was an enemy alien in a country that didn't fully accept her, she willingly accepted him when she became pregnant with his child. This time, the father was thrilled with the news and wanted to bring her home to his working-class family. They were an unlikely couple on an impossible mission to become whole in a broken world.

7

REPATRIATION

After the repatriation of German POWs began in 1946, Heinz Wiesner returned to Berlin in late 1947 and Mary soon followed. The German Consulate on Belgrave Square issued her a German passport, and so she ceased to be a stateless person in England and received financial assistance from the Jewish Refugee Committee to pay expenses associated with her return to Germany.

In 1948, I returned to the Fatherland. There wasn't much to pack, just our clothing, a few books, a few sentimental articles, and, of course, our passports with visas. I don't know how the Germans figured out that I was still a German citizen since I was made stateless in 1938. Peterle, of course, was British. They sent us with a trainload of repatriated soldiers, and I was the only woman with a little boy among 100s of soldiers. Neither of us complained. We never had so much attention. Peter spent the journey being bounced from lap to lap, laughing all the way back to Berlin. There was my Prince Charming, standing in a gloomy, partially destroyed railway station. We took a streetcar, then walked to where his family lived. I was acquainted with Berlin, also parts of East Berlin where there were many four-story walk-ups, like the one where I had lived with my family. I wasn't prepared for the Berlin that had been through heavy air raids. It was a mess which resulted in an enormous housing shortage, as I was to find out. After climbing four stories, we came to the Wiesner family apartment where we were greeted with much enthusiasm, especially for my little Peter, who was taken into everyone's arms. My heart sank when I saw the size of the apartment. Everything was small, but spotlessly clean. How were we going to fit into it? Father, mother, Heinz's younger sister, Heinz, Peterle, and I, not to mention the baby that was due in five months. Right there the image of Prince Charming, and the things he would do, crumbled. I was too young and too impatient to look at this merely as a steppingstone. And I knew that Heinz was not too happy either. He couldn't find a job for a while and his father carried the whole family, doing some menial labor. Up to this point, I might have been spoiled, getting my way. But this time was different. I simply couldn't see myself out of this situation. After Heinz had taken me to the registrar to make our union legal, my mother-in-law gave us a little wedding reception in our small room, and all I remember is that my chronic state of heartburn reached an acute state after eating too many sour herrings. Nothing was our own. Heinz had to borrow a suit from a friend, who was also our best man, and I had to borrow a hat from Anna, my mother-in-law. I am sure that this was not the type of wedding my mother had hoped for me. But I became a Mrs.

Mary had only a few facts about Heinz's parents, Anna and Erich, his two sisters, Margot and Dorchen, and his older brother, Kurt, who was killed in the war. Long after her death, I tried to find out more through online German public records, including birth and marriage records, census data, and military service prior to World War I. Failing at that, I have relied on what my mother told me about Heinz and his family and what I saw and heard as a child.

The Wiesner family lived in a working-class neighborhood in the Russian sector of occupied East Berlin that had partially survived the Allied bombing. Their apartment was in a block of four-story buildings on 50 Ebertystrasse in the Friedrichshain section. Behind the building was a small courtyard where kids played hopscotch and hide-and-seek or jumped rope, stopping only to pee under a tree, when necessary, well within sight of their mothers who kept watch from the windows above. Occasionally, a beggar appeared in the courtyard playing an accordion for pfennigs pitched from windows.

Mothers shouted out to call their kids in for lunch, which was usually a *Stulle* [open-face sandwich] spread with jam or bacon grease with onion and salt.

Omi Anna did her best to keep the small apartment spotless and to cook meals with whatever ingredients could be mustered. Heinz's sister, Margot, and her husband, who had their own apartment, were members of the East German Socialist Unity Party. They may have used their influence to provide perks for the family. We hardly saw them. Mary had a tough time adjusting to life among the proletariat.

My new family tried to be nice to me, but they were not the kind of people I had hoped for. They were so typical East Berliner, not only because they distorted the German language, which I found upsetting, but also because I found them (or their background) crude and outright insensitive. If my parents had seen me then, both would have died of instant heart failure. My only happy thought was little Peter. I kept praying for a little sister for him. Anna was the type of East Berliner who could have been best described by Zille, the German caricaturist. The only difference is that Zille would have drawn lovingly and with understanding, whereas I had few kind words to say about her. We competed for Heinz, and she would report to him all the faults she could find in me. Although I found her difficult to take, I realized that she did love Peter as if she were his real grandmother. My father-in-law, Erich, was less crude than the rest of the family. He was inoffensive and mild spoken and had nothing to say in the household which was dominated by Anna. I really liked him. He worked long hours, came home after a few beers and then cried in front of the picture of his oldest son, Kurt, who died in his arms on the Russian front where they had served together. Dorchen, my 14-year-old sister-in-law, was okay. She spent much of her free time playing with Peterle and teaching him German. Heinz and I had absolutely no privacy and consequently lost communication. It was sad to see Heinz change from the vigorous young man I met in England to an unhappy burdened person within a year. The only thing that seemed to console him was his many glasses of beer and schnapps. While he was drinking, I spent endless hours crying in the toilet, the only private spot available. I was once caught crying by Peterle, who asked with great concern whether I drank too much water when he saw the tears streaming out of my eyes.

The birth of my sister, Monika, during the Berlin Airlift in 1948 provided a needed diversion as well as a new set of challenges for life in a small apartment. Monika was born in the Jüdisches Krankenhaus in the French Sector where Mary's father had died. Miraculously, the main building of the hospital, built in 1914, survived the war.[1] Mary's description of Monika's birth again evoked the joy that she once ascribed to my birth and to her own.

The labor pains made me forget my unfortunate circumstances. Again, I was involved in the most beautiful experience of giving birth. Again, no pre-natal care, except for seeing a doctor once who told me that he couldn't hear the fetal heartbeat. He had me worried for three months and most of all during the last stages of labor. When my labor began, Heinz took me to the Jewish Hospital where my father had spent his last days. I had to stand, or hobble from one leg to the other, all the way. As soon as I was admitted, my pains stopped. My uterus had stopped contracting and it took just one injection to continue full labor. A couple of pains, and then came the enormous shaking of my body, exit-demanding final pain accompanied by a giant scream, pain and joy intermingled, a tiny head and then little body came slithering out. I sat up to find out if my baby was all right. Dear God, thank you, I had my little girl. There was nothing wrong with her, heartbeat was fine, and she cried. Peterle, you had a sister, and I had my little girl. She was named Monika, a name taken from a novel I had read some time ago. Her middle name, Gertrud, was in memory of my mother. This happy event did little to change my relationship with my husband and his family. I still couldn't adjust to their way of life or the way they expressed themselves. Heinz took little notice of his new baby, but I couldn't hold this against him because many young fathers do the same. Heinz preferred to dress up Peterle, take him for walks, show him off in the neighborhood, always proclaiming that Peter was his son, whom he "made" in England. With Monika's arrival, we emptied the wicker laundry basket, lined it with some pretty material, put it on the stove in the kitchen, the only empty space available, and called it the nursery.

With a new baby in the house, the total number in the household was seven, with no escape from the din of fussing and bickering in dark, close quarters. A window in the front bedroom faced the street. The adjacent kitchen and back bedroom, which doubled as a living room, had small windows facing the courtyard. There was a toilet with a sink, but no bathtub. A lot of personal scrubbing took place in the wash basin in the kitchen. Anna Wiesner made sure the place was shipshape.

Mary knew better than to cross my "Omi" Anna. She respected her mother-in-law's fortitude under adversity but resented her intrusiveness. Anna's legendary common sense prevailed when Monika became sick due to malnutrition. She kept Monika out of the hospital and gave her improvised sugar water and flour pap as a nutritional substitute when breastfeeding failed and cow's milk was unavailable. Thanks to her grandmother, Monika recovered.

There was much talk about the Berlin Airlift that began on June 26, 1948, two days after Monika was born, and lasted for nearly a year. Everything was rationed and things brightened up when packages arrived from relatives in America packed with Hershey chocolates and Carnation condensed milk. That summer, we relocated to a farm outside Berlin where Heinz found work through a friend. Then we returned to Berlin to live with Heinz's parents again. Conditions gradually improved.

As soon as she could after arriving in Germany, Mary looked up her cousin, Irene, who had survived the war in Berlin to find out if there was anything else she knew about what happened to her mother and the rest of the family. She hoped Irene could tell her what had happened to her friend Thea-Margot and her husband, Edgar Metzger before they were deported, and about Ernst Champanier, who figured prominently in her wartime correspondence. For some reason, she never mentioned Ernst in her stories and writings, nor is there any evidence that she corresponded with him after the war. I wonder whether she was aware that he was a concentration camp survivor and emigrated to England in 1948 shortly after she returned to Berlin.

Given his reported influence during her teenage years, I sought information about Ernst Champanier that might explain why Mary did not keep in touch with him despite his close friendship with her parents. What I found out was that he was born in about 1908, the son of a cantor, Julius Champagner, from Breslau whose name was spelled differently. After Ernst was deported from Berlin to Riga in 1942, he was forced to work for Organisation Todt in Nittau named for its founder, Fritz Todt. He was also assigned to the Ghetto hospital in Riga, and then to a dental laboratory near the Kaiserwald concentration camp. Liberated by the Russian Army, Ernst came to the UK in 1948 to join his half-sister, Edith Rosenthal, who went there in 1939. Since he was very critical of the German-Jewish bourgeoisie, he did not get in touch with the refugee community in the UK. He was active in the anthroposophical community and supported the Red Cross as well as the International Friendship League that sent parcels to Germany after the war. He died in England in 2003 where he was also known as Ernst Mitchell.[2]

In early 1950, Mother took Monika and me to visit her cousin, Irene, at her apartment in West Berlin a short time before she left for America to joint her mother and sister's family in New Hampshire. She explained that one never visits empty-handed, so we went to a flower shop and picked out carnations. After Irene greeted us at the door with affectionate hugs, she placed the flowers in a vase and offered us some cookies and candies. I was distracted by her solid Victorian-era furniture and a grandfather clock that chimed on the hour.

Irene understood and sympathized with Mary's situation. She didn't judge her for having married outside of Judaism since she herself was the product of a mixed marriage. Irene represented a role model, an independent and unmarried woman not hampered by religion or ethnicity, who encouraged her to think about building a new life in America. By nature, Irene was stoical and good natured, qualities that contributed to her survival during the war, as did her non-Jewish looks and Aryan surname.

Mary often talked about her relatives in America, and held out the hope that we, too, might someday live in America to escape the widespread hardships and the grim residues of war in plain sight all around us. I remember our trolley ride through a neighborhood that had been partially cleared but was still dotted with standing ruins. As we rattled through a long stretch of cleared city blocks, huge electric transmission towers with drooping power lines receded into the distance and disappeared. After arriving in our neighborhood within walking distance of our apartment, I pointed out the rubble spilled into the street. With a fearful look, my mother reminded me not to play there because of the possibility of tripping unexploded bombs. Wherever we went, amputees hobbled on crutches among the crowds as daily reminders of the war.

I learned that the German word, *gefallen*, referred to soldiers who perished. The bedroom bureau was where the photo of Heinz's older brother, Kurt, was enshrined. It seems that Kurt had been the favorite son, a fact that helped drive Heinz to drink.

Anna and Erich continued to provide a steadying presence in the household. While *Omi* [Grandma] ran the household without fuss, *Opa* [Grandpa] was less of a disciplinarian. He was easy on me after repeated toilet training failures and took me on my first excursions into the world riding on the back of his bike. I didn't mind the bumpy cobblestones that made the bike rattle.

Heinz spent a lot of time drinking in the *Kneipe* [a small bar that doesn't serve food] downstairs and bragged that the owner was his good friend. Several times my mother sent me there to fetch him so that he wouldn't squander more money on beer and schnapps. I came to detest the reek of his beery breath. When drunk, Heinz would ask me which parent I loved the most. He called me "the little Englishman" and on one occasion made defensive remarks about my mother's resourceful Jewish connections. I became increasingly aware of the conflicts in our family at that time. I called my mother "Mutti" but don't remember addressing my stepfather as "Vati" or "Papa" and don't recall my mother referring to him as such, either in his presence or during his frequent absences. For me, he was just "Heinz."

One time, Heinz came home drunk, and in a foul mood picked me up and threw me against the bedroom wall. I was more stunned than upset at this unexpected outburst. As Mutti cleaned my scraped thigh, she said that this would never happen again, and gave me a few pfennigs for a Kasper puppet show in the courtyard. I felt numb, inattentive, alone.

The holidays provided a diversion. The first Christmas I remember was in 1949. A few days before, Heinz previewed some shiny toys and asked me which of these I wanted for Christmas. I pointed out a red car. On Christmas Eve, Opa dressed as Saint Nicholas scaring the daylights out of me. The toys I had seen several days before did not reappear. Mutti explained that Heinz had to sell them because our family needed the cash. By this time, I had become inured to the haphazard aspects of Heinz's intentions. He was prone to make promises he couldn't keep.

As their marriage devolved, Mutti became increasingly desperate and didn't know where to turn. Instead of putting up a fight, she stifled her anger and sought out a scapegoat, which turned out to be her beloved teddy bear that had been with her since she left Berlin on the Kindertransport.

He survived the air attack over London but came to a sad end after the war. One day in 1949, after a terrible argument with my husband, I took my beloved Teddy in a state of rage and cremated him in the kitchen stove.

I didn't know at the time that Mutt and Heinz were involved the black market to make ends meet. After we arrived in America, Mutti told us the story about "liberating" beef recounted in her autobiographical notes.

Our situation improved when Heinz managed to find work at a nearby slaughterhouse. With this steady work came the temptation of the black market, which boiled down to stealing. It was all right to steal from the Russians, the archenemy who raped women when they entered Berlin in 1945. Nobody seemed to be concerned with being caught, which would have meant deportation to a Russian labor camp. Meat from the slaughterhouse, near where we lived, was taken from refrigerators, put into sacks, placed below a grate leading into the street for later pickup. Later in the middle of the night, Heinz would unscrew the grate and pull the meat up using a rope, bring it home to be repackaged in laundry baskets for sale in West Berlin. This was a risky undertaking, but fortunately neither Heinz nor his friends were caught. For them, it was worth the risk because of the money to be made. Heinz started buying furniture in anticipation of moving to a place of our own. He even bought me two fancy dresses. We then moved into our very own apartment in East Berlin which we managed to get because of my being Jewish.

Moving into their own apartment didn't help Mary and Heinz work things out. Their new privacy only accentuated their differences. For the first time, we had the outer trappings of an intact family life. We had a new Rundfunken radio that mysteriously appeared in our lives. It had a green-eyed tuner that symbolized our new station in life. Mutti was offered a job, she claimed, because of having made up a story that she had been an active communist in England. While she worked, I went to a pleasant state-run nursery school while my sister was watched by her grandparents. I remember lying awake during nap time and learning how to pick up a pencil using the toes on my right foot.

Mary was approached by Communist Party members who invited her to attend training sessions, as her sister-in-law, Margot, had done. She got cold feet when they asked her to become initiated. Living conditions improved slightly although food continued to be rationed. When the Socialist Unity Party, formed in 1949, increased its political hold in the Russian sector, there was an exodus to the other sectors of West Berlin controlled by the British, French, and Americans. Mary and Heinz talked about getting out of East Berlin, with the possibility of emigrating to America, but by this time, Mary thought about ending their marriage.

I don't remember being overjoyed having our own apartment and don't recall the street name. Even the new furniture didn't mean much. This is because Heinz started to drink heavily. Instead of coming home for dinner, he would stay out late, come home drunk and make a commotion, waking up the children. No longer under the watchful eye of his mother, he could do as he pleased. I was afraid of him because I had no experience in coping with alcoholism. Thank God, he didn't abuse the children. Had he tried, I would have turned into a wildcat. I never let him know I was afraid of him and did my share of griping and lecturing. Our relationship ended as far as I was concerned, but Heinz claimed that I would never divorce him. Little did he know that

I was searching for an opportunity to leave. But where were we to go? At that time, East Berlin was being shut off from the West. Barricades, which eventually led to the Wall, blocked traffic between East and West. I managed to persuade Heinz to risk crossing into West Berlin on the promise that we might emigrate to the United States with the help of my cousin in California. Little did he know that he didn't figure in my plans.

Leaving East Berlin became risky. The communist regime increased its grip on people's lives through the pre-war system of registration and its emerging network of neighborhood informants. Travel to the west sector was forbidden. Occasionally, the East German police boarded subway trains from West Berlin that went through the east sector, checked identification, and arrested those suspected of having moved illegally to the West. Clearly, it was time to get out.

8

FLEEING BERLIN

In 1951, there were still ways to leave East Berlin despite the checkpoints at border crossings. Based on what he knew through his network of friends, Heinz arranged our "escape" to West Berlin, possibly through bribery according to my mother.

> I found myself packing again, mostly clothes and a few household articles. I don't remember what happened to our furniture. Heinz had previously inspected all the crossing points into West Berlin, got hold of a vehicle and crossed over without incident. People in West Berlin cheered us as we left the last strip of East Berlin asphalt behind us. Initially, we stayed with friends of Heinz, a young couple with two small children, who had also fled from East Berlin. We all lived in one small room, four adults and four children. Then we moved in with an old lady. The children slept in her bedroom. Heinz and I slept in the hall.

Our landlady, Frau Schombe, was a kind elderly lady required by law to rent space because of the housing shortage. Monika and I shared her old-fashioned, curtained bedroom, as well as the bedpan therein. In one corner of the room was a grandfather clock that clicked off the seconds and chimed on the hour. In an adjoining room was a couple who fought constantly amidst their baby's cries, which didn't penetrate the old lady's ears because she was partially deaf. At Christmas time, Frau Schombe baked a stollen and decorated her Christmas tree with fancy glass decorations and candles that were carefully mounted on the branches. She let me pick out "Silent Night" on her foot-operated organ next to her bed. To add to the festivities, Mutti brought my favorite treat, marzipan. After Christmas day, Heinz went on a drinking spree and the festivities turned sour. It seemed to me that the entire neighborhood smelled of beer.

When I started first grade, Mutti registered me as Peter Krotoczynski, the name on my British passport, which I learned to spell soon after I learned the alphabet. She handed me a *Schultüte,* the cardboard cone filled with candies traditionally given to German kids on the first day of first grade to sweeten the onslaught of formal education. That year I got a taste of *Pauken,* the German word for drilling knowledge into students. My first-grade teacher was a stern man, whose pedagogy clearly was not based on those progressive Pestalozzi learning theories that had figured in Mary's early education. He said that ballpoint pens were the work of the devil and exalted the elegant fountain pen. In school we used old dip pens that required both deft dipping and assiduous drip avoidance. This antiquated method was still an improvement over using my finger to write imaginary words in the air as I did at home where there was little access to pens and paper.

When not in school, I schemed about how to get out in the world on my own. One day, I rented a bike for 50 pfennigs without parental permission, bruised my knees after several falls, and received a spanking from Heinz after confessing my adventurous misdeed, but there were other moments that didn't involve discipline. I recall my stepfather talking about his experience as a mechanic in a *Panzerabteilung* [tank battalion] during the war. He pointed to the scars on his neck and explained that he had been wounded while picking mines. Mutti explained that Heinz and the other soldiers on his detail were glad to have been captured by the British. As much as Heinz was fed-up with war, he was still up for discussing the relative merits of the British and German tanks and other weapons used during the conflict.

On one occasion, Heinz took our family for an outing to a patchwork of lakes surrounded by forests in the western part of Berlin. On a boat ride on the Wannsee, I was thrilled with the water swirling in the wake while some drunken adults sang, "*Wir wollen Kaiser Wilhelm wieder haben*" as if having Kaiser Wilhelm back again would make things better. Neither Mutti nor Heinz had jobs. Our family received welfare stipends, but not enough to cover all basic expenses. Extra money trickled in thanks to Mutti's entrepreneurship. Her command of English made it easy for her to deal with American soldiers who supplied her with cigarettes that she resold on the black market.

> Skirting the law seemed justified. We were not allowed to look for jobs until we were screened to make sure we weren't communists. I spent a lot of time in government agencies waiting to become a recognized West Berlin citizen. Heinz would not go with me, and I don't know how he spent his days, but I did know how he came home, drunk as before, anytime he pleased. I was exhausted waiting for him, trying to dampen the noises that would otherwise wake the neighborhood. When I didn't answer his gorilla calls, he screamed all the louder. I was on the verge of collapse.

When cousin Irene departed for America earlier on in 1950, Mary was left with no family in Berlin to turn to for emotional and financial support. Her unrelenting feelings of sadness from the loss of loved ones in the Holocaust stoked her emotional turmoil and strengthened her resolve to leave Heinz Wiesner. Monika and I accompanied Mutti on visits to Jewish agencies, where she sought legal advice on dissolving her marriage and gaining full custody of her daughter. One evening at the end of the summer in 1952, she took us to Weissensee Cemetery in East Berlin, to visit her father's grave. Crying and pointing to the sky, she told us that she could see her mother's face in the full moon looking down on us. For the first time, I realized that there was something terribly wrong with her, something beyond her control. Days later, Mutti sought treatment for clinical depression at the Jewish Hospital and took us back to East Berlin for a place to stay.

> I took Peter and Monika to a Jewish Home for children in East Berlin, the only place I knew they would be safe and well treated. I was disoriented and relied on Peter, then aged seven, to get us there. The Berlin Wall wasn't up at this time but there was a danger of being arrested by the East Berlin police for having fled the East Sector. I was

lucky. The children were accepted at the home with open arms as soon as the management became aware of my condition. Afraid to take the streetcar, I walked several miles to the Jewish Hospital back in West Berlin where Monika had been born.

The Jewish home for children was in the Pankov neighborhood of Niederschönhausen in the Russian Sector.[1] This *Kinderheim* [orphanage] was in a large family residence, part of a complex that included an old age home. Monika and I spent about nine months there, from September 1952 to June 1953. For the first time in our lives, Monika and I were away from Mutti for an extended period. This would be one of many separations in the years to come.

Not long after our arrival, I began second grade at the local public school. My teacher was a nice soft-spoken young woman, who taught us about Comrade Lenin, President Wilhelm Pieck, and the virtues of communism. She didn't impose the stern discipline I encountered as a first grader in West Berlin. One day, she announced that our class could win a trip to the Black Forest by learning the tenets of communism by heart, but we never made it there because for some reason we didn't qualify. For revenge, my disappointed schoolmates and I repeated dirty little rhymes about the Young Pioneers, the communist equivalent of the Boy Scouts.

I didn't see much of four-year old Monika who was grouped with the preschoolers. I spent most of my time with the older children but had some time for myself on my own. The staff at the orphanage prepared us for possible emigration to Israel. We learned about Jewish culture, danced the Hora, and sang Jewish songs like the Israeli national anthem, "Hatikvah." I participated in exercises to prepare for emigration to the Promised Land. My favorite was walking on a steel barrel to improve my balance.

I learned about the vagaries of "justice" when the headmaster's dog sank its teeth into my forearm after I tried to pet it. Although his pooch was not punished for biting me, the orphanage cat was "euthanized" several days later for having killed several birds. For me, this was an object lesson about the politics of justice. The scar from that bite became the identifying mark listed in my passport when it was renewed.

By this time, I was aware of the uncertainty of our family's situation. Mutti took me aside and told me more about my British parentage, and I came to realize that "Herr Wiesner," as she then called him with disdain, was to be avoided and that my real father was somewhere else. Our stepfather ceased to be part of our immediate family and Mutti kept our whereabouts a secret. This meant we also lost connection with Monika's grandparents, whom we missed. Since our stay in the Jewish *Kinderheim* gave us a measure of stability, Monika and I took these changes in stride. When Mutti assured us that we would be fine, I still believed her but with some hesitation. I don't recall seeing much of her during that time and thought she feared being stopped by police in East Berlin. At that time, I didn't know that she had been hospitalized.

Years later, she wrote about the quality of the care she received in the Jewish Hospital while we were in the orphanage.

> The hospital provided good care, rest and regular meals. Heinz was not allowed to visit. After four weeks, I was transferred to a psychiatric rest home in the suburbs surrounded by a beautiful lawn and tall trees. My psychiatrist, a young man, gave me a lot of his time. I was plagued by ambivalence, whether to leave Heinz. By now, he could visit me and was on his best behavior, full of promises. But I decided to go through with my original plan to leave him. The doctor helped me to work through my problems.

Notes from interviews by psychiatrists and social workers, available through the *Wiedergutmachung* [reparations] office of the German government, provide a lengthy summary of Mary's troubled life, including problems with her marriage and depression related to the loss of her parents and family. When she discussed her years in England, she didn't mention the well-established fact that the Cohens sheltered her after her arrival in London. Instead, she told a psychiatrist that her Uncle Charlie refused to take her in but eventually did. Given that Charlie died in 1936, this story had no factual basis and never appeared in her writings and correspondence. To my knowledge, Mary was never in touch with the surviving members of Charlie's family while she was in England.

Based on her own account of her sessions with this psychiatrist, her primary concern was the breakup of her marriage with no place to go.

> I resolved to leave Heinz, taking Monika and Peter with me. There was no use talking or reasoning with him. I had done that in the past with no results. I simply decided to run away – disappear into the vast city, which I did. It was either courage or desperation that drove me. I didn't know a soul in West Berlin. I took 40 of the 80 Deutschmarks, our monthly allowance as refugees from East Berlin, to find a place to live. With luck, I rented a small room and managed to persuade the people not to register us with the police because I didn't want my husband to find us. And he didn't.

After her discharge from the psychiatric home, Mutti retrieved us from the Kinderheim. We stayed with her in her hiding place, a small room in Charlottenburg, and tagged along while she looked for work. That summer she was hired as a counselor in an overnight camp in Grunewald for Jewish children, including her own. We packed our things and moved into the camp dormitory. The Jewish camp was my first introduction to the artifacts of luxurious living. There was access to a swimming pool on an estate, festivities under Japanese lanterns, Neapolitan ice cream served on wafers. I imagined how the rich lived when we took walks in Grunewald where huge houses and landscaped gardens were barricaded by massive stone walls and ornate iron gates.

At the camp, Mutti was popular with the kids because she knew how to use her sonorous voice in games and storytelling. She had them spellbound with her humorous stories. At ease as the center of attention, she was immersed in the excitement of splashing water and giggling children waiting their turn to have their hair dried by her. I was jealous to see her charms bestowed on other children.

My opportunity to bask in her presence at the camp was cut short when my allergic reaction to a bee sting caused me to be hospitalized for a week. When the camp vacation was over, we went back to our one-room hiding place in Charlottenburg. We didn't know what would come next. Mutti had to think about enrolling us in school and finding someone to mind us so that she could work. Time was running out. She was in a bind

– no job, no apartment, no immediate prospects, no relatives in a position to provide immediate help. In addition, she had on her shoulders the challenging tasks involved in preparing for immigration to America. First, she needed to get her papers in order and to earn money. Not able to find work, she went to state agencies and Jewish relief organizations in the same neighborhoods where she had once lived as a girl.

Strapped for cash, Mutti resorted to old-fashioned fundraising with a couple of Polish-Jewish "schnorrers" who went door-to-door with sob stories to elicit donations from rich German Jews who had somehow managed to reemerge from the war intact. When word of this unorthodox "enterprise" got around, the head of the Jewish Community, Heinz Galinski, warned her to desist or risk being ostracized if she continued her stunts. In private, she muttered, "*Er kann mir den Puckel runter rutschen*" [He can slide down my back], or in less polite language, "Kiss my ass." However, she did comply with his directive.

Mutti did what she could to provide us with diversions. We went *spazieren* [for a walk] along festive Kurfürstendamm on a wintery day one late November, with Christmas not far away. On our way to the Berlin Zoo, we stopped at the famous Café Kranzler and discussed over hot chocolate how Knautschke, the zoo's hippopotamus, devoured the rotten tomatoes that onlookers threw into his huge mouth. On another outing along the Ku'damm, we gazed at the ruins of the Kaiser Wilhelm Memorial Church that served as a grim reminder of the Allied bombing. We also happened upon a crowd gathered around a strange attraction, the carcass of a sperm whale, covered with pitch, which had been transported to Berlin from the Baltic Sea. We joined in, paying pfennigs to gawk at and touch the dead Leviathan. Mutti also took us on excursions to Grunewald where we walked through the pungent pines to pick the few wild strawberries we could find. There were trips to Berlin Zoo and afternoons at the movies to see Westerns and Disney films, including *Bambi*, which made me think tearfully of my own mother's vulnerability.

Mutti loved the circus and so we went to see the one-ring shows when we could. I was fascinated by the lion tamer and the docile elephants that made their rounds linking their trunks and tails. She would tap us on the shoulder and tell us to watch the chimps. "*Guck mal den Affen an,*" she'd say so we wouldn't miss the ringmaster throwing the chimp a banana.

But one time, the circus routine was different. After the acrobats finished, the ring master announced that anyone in the crowd could win 50 Deutschmarks if he or she could stay on the circus "pony" after completing a circle around the ring. As the clowns watched on, Mutti rose to her feet and volunteered. A minute later, she mounted the horse and strapped in, connected to a rope suspended from the tent ceiling. It didn't take long for her to fall off when at the ringmaster's command the horse took off like a shot. Our poor mother had bruise marks for weeks, but no 50 Deutschmarks. Afterwards, she talked about her performance with her abounding sense of humor to cover up the stark reality that our finances had hit bottom.

> Our last evening together was Christmas Eve. I took the children for a walk along Kurfürstendamm, Berlin's main street. All we had between us was 50 pfennigs. We brazenly entered one of the better restaurants and ordered a bowl of soup, to be shared by Peter and Monika, and while Monika waited her turn, she went over to the next table which was occupied by three young American soldiers. Little Monika was such a charmer. the language barrier didn't bother her. When I ordered her back to our table, apologizing in English (Mama was a charmer, too), it was too late, or rather just in time. We were invited to the best meal we ever had. But this was not all. We engaged in a lively conversation. Opposite me sat a dark-haired soldier, who introduced himself to me as Al whom I liked best of the trio. I told him that X-mas wasn't really our holiday, and his eyes lit up and he told me that he was Jewish, too. We almost felt like relatives and exchanged addresses. Meeting Al, who became a dear friend, and later my lover, was a godsend.

Despite the good fortune of meeting a man she considered a "godsend," Mutti was still broke, unemployed and lacked the papers and access to childcare that would enable her to take a regular job. For that reason, she placed Monika and me in Haus Michael, a Lutheran-run home for children in Lichterfelde in West Berlin

This was no life for the children, running and hiding and not enough food to eat. Not being a West German citizen, I was not allowed to take a job that would have enabled me to provide for them. The thought of parting from Peter and Monika broke my heart, but I had to consider the children's well-being first, and so I had them placed in another orphanage until I was able to offer them a half-way decent life. After the holidays, the process of placing the children began. They were put in a hospital for quarantine. Peter was cleared in a week, but my poor Monika stayed for three weeks because she never had any childhood diseases. It was so sad to see her little face through a glass window. I was not allowed to talk to her. She never cried or carried on, just looked so sad. Finally, she could join her brother in their new home, Haus Michael. I managed to find a room within walking distance. Visiting hours were once a week, but I showed up at least two or three times a week.

Haus Michael consisted of two residential houses for about 30 children. The main building housed the boys. The girls' dormitory was across a courtyard that was used as a play area. Herr Alberstedt, the orphanage supervisor, had separate living quarters in the main building for his family, including his little blond daughter, whom we rarely saw. The boys were distributed in the bedrooms upstairs. I tried to see Monika as often as I could during common play times outside in the courtyard between our two buildings. She told me that one of the nursemaids in her dormitory kept an artificial nose in a glass at night.

The orphanage was held together by routines. We made our beds in the mornings, folded our pajamas under the pillows, and lined up in a row for breakfast. Sundays, we got into starched plaid shirts and polished shoes for church where the droning organ heightened the occasion. In this Lutheran place of worship, I sat on a hard pew and listened to the minister lead the congregation in prayers and hymns about God and Jesus. Soon my eyes were distracted by the stained glass windows behind the pulpit. I felt out of place and squirmed. I knew I was Jewish but didn't know exactly what that entailed.

The church bells pealed as we exited the church. One Sunday, a flock of cranes flew above the rooftops, their bugle calls echoing through the open sky as the wind rustled through the trees. When we passed through a small city park on the way home, I was taken by the colors of the pansies, and I took a deep breath to smell and taste the dark, musty soil in the spring air. Back at Haus Michael, we lined up excitedly for *Mittagessen* [lunch], featuring *Blutwurst* [blood sausage]. I didn't like the idea of this German delicacy, but when I tried it, I enjoyed the sweet taste without asking further questions.

The orphanage gave me opportunities to be with kids my own age. I got into occasional spats, climbed trees, and competed to see who could toss the ubiquitous horse chestnuts the furthest. My companions and I fought strange boys on the nearby meadow for imaginary turf with homemade bows from tree branches and arrows made from dried-out reeds. I participated in pranks, like stealing berries from the dentist's garden next door. Our gang of little rascals included Siegfried Kirschner, the toughest kid in the orphanage, who taught me how to siphon sips of milk from the ten-liter cans that we were charged with hauling from the local dairy to Haus Michael.

There were also tender moments when we tried, unsuccessfully, to "rehabilitate" a retarded boy in our group, prone to hurling feces against the wall and even at people. In vain, we tried to teach him to play checkers while waiting for the total solar eclipse on June 30, 1954.

One fine day, I made a bid for freedom. I went AWOL with a boy named Franz to visit the spot where inventor and aviation pioneer, Otto Lilienthal, tested gliders on a 49-foot hill that he had built near his home in Lichterfelde. It is known, for obvious reasons, as *Fliegeberg* [Fly Hill] and now serves as a monument to the glider king who died in 1896 testing a glider in the Rhinow Hills. After paying homage to Lilienthal, we ate some red apples lifted from a nearby orchard and returned to Haus Michael before sundown without receiving the anticipated punishment. In the dead of winter, I went AWOL again with two friends to visit Mutti, whose room was about a half-hour walk away. She welcomed us with hugs and kisses and immediately put us in bed to warm our frozen feet. Mutti was a grand hostess, serving us hot chocolate and cookies in bed. Several hours later, she escorted us back to Haus Michael where she mollified Herr Alberstedt by praising our good behavior.

My reputation as a prankster made me a marked boy. One time, I was called into the office of Herr Alberstedt, the orphanage supervisor who falsely accused me of destroying the basement toilet by pushing a boulder down cement steps. While I was being scolded, I was transfixed by the enormous painting behind Alberstedt, a romantic landscape of a stream in the woods, which enabled me to be oblivious to his stream of unfounded accusations. I escaped into the painting scene and in my imagination, I skipped rocks on the painted stream that disappeared into the mysterious forest.

Punishment came later as I found out when I got the measles. Herr Alberstedt put me in a makeshift isolation ward in the same basement where my alleged crime occurred, guarded by a nasty, snarling German Shepherd called Senta, who stood guard outside the door to make sure I wouldn't flee my quarantine. That same year on St. Nicholas Day, all the children in Haus Michael put their shoes out to receive the traditional treats that would be left by St. Nicholas. But while the other kids found treats in their shoes, mine were filled with coal.

The time spent in orphanages, one in East Berlin and one in the West, normalized our separation from our mother. Although Haus Michael was not an overly friendly place, I was not unhappy there since we visited with Mutti on a regular basis. I liked being with the kids and got along with them. Access to ping-pong and chess was a plus. No one there interfered with my inner life. They did not have the key to my fears.

In 1954, our second year at Haus Michael, Monika started the first grade. We didn't go to the same elementary school. Along with three boys from the orphanage, I attended the Giesendorfer Grundschule for third and fourth grade. As the only dark-complexioned kid in my class, I was called "Schwarzer Peter" behind my back. I tried to shrug it off, avoided direct contact with other kids and did not make friends at school.

My surname, Krotoczynski, made me stick out in a country not favorably disposed to Poland and Polish Jews. One time on my way to school, I was shot in the leg with a BB gun. Even though there was no way of disguising my non-German heritage, Mutti tried to help me out by giving me Lederhosen that I dutifully polished with bacon grease to achieve the standard Teutonic shine and hardness so that I could pass for *ein echter Deutsche Junge* [a genuine German lad].

During religious class in fourth grade, my teacher, Frau Fischer, taught us that the Jews killed Jesus. I was convinced that she believed I shared the guilt because I was Jewish. She also complained frequently about the occupying Americans, particularly their disapproval of the German national anthem, *Deutschland über Alles* [Germany Above All], which she had us sing just to spite the Yanks. When I complained to Mutti, she arranged a conference with Herr Alberstedt and the school principal to complain about Frau Fischer's antisemitism. This had the desired effect. Much to my surprise, I was not singled out for retribution by Frau Fischer, who was careful with me from that point on.

Although Monika and I were becoming well-adjusted to life apart from our mother, we longed to be with her and were aware of the stigma of being in an orphanage. We didn't see Heinz during our two-year stint at the orphanage since he didn't know our whereabouts.

We saw Mutti as frequently as the rules allowed. She included us in her life as a single person, happily introducing us to her new circle of friends and acquaintances, including people from the Jewish Community and students at the Freie Universität Berlin, a large public university located in Dahlem. There was also a new wrinkle. Among her friends was the GI "Onkel" Al who had rescued us in the restaurant on Kurfürstendamm on Christmas Eve. I was confused by this man's sudden presence in our lives. We saw him only a few times. Since he didn't speak German, it was hard to get to know him even though the way Mutti spoke of him made it clear she was smitten by him.

My new friend Al was transferred from his old address to large barracks close by, halfway between Haus Michael and my street. I saw Al whenever possible and my fear of Heinz finding us gradually disappeared. I was about to spend one and a half pretty good years. The children adjusted, were safe and cared for, and I could see them almost any time. Al always had a good supply of candy and chocolates, which were a great treat. But I did my share of crying, usually on my way home after a visit with Peter and Monika.

Mutti told amusing stories about the "Ami" GI's, including their penchant for doling out nylon stockings and chocolates. We made fun of American English with the nonsense rhyme, "How do you do, *mit einem Gummi Schuh*" [with a rubber boot]. I was aware that Mutti continued dealing in black market sales of American Army PX cigarettes supplied by her GI contacts. She knew the importance of networking to make a better life for us. Her notebook was full of appointments with government officials and potential employers. She remained in close touch with people at the Jewish Community and her efforts made a difference.

> Now I was able to continue the process of becoming a West German citizen. After endless trips, filling out stacks of papers and sitting in crowded rooms, I finally became a citizen for the first time. As a West German citizen, I was able to look for jobs and managed to find two very nice, well-paid jobs.

Mutti found her first nursing job at Krankenhaus Bethel Berlin, a hospital within walking distance of Haus Michael. Then several months later, she found a better-paying job as a qualified nurse (RN equivalent) for the British Army in Grunewald, thanks to her knowledge of English.

> Nobody bothered to investigate that the certificate I produced was not my State Final. Anyway, I worked in a center taking care of the families of British soldiers and officers. There were two other German nurses and a doctor, also German. He was an old army doctor, good natured and mostly intoxicated owing to the generous presents from our patients. The girls and I had to rely on our own nursing knowledge a good part of the time when the good doctor stretched out or passed out in the back room.

Mutti took us to her workplace one weekend day, where she proudly introduced us to the doctor and other nurses. We walked around Grunewald's woods and lakes, and then took a bus through a wealthy residential area with large estates and gardens, some of them rented by the American and British occupying forces. At the end of the day, Mutti brought us back to Haus Michael.

On my eighth birthday, Mutti bought me a leather briefcase. She thought having the right trappings underscored one's commitment to an education that would someday lead to a successful professional life, the kind she never had. By that time, I had set my goal to attend *Gymnasium*, an academic high school that would prepare me to pass the Abitur, the qualification exam needed for acceptance to a university.

Mary made friends easily and talked a lot about them. One time, she took us to an encampment with friends at the Freie Universität. To relieve our boredom, one of her pals took us for a short ride in a canoe on the Krumme Lanke, one of the smaller lakes in Grunewald. On some weekends, we stayed overnight with Mutti in her little room where she prepared us hot chocolate before bed and cooked a full English breakfast with eggs, bacon and all the trimmings in the morning. She read us fairy tales in a voice that believed in them, and often spoke about leaving for America soon.

In preparation for our exodus, Mutti taught us a little English. She signed us up for a summer vacation program that placed Jewish children with Jewish families in the US military. Very soon, Monika and I were on our way out of Berlin with a busload of children headed through East Germany to Frankfurt where we were met by our host families. My host family, named Lion, lived in an off-base apartment complex on the outskirts of Frankfurt am Main. The father was a US Army officer and the mother spoke fluent German. She was an amateur photographer, who took lighthearted photographs of me clowning with a potted plant on my head. I spent pleasant hours entertaining the couple's toddler and took bike excursions into a neighborhood where I met some local German kids who wondered why I would be staying with an American family. On the next day, I crashed the bike that belonged to the family's housekeeper. Much to my surprise, my hosts minimized the incident and said it would be no problem getting it fixed.

The Lions took me to see a movie of the Harlem Globetrotters, to the Frankfurter Zoo, and to meet up with the family that hosted my sister. Mrs. Lion told me that my sister's host family wanted to adopt Monika and that she succeeded in discouraging them from contacting our mother regarding their proposal. After I returned to Berlin, Mrs. Lion sent a follow-up letter that made no mention of my sister's host family.

Dear Mrs. Wiesner

Thank you for your card. I hope Peter had a good trip home. I had already thought of finding someone else to keep him till the 31st but all my acquaintances have very small children, so it was not feasible. I am glad to hear that you plan to take him out of the children's home. It will certainly be much better for him even if it means added problems in other respects. I hope you will all be able to go to the States very soon. We did not visit Monika as that Sunday turned out to fall on my husband's birthday. In a few days, we shall leave for a trip to Italy where I have many relatives I have never seen. If that doesn't fit in with my "Jewish background" let me explain that my father is French Italian, so I am only half Jewish. My parents were divorced when I was very young, so I am acquainted with such a situation. However, it did not affect me very much as my parents remained always on very friendly terms even after both remarried and so I am still very close to both. Hoping you enjoy the enclosed pictures.

Increasingly, Mutti was drawn to the English-speaking world, keeping up correspondence with those she had known in England. This included my biological father, who had written her a few times after she left him. She never kept those letters, but in April 1954, Mutti wrote him about our plans to immigrate to the United States and how he could help us make that happen.

> Dear Denis,
>
> I hope you have received my last letter, also my card for your birthday. Overall, I am a good correspondent, but today I write to you seeking a favor. As I have told you previously, I intend to go to the States. Well, this plan seems to materialize sooner than expected. I was able to start work at the end of last month, but I have not earned more than to cover living expenses. Now the Consul is asking for the money for the visas. It is quite a handsome sum: 105 Marks a head, which means about nine Pounds. For Monika I get the visa money from her father, for myself I can just about manage, and for Peter I am at a loss. Could you possibly help? I know it is asking a lot, but if you should by any chance spare it, I would be more than pleased. As you know, I was receiving poor law assistance all the time, which is not even enough to live on. Otherwise, I would have saved some money working. I have never asked you for money outright, but I have no one to turn to. When we are in America I hope not to have to beg again, except for sums we are entitled to. You will help me furnish Peter's education, will you? I feel it would be a great sin not to give the boy a good education, since he is intelligent above the average. How have you been keeping? How is your film progressing? I do hope that this first film will open all the doors for a good future for you. In California, I would be living right close to Hollywood and with good luck I might get involved in the film industry myself. People keep telling me I have some talent, which I don't really believe myself, but one never knows one's luck. If all goes well, we might sail for California in early June, if not in July '54. Well, Denis dear, I hope you are keeping fine, and I would be glad to hear from you soon, even if you are not in a position just now to help me out with the visa money. With love from Marie and Peter.

Denis never replied to Mary's letter, because he never received it. In 2014, his sister, Monica, sent it to me after discovering it among her mother's papers. She offered an explanation as to why her own mother might have kept the letter from Denis.

Mothers were very protective of their sons (not girls!) and so it was with mine. A letter arrived at her house addressed to Denis, which to her shame, she opened and read and never gave it to Denis. I found it among her papers when she died. I was greatly shocked. This was so many years after that I was unable to do anything about it. But I decided not to tell Denis as he would have been greatly upset. I now send it to you so that you will know that he was not as dreadfully callous at ignoring Mary's cry for help regarding the visa. I am also sending you a photo of you when you were about six, also another of you as a baby.

However, in October 1954, Mutti did receive a letter from Denis, only months before we left Germany. In it he discussed his budding film career and his frustration with the industry.

Thank you for your letter, I was surprised to hear that you are nursing again and not apparently hating it. You do not say much about what is happening to Peter and your daughter, or if you still intend to go to the States. My film is finished, and I am waiting for its first showing which will take months. I doubt if I shall get any money from it, as it will only be shown at the Edinburgh Festival, Cannes, Brussels, and perhaps Berlin! So you may see it. I am exhausted and utterly fed up with working for nothing. I have written eight plays now and one film, all of which will have been shown to the public and yet I have had no money from any of them! I have made up my mind that in future I shall write only for money. The BBC have offered to buy my scripts if they are of general interest. I would very much like to hear from you of any interesting subject or any material whatever which you think might be useful to me concerning life in Germany. If I write a script, for example, about a family in Berlin, I will give you half of what I receive here, and anything that you can get in Germany we could also share. Facts are really what I need about day-to-day life, so if you have time, please write to me when I have sent you my new address. (I am leaving here on August 30.) For the present, all my best. Denis.

This letter, of course, made no reference to the correspondence that Denis's mother withheld. It must have felt odd for Mary to hear how far removed he was from the reality of our lives in Germany. I don't know if she answered his letter, but apparently, she did not write again about our plans to immigrate to the United States because we later learned that Denis came to Berlin looking for us in 1955, a year after we left. Mutti never talked to me about any communication with him. I was nine years old, and it was probably for the best. Monika's father was out of sight and my "real" father was an imaginary figure. When I asked my mother about him, she said that he lived in England and told me that England is a wonderful country and that the English were decent people, but that they have an odd sense of humor that takes some time to understand.

Mutti's description of the English made me think about my heritage. I knew, of course, that my olive skin and black hair didn't fit the Aryan look. My sense of Jewish identity gradually came into focus after Mutti's divorce from Heinz left her free to reclaim her Jewish heritage. I grew to understand that my identity was closely aligned with hers after I learned that Jewishness is conferred on a child through the mother. We began to hear about her own parents, and she showed us the few photos she had of them. Mutti involved us in lighting candles for Shabbat and taught us some simple Hebrew prayers. She also showed me the book on Palestine that was given to her when she graduated from the Jewish Girls School.

I remember our going to a dilapidated synagogue where we waited in the courtyard for the service to begin. We heard distant thunder and wondered whether it would rain. Mutti had two competing explanations for thunder, one was the German expression, *Der liebe Gott schimpft* [the dear God scolds]. The other one, designed to dispel our fears, was that thunder is merely a form of celestial bowling.

After we entered the synagogue, a bearded rabbi conducted the service in Hebrew. I recognized a few words that Mutti had taught us. After we left the synagogue, she said that something terrible had happened to her parents, then she cried and told me never to ask any questions if I should see anyone with numbers tattooed on their arms.

9

MUTTI'S QUEST FOR HER LOST PAST

Mutti never stopped trying to uncover more about what happened to her family and friends during the Holocaust. First and foremost were her efforts to learn the detailed circumstances of her own mother's deportation and murder. All she knew was based on a letter she received in October 1952 from the Jewish Restitution Successor Organization confirming that Gertrud Krotoczynski went to Riga on November 27, 1941, and was presumed to be dead. Since there was no specific information about how she died or where she was buried, Mutti speculated.

My mother went smiling on the way of deportation. Perhaps she wanted to die. She had nothing to live for. I have a photo of my mother shortly before my father died. The expression in her eyes is almost haunting. And I detect in her faraway and "strange" smile, perhaps the early sign of escape if not insanity. My impression could have been stimulated by the report of the Rabbi whose children mother took care of after father's death who reported my mother's unusual "smiling" and that she appeared to act "removed." This type of behavior the Rabbi interpreted as "insanity." If this should have been a fact, I would be grateful. Much would have been spared for her. Despite all the hardships , including my father's illness and financial difficulties, I do remember my mother as a happy person, who sang most of the days and had a good sense of humor. She was even-tempered and never complained. I never saw cry. I shall never know how my mother spent the last days prior to her deportation, how she felt and what thoughts were with her. I can just presume. If she did know deportation and death was awaiting her, was it not possible that she did "smile" and act removed? She had nothing to lose anymore. Her beloved husband had his grave. Her beloved child was safe in England. Mother's own life had become empty and meaningless, and there did not seem to be an end to Nazi rule. I presume mother was not only prepared to die, but she wanted to die, because it was beyond her human tolerance to bear her existence. I just pray to the Almighty that mother didn't have to suffer while she was held captive in a camp before the final act of inhumanity. If she did go insane, it might have been easier for her. But is insanity insulation against pain?

During the 1950s when Mary was in Berlin, there were no readily accessible records of deportation and extermination. All Mutti knew at that time was that she lost five of her maternal aunts and one uncle by marriage.[1] She focused most of her attention on finding the relatives who survived. Before her cousin Irene left Berlin for America in 1950, she provided her with the information needed for contacting those who had left Germany before the war.

Mutti was desperate to find out what happened to her best friend, Thea, who had lived nearby her family in East Berlin. It had been about a decade since Mutti received word from her through the Red Cross in 1941, announcing her marriage to Edgar Steinmetz, whose parents, Alexander and Ella Steinmetz, were close friends of Mutti's parents. All that Irene could confirm was that Thea and Edgar were conscripted as forced laborers in Berlin before being deported.

In 1953, Mutti was finally in touch with Edgar Steinmetz through the Jewish Community where she also learned that Thea had died in Auschwitz. She wanted to find out from the surviving husband exactly what had happened to her friend. When she met Edgar at a restaurant in West Berlin, he told her that he was forced by the Nazis in 1941 to work as a qualified technician for Siemens-Chuckert, an electrical engineering company on Schöneberger Straße in Berlin. Thea also became a forced worker elsewhere. In February 1943, the Gestapo arrested Edgar and Thea, and deported them to Auschwitz where Edgar worked as a supervising electrician, making use of the professional qualifications and experience that he had gained in Berlin.

I don't know to what extent Edgar discussed with Mutti the events leading up to their deportation to Auschwitz or the details about where he and Thea were housed or how often he could be with her. Although his job as an electrician increased their chances of survival, he was unable to shield her from the horrific living conditions. Edgar reported that she went insane, unable to process the reality of unrelenting extermination. It is likely that Edgar wanted to spare Mutti from knowing all the details about Thea's suffering and death.

When Edgar told Mutti of how her best friend wasted away, there must have been a long silence, especially after he told her that he thought pulling the gas chamber switch was a form of mercy killing. In her writings, she seemed to blame Edgar for complicity in her friend's death because of his role as an electrician facilitating the killing process. She was appalled by his detached demeanor and suspected that he may have been a capo, a prisoner functionary assigned to supervise forced laborers. What he told her made it impossible for her to have anything more to do with him, even though she knew she didn't have the moral authority to judge him.

My own research yielded additional information about Edgar's role as head of the inmate electricians at Auschwitz. In 1959, almost a decade after Mutti met with him, Edgar testified at a tribunal in Berlin about the operational and technical aspects of the extermination facilities at Auschwitz-Birkenau. In 1970, he gave additional testimony regarding details about the design and operation of the death chambers, including the involvement of German companies, notably Siemens, which supplied and supported the operations.

Edgar's role at Auschwitz is discussed in a book written by his Auschwitz coworker, Bruno Baum, who had also worked with Edgar at Siemens in Berlin before he was deported. Baum referred to Edgar's testimony concerning the technical support he provided for the design and implementation of the power systems required for the extermination facilities at Auschwitz-Birkenau.[2]

Mutti was also able to reconnect with Jenny Stanesco, her close friend from the Mädchenschule. After receiving a brief Red Cross message from Jenny after the outbreak of war, she didn't hear from her until after the defeat of Germany. Jenny wrote that she had attended a music conservatory in Brussels with the hope of building a career in classical music. She never did become a concert violinist, as she had hoped, and ended up playing Hungarian and gypsy music in high-class coffee houses. Jenny and Mutti kept up a life-long correspondence but never saw each other again.

Mutti corresponded with Rudi Sabor, her teacher at the Mädchenschule who made a dramatic escape from Berlin to London in 1939 just months after she left on the Kindertransport. He was tipped off by a German friend, a member of the SS, that he would be arrested at his home by the Gestapo in 30 minutes. Rudi left home immediately and made a daring escape by riding for two days and nights on a Stadtbahn train until his visa for England was available. After six months in a British camp for enemy aliens, he joined his fiancée, Emmi Veit, and settled in London where he became an eminent music scholar and teacher.[3]

Writing in English in 1951, Rudi offered advice and support to Mutti as he had done at the Mädchenschule. Despite the horrors of the past years, they both still had a love of German culture built on the likes of Goethe, Schiller, Beethoven, and Wagner. In addressing several letters to her, he used the name, Kunigunde. There are characters in song and literature, as well as saints and queens named Kunigunde. Perhaps a reference to one of these may have had special meaning for Mary and Rudi.

My dear Kunigunde,

In thoughts, as often before, I have written to you more than once. When it came to sitting down to it, many things interfered. Now I am on holiday, and have a machine on loan, and the sun is shining. I am not any more on the threshold of senility, but at 38 have entered decrepit old age, so nothing will stop me from writing to my old (?) friend.

As so often before, yours – apart from TJO and her mother – was the only birthday letter, treasured for its keeping faith, thank you, and there is also a letter from January with the Sybille (Michelangelo). How well remembered.

Mary dear, whatever ails you, I implore you, don't let it depress you so much, that you, as you say, see this cynical side of life exclusively. I know, just as well as you, that in Hölderlin's words, *"Nicht alle Blutenträume reiften."*[4] But this is how things are, and how little we can do to change it. What remains is not too little, you remember don't you? You possess the magic key which will unlock the world of tones, of rhymes, of nature to you. You see, we ourselves count for so little. We live presumably once only, and what we do today, has been forgotten, at best, the day after yesterday, but to some of us is given the power of conjuring up in the course of a day or a night, the hour of fulfillment, die Zauberstunde, the "Kairos," the important moment, spent with Beethoven, Goethe, Grunewald, memories, a dear face from the past or the present, children's dreamy eyes, a blossoming tree. See, all this is yours. How rich we really are. Write again dear, even if I cannot say much. But you know, don't you, that deep within my thoughts, Auguststraße [location of the Girls School], Klobbicke [a small, picturesque hamlet in Brandenburg] and our songs, are three times as important as the outer trappings of mellow, old age. With love to Peter, Monika and Heinz, and as much of it as you like, take for yourself.

In his letter, Rudi included his own short poem to Mary written in German, *"Anlässlich einer zurückgekehrten Sybille"* [On the Occasion of a Returned Sibyl]. In it, he marvels at how she guarded the image of Michelangelo's Sibyl through the stormy 13 years since they had been in Germany. Upon seeing the image Mary enclosed her letter, he writes the line, *"Wie rührt die Trauer, die es hergeführt."* [How touched I am by the mourning it stirs].

Throughout his career, Rudi wrote about how an appreciation of German culture could transcend German nationalism and personal loss. A noted music scholar, Rudi published several books about Wagner in which he sought to extricate Wagner's legacy from its appropriation by the Nazis. I don't know how Mother reacted to Rudi's feelings about the redeeming value of German culture, but I found an inscribed copy of Rudi's book, *The Real Wagner*, among her books.[5]

10

AMERICA, THE PROMISED LAND

Even as Mary delved into the past, her attention was riveted on obtaining the documents needed for going to America. She received help from the Berlin Jewish Community as well the Berlin division of the Hebrew Immigration Aid Society (HIAS). A letter from HIAS, dated December 9, 1953, confirmed that plans for our emigration were well underway. Much of her conversation revolved around our cousins, Albert and Estelle Stanley, who had agreed to become our sponsors. A major obstacle was to finalize her divorce from Heinz and to gain full custody of Monika, so that she could go to America without his permission.

It was more difficult than I thought getting a divorce because Heinz wasn't willing. He concocted all kinds of stories which could never be proved. In turn, I played his game accusing him of things which I don't remember now. I was afraid that he might find out about Al, although he didn't know where I lived. All the bickering was via lawyers, and I don't remember any court scenes. Finally, the divorce was granted by supposed mutual consent. But more feathers flew when it came to the custody of Monika (he never adopted Peter). I came up with the theory that when Heinz marries again, he would most likely marry a non-Jewish woman who might not be able to be a good mother to the little Jewish girl, especially if there were to be arguments with Heinz. I used this far-fetched theory only because the postwar Germans were trying very hard to "make good" to the Jewish people. Thank God, they granted me custody and gave Heinz the usual visitation rights. But this was not the end of dirty fighting. Meanwhile, my cousin in California had made all the necessary arrangements for our immigration. However, one obstacle remained. Heinz would not give his consent for Monika to go to America because this would violate his visitation right. His attitude was "over my dead body" and I thought this put an end to my dream of going to America. I was miserable. Al was sent back to America around this time, back to his wife, whom I found out about from one of his friends after he left. I had no one to comfort me.

"Onkel Al" was the "nice Jewish boy" Mutti might have married who would have met her dead parents' approval if he hadn't been married already. Mutti later told me that she felt betrayed because Al didn't tell her about his being married and didn't have the decency to say goodbye before he left. She never tried to contact him afterwards. Marrying within the tribe wasn't meant to be. Meanwhile, Mutti was equally ruthless in dealing with Heinz after he landed in prison.

Then I received a letter from Heinz. He was in jail and asked me to visit him. He told me that he was involved in a theft and that his buddies had betrayed him. He thought that seeing him in jail would soften my feelings toward him. It did just the opposite. I found out that being in jail stripped him of certain rights, including signing the immigration permit for Monika. Instead, the permit was signed by the court, and I had to get out of Berlin in a hurry. Today, dear Heinz, I ask your forgiveness. I know it was a dirty trick, but I had to do it. I had to get out of Berlin without saying goodbye. While our last immigration papers were on their way, Heinz was released from jail. His visitation day fell shortly before our departure to America, and I drummed into the children not a whisper about going to America. Peter was old enough to understand, but I was worried about Monika, but thank God, they didn't say a word. Two days later we were off to America with a couple of suitcases. Goodbye, Berlin; no one saw us off, but again, I know for sure, a father was crying because he would never see his little girl again.

Soon after Mutti found out that she had permission to take Monika to America, she announced our imminent departure. "Kids, we are leaving for America soon!" To celebrate this good news, she brought us two huge, juicy red apples that we consumed while sitting on the front door ledge of Haus Michael while my friends asked questions about America that I could not answer. Mutti stood by with muted excitement and uncertainty.

I tried to imagine what it would be like to be there. I wondered about the mighty Mississippi after our American relatives sent me a shiny red steamboat toy made of hard plastic. I conjured images from cowboy movies as well as newsreels depicting typical scenes of America, including the New York Harbor, skyscrapers, traffic, and pedestrians in Times Square. I had watched a documentary film at Haus Michael about Navajos peacefully tending their animals and expected to see bucolic scenes in America.

On the day of our flight, Mutti made sure we were properly dressed. She handed me my updated dark blue British passport, with my name, Peter Krotoczynski, carefully printed in its oval window, plus my photo inside with meticulously combed hair and a tooth missing. My mother and sister had their West German passports. All we had to do was board a plane at Tempelhof. Mutti was apprehensive and afraid something would go wrong.

> And so I was on the way to the land of milk and honey. I didn't think I would miss Berlin. I had high hopes and expectations based on what my father had told me. America was God's country which would solve every problem of ours and hand us a few things on a silver platter. And there would be our sponsor, cousin Albert, and his wife who would help us on arrival. We left on November 14, 1954, flying from Berlin to Hannover in a DC-3 and then taking a bus to a refugee camp in Bremerhaven for quarantine. There we were, with hundreds of other refugees squeezed into huge barracks. To my way of thinking and dreaming, this is not the way things were supposed to be. I was sick of being a refugee. Peter and Monika, however, took this in stride because for them this was an adventure, and they were finally "at home" with me away from the orphanage.

We spent two weeks in the dingy refugee camp. To pass the time, Mutti taught us some English, starting with numbers and the names of things we liked. She took us for an outing by bus to Bremen where we bought shoes. The days dragged on. At night, some of the adults played cards. The camp screened old Hollywood movies with love scenes that I found boring and incomprehensible. Mutti was depressed, unable to answer our many questions about America and what life there would be like. Finally, our departure date arrived. We loaded our four suitcases on a bus and headed for the harbor in pouring rain.

We finally boarded the *Olympia*, one of the ships owned by Aristotle Onassis and hardly a luxury liner. Hundreds of people squeezed into this small passenger ship. That evening, after we headed for Ireland into foul weather and rough seas, Mutti was one of the few hardy people still in the dining room when the rocking boat sent most of the diners, including bilious me, heaving and zigzagging downstairs to the sleeping quarters. Monika and I were the only children on board and were allowed to stay with Mutti in a dormitory where a dozen women bunked.

The following day, our ship anchored off the west coast of Ireland where several shy, scared-looking teenage girls arrived by tugboat to board. Mutti's crisp British English and outgoing personality enabled her to calm and comfort the newcomers. I did my best not to notice them or the other women walking around in their white slips and took off to explore the ship on my own.

Although the women chattered a lot and tried to make me feel at ease, I was constantly looking for ways to slip out to check the innards of the ship's hull and its on-deck diversions. Later during the voyage, I played ping-pong with some Canadian soldiers who were also looking for ways to while away the time. I didn't notice that Mutti couldn't shake off her depression.

> The children seemed to enjoy the trip, aside from the seasickness when we crossed the Channel. Peter became the well-admired ping-pong champion, and I still remember him in his little half-length blue coat, barely reaching up to the table, playing in all-weather on the deck, chasing after ping-pong balls headed into the ocean. Monika got

busy charming the captain of the ship out of many dollars for the Bingo games. Only Mama was not very happy, her dreams of the land of milk and honey soured.

Despite cramped quarters and occasional boredom, I was taken by the romance and adventure of the open seas. I explored every part of the ship and snuck into the hold to peek at the mighty diesel engines that gave off a heavy smell and deafening roar. I climbed the rigging where I saw the waves and sky change daily with the wind and weather. I thought little about Mutti and her apprehensions, freed from such thoughts by the spectacular display of nature's power and mystery that held the key to our immediate future.

For several days, our ship sliced through monstrous gray-blue waves that splashed across the bow and rocked the boat so that the sky disappeared and then traded places with the ocean that fell from view. Days later, the undulating sea turned calm, almost flat, and so my attention turned to the unrelenting cries of the gulls following in the ship's wake.

Our voyage on the open seas was punctuated by numerous fire drill exercises. Passengers lined up on deck with their life jackets, waiting for the all clear. I worried whether the frequency of these indicated the ship's lack of seaworthiness.

Mutti's depression became apparent. I was surprised that she didn't share our sense of adventure. I had my fill of Jerry Lewis and Dean Martin movies, topped off by doses of Tom and Jerry mayhem. It was fun complaining about the dark American Hershey bars, which compared unfavorably to Tobler milk chocolate, but I wanted them anyway. What does it say about a country if it can't compete with Swiss chocolate?

By the ninth day of the voyage, I was restless as were the other passengers, yearning to see land. Finally, we sighted the Canadian coast, a swath of snow-dusted pine forest stretched along the shore. Our ship made a stop at Halifax to let off the Canadian soldiers. Then we headed south to the United States, and a day later, the Olympia entered New York Harbor shortly before daybreak on November 26, 1954. We were on the wrong side of the ship to see the Statue of Liberty but caught a glimpse of New York's skyscrapers shortly before we docked. Mutti was sullen, didn't say much.

Although our passports were stamped, "Admitted by Department of Justice, New York," our arrival port was in Hoboken, New Jersey. Going through customs on board took much less time than expected. The HIAS people sent us to Penn Station in a taxi that drove through dirty New Jersey streets lined with grim four-story walk-ups and dilapidated stores.

At Penn Station, we waited for several hours to board a train for Chicago. Mutti bought us candy and comic books that we clutched tightly before boarding the train. She warned us that we would spend many hours on this "milk train" and so we sat and squirmed as the flat winter landscapes of Ohio and Indiana whizzed by. We noticed huge television antennas on the roofs of modest clapboard houses along the tracks and wondered how poor people could afford television. With time to kill, we tried to make sense of the American comics with Mutti's help and played with American coins. I traded Monika a few of her dimes for my larger nickels, a business practice that didn't meet Mother's approval.

In Chicago, we boarded the El Capitan with "full-length dome cars" for panoramic glimpses of America. To my disappointment, we missed seeing the Mississippi when we crossed it in the dead of night. By the time we stopped at Albuquerque, the bright semiarid landscape of New Mexico illuminated my imagination about cowboys and Indians. Then suddenly we saw our first real American Indian, a man in full headdress, who boarded the train to sell ice cream to the passengers, a sad and humiliating sight that had nothing to do with the noble and fierce Indians featured in cowboy movies. He didn't even measure up to the dignity of the impoverished Navajos tending their animals in the documentary shown at Haus Michael. What did impress me were the vivid colors of the desert landscape, the streaks of yellow and orange against the turquoise sky. There was nothing quite like it in drab Berlin. I was only dimly aware that my excitement was out of step with the apprehension felt by our mother.

> The closer we came to Los Angeles, the more my fear of the unknown became uncontrollable. I kept praying that we wouldn't ever get there, but I knew we would. Fortunately, Peter and Monika enjoyed the journey. My little charmer made friends with the man at the food counter and managed to get a good ice cream supply for herself and her brother (we ran out of money by this time). I will never forget the night sky over Arizona. I never saw such bright stars. They only confirmed my fear of this unknown life in a new country. I wished my father had never spoken of the land of milk and honey.

On November 28, 1954, in the morning, our train arrived at Union Station in downtown Los Angeles. While we waited for our luggage, two Mexican American porters, speaking Spanish to each other, helped us with our bags as we made our way to the waiting area. I also saw an African American woman pushing a cart with cleaning supplies.

Waiting for us at the train station was our cousin, Albert Stanley, who recognized us from the photos Mutti sent him. He was well into his mid-seventies with looks that resembled Mother. Albert didn't know any German and so Mutti spoke to him in English while he drove us to Santa Monica. As I tuned out the rhythm of their voices, my attention shifted to the large American cars passing us on all sides. Tall, slender palm trees swayed against the backdrop of the light blue sky. Billboards of smiling people whizzed by as we drove west on Olympic Boulevard. I was stunned by the sun's brightness and the jagged sharp shadows cast by palm trees, and by the abundance of colorful flowers and the rich earth tones of the Spanish architecture. When I heard the whirr of lawn sprinklers, I noticed the landscape workers tending the lawns surrounding Santa Monica City Hall. They were all dark skinned. Mutti later told us about the prejudice against Negroes and Mexicans that became readily obvious the more we became acquainted with American culture.

Since we arrived with only a few clothes, Albert took us to buy used jeans, sneakers, and t-shirts at Goodwill. I was taken aback by this but didn't say a word. No matter how poor we had been in Germany, we had never received musty used clothing. Albert's wife, Estelle, made sure that our next set of clothes were bought new from J.C. Penney.

Cousin Albert put us up at the motel he owned, the Kensington Motel on 1746 Ocean Avenue in Santa Monica. Albert and Estelle had a nicely decorated apartment in one of the landscaped bungalow houses towards the rear of the property behind the smaller units, with a view of Santa Monica Pier and a glimpse of the ocean waves from their kitchen. We were given an apartment in another building across from them. It was one of a series of four-unit light brown stucco bungalows organized around a central courtyard and walkway. In the middle of the courtyard was a small, oval swimming pool surrounded by small blue and white tiles. Albert had planted extensive flower beds around each bungalow. The sign outside read in neon, "98 modern units."

Our apartment had a creaky Murphy bed that swung out of the closet. Close by were a couch and a television. Monika and I loved to make the Murphy bed so we could lift it up with a push, then hear it spring back against the wall with a loud thud. There was a kitchenette with a refrigerator, gas stove, and small breakfast table. Some of the furniture dated back to the 1930s and 1940s. An upright Hoover vacuum cleaner could be borrowed from the front office where clean towels were also readily available.

Monika and I were shy when introduced to Albert and Estelle because we couldn't communicate in English, but we wasted no time in getting used to our new surroundings, including the routines of this apartment hotel. Taking a swim in the pool and going to the beach became part of our routine.

Mutti enrolled us in Madison Elementary School on 1018 Arizona Avenue, Monika in the first grade and me in the fourth. The principal suggested that I use the family name, Wiesner, instead of my difficult-to-spell surname. Having the same last name as my mother and sister was fine with me.

Mutti found work in a nursing home, and we settled into a routine that included after-school activities. California's warm climate added a sense of displacement to our first Christmas without snow. Our mother's fluent English helped us sing American versions of the Christmas carols we already knew. We relished the novelty of swimming in December, not only in the hotel's heated pool but also in the frigid Pacific.

While Monika and I became engrossed in the novelties of our new country, Mutti struggled emotionally.

The children appeared to take everything in stride, but Mama? I simply was not happy, destroyed by my own dreams and expectations for which I shouldn't have blamed anybody. I would have liked many things but was afraid to ask. I tried showing gratitude, but it was insincere. I was incapable of accepting anything graciously, like armloads of used clothing. When I was taken to the supermarket, I was so overwhelmed at the sight of so much food. Instead of enjoying the abundance, I felt hostility and grieved for the people who had starved to death in concentration camps. I also didn't like the idea that we were treated to all our groceries. Although I felt exhausted, I wanted to go to work, which I did five days after our arrival. Cousin Albert knew someone who owned a sanitarium nearby who offered me a job from 7 a.m. to 3 p.m. These hours were acceptable. Peter was old enough to supervise breakfast for Monika and to make sure they caught the bus in time for school. In the afternoon, we were home at the same time.

No more Nurse Mary like in England, but just plain Nurse. Working in the sanitarium, I was never so confused in my life. Everything was so different. I couldn't even find the light switch. Worst of all were the patients' beds, operated by two handles plus a steel bar below. Whoever invented those beds did not have the comfort of the patient in mind. Not even a cat could get comfortable in them. I had to think of the loving care we gave our patients in England when two nurses would use three pillows plus leg supports. We adjusted these pillows until our patient was comfortably settled. But here in the sanitarium the nurse put the patient in the center of the bed and started cranking the handles. Before long, the patient looked a mess, leaning to one side at a 90-degree angle. I had to take care of six to eight patients during my shift. It was not easy to give good care to all my patients since they were handicapped by chronic illness and senility. Plus, having two patients per room meant that I had to be in four rooms at a time, to my way of nursing. I was used to large wards where I was able to keep an eye on all my patients, even when I was busy attending them individually. My reassuring voice was a comfort to the patient who was waiting for my attention. I did my best taking good care of the patients in the sanitarium. It wasn't easy meeting set schedules. Each patient had to be thoroughly washed and dressed. Medical procedures had to be taken care of. They had to be in their wheelchair by lunch time. I did not skip on anything, including hairdos. You could recognize my patients by their braids or combed straight-down hair.

Unaware of Mutti's job challenges, Monika and I readily learned English while memories of Berlin receded in the California sunshine. We were diverted by the novelties of our new life in America while sadly Mutti's depression kindled her resentment against our sponsors.

They seemed very happy to get their refugees from Germany. Albert told everybody it took him 16 years to get me over to America, counting his fruitless efforts in the 1930s. I had the feeling they brought us over mainly to brag to their friends. Despite their generosity, I just couldn't feel close to them. Being a refugee again in a new country struck me as a repetition of what I went through in England after arriving in 1939. Only this time I came of my free will, yet I didn't feel free. Burdened by the past, I couldn't shake it. I couldn't forget that my father died prematurely and that my mother was left to die in a concentration camp in 1941.

Mutti didn't know at the time that her mother had been shot upon arrival in Latvia by train and was presumably buried in a mass grave in Rumbula Forest outside of Riga. The uncertainty surrounding her mother's death and her own survivor's guilt fueled speculation that more could have been done by relatives to save her parents.

I was plagued with the old feeling of guilt that I had survived. I also blamed my cousins for not having tried harder to get my parents out of Germany when it was still possible. I kept rereading old correspondence of my parents in which they tried to convince my

American cousins about the gravity of the situation in Germany. Even when entry in the United States was not possible, they might have gone to other countries such as Chile, Bolivia and China, which still granted entry visas. The big obstacle then for my parents was money. They were too proud to ask for it, and when finally a Jewish organization asked for them, it was too late. The borders were closed. Although I had no positive proof, I blamed my cousins for the lack of genuine concern to raise $800, the amount needed for two visas to Shanghai to save two lives, or at least to allow them to die in dignity.

I hadn't been fully aware of what was behind Mutti's feelings towards Albert and was dumfounded by these accusations but kept my own counsel. Fleeing to Shanghai, widely regarded as a problematic because of poor living conditions there, was not an option for her parents because of her father's deteriorating health. It was a matter of happenstance that her family could not help. Her elderly uncles and aunts in Berlin were in the same predicament as her parents, with no money to spare and no place to go. Once war broke out, the cousins who managed to flee were no position to help either. Mutti later admitted she didn't have any idea of what else they could have done to enable her family to emigrate before the war, but there was simply no way for her feelings of loss and guilt to be quelled.

Mutti did try to reconcile the death of her mother with guilt about her own survival, but she needed to focus on the everyday tasks of getting her children off to school and herself to work at the sanitarium. After cereal for breakfast, we would board the Santa Monica Blue Bus that stopped on Ocean Avenue, across the street from the Kensington. I wore my jeans and striped t-shirt, and Monika wore a crinkled dress with sash. We had student bus passes around our necks that the driver punched, also tickets for our cafeteria lunch that were punched later. After school, we checked out sports equipment at the school's supervised playground, and then went home to meet Mutti when she got off work. I bought a bike from the school janitor for $3 that provided me with mobility to explore the streets of Santa Monica. A mechanic at the gas station near the Santa Monica Pier showed me how to change a bike tire and let me use his tools to do simple repairs.

Monika, then six years old, has only vague recollections of bewilderment during her first days in Madison Elementary. She recalls that one day she decided to go home on her own. She caught the city bus at school and by mistake got off too soon on Ocean Avenue. She couldn't find where she lived and so walked back to school to get help. A person in the school office drove her home to the Kensington. Many years later Monika recounted a single incident.

> First grade … I didn't really know what was going on, but I was adjusting. After a while, a new girl, Zelda, came to class. She was Black and appeared to be scared just I had been. So I befriended her. We sat together.

Since I was three years older than Monika, my adjustment posed fewer challenges. Unlike Monika, I had already learned how to read in Germany. My fourth-grade teacher, Mrs. Fischer, introduced me to the class as well as to the system of using gold stars to reward good spelling. Hans, a blond German boy in class, was helpful during my orientation period, but that stopped when his parents told him not associate with me because they didn't want him to continue speaking German. His hesitancy in telling me made me suspect that there were other reasons.

During the first few months, I read children's books to build up my English vocabulary. By the end of the school year, I caught up with reading, writing, and spelling. Having experienced the regimentation and rigor of the German system made it easy to navigate the relaxed and nurturing environment of my new school. Whereas I relished independence, Monika was young enough to be dependent on Mutti for guidance.

Americanization took its course – hands over heart, pledge of allegiance, singing the odd lyrics of the Star-Spangled Banner. I learned all about the pilgrims, cowboys and Indians, the American Revolution, the Erie Canal, and how to square dance. Do-si-do! The all-purpose second-person English pronoun "you" replaced the informal German "du" and formal "Sie." American slang came naturally through playmates. I learned the hard way that kids were "only kidding" when they called you a Nazi. The principal urged Mutti to teach her son about democracy after I punched a kid for mistaking me as a member of the "master race." It didn't take long to learn the ropes of getting along with American kids by not taking ritual insults seriously. My adjustment to social norms included standing by quietly while kids chanted ugly racial epithets while playing basketball after school.

Apart from the challenges of adjusting to a new situation, our first year in America was marvelous. There were many new sights in sunny Santa Monica – exotic plants, magical hummingbirds, NS Man of War jellyfish. Then there were the Muscle Beach characters with tattoos, who played ping-pong, lifted weights and did acrobatics against the backdrop of the mighty Pacific

Monika and I took to American food readily. We ate corn flakes and shredded wheat, toasted white bread, soft drinks, hamburgers, plenty of readily available ice cream which was only an occasional treat in Germany. Monika developed a taste for tuna salad sandwiches and Cokes. In the front office, Albert kept candy that he bestowed gratis when Monika and I came in with a quarter to buy. We were particularly fond of Abba Zabba taffy with a peanut butter center.

There were plenty of amusements in Santa Monica and adjacent Ocean Park just a mile south. We attended Saturday matinees for kids at the Criterion in downtown Santa Monica. Within walking distance was the Santa Monica Pier. When it first opened in 1909, it had two parts. One carried sewer pipes out to sea and later accommodated fishermen and sightseers. The other abutting it was Pleasure Pier that featured amusements and entertainment, including the Hippodrome building that housed a Charles Looff Carousel and later one from the Philadelphia Toboggan Company.

Monika and I learned to roller skate in the pier's ballroom and occasionally ventured out with Mutti to play pinball in the arcades, where we would pile into a photo booth to document our presence. The end of the pier jutted out into the ocean providing boat launches and fishing spots. I found my angling spot on the rafters under the pier where I reeled in my share of seaweed as well as the occasional perch or mackerel that I would throw back.

I liked the informality of American life and the generosity of the people. For us, America was a consumer heaven of sweets and toys available through small convenience stores. One downside of this mercantile extravaganza was the widespread litter that would not have been tolerated in Germany.

While living at the Kensington we got to know Albert and Estelle's family. Their two sons, Albert Junior and Max, had families of their own. In the playroom set up in their grandparents' apartment, we played with two of the Stanley's young grandchildren, Steve and Dinah. Estelle had a photo of Max, an engineer and test pilot for Northrop, standing in front of the experimental Flying Wing. We went to visit Max's family, who lived in a hillside house in upscale Pacific Palisades, north of Santa Monica. Since my English still felt inadequate in settings like this, I didn't interact much, and instead looked around Max's house, impressed by its size and high-quality furnishings. The house had huge windows with vistas of the colorful landscaped grounds. I descended on their piano and picked out a few German tunes.

We also visited Mutti's maternal relatives who lived in the mostly Jewish Fairfax area in Los Angeles, a half-hour bus ride from Santa Monica. Unlike the Stanleys, who were thoroughly American, these German-speaking cousins left Berlin in 1938 and brought with them memories of the Berlin *mishpachah*. They knew Mutti, their youngest cousin, when she was still a child. We quickly became the stateside poor relations under their watchful eye, following the pattern established in Germany. Occasionally hearing the German chatter of our Berlin relatives did not distract from our intense Americanization.

At home, Monika and I recited TV commercial jingles and mastered the technique of jarring our little Admiral TV set to stabilize the image, then twisting the knobs to adjust vertical and horizontal holds. The omnipresent jingles and slogans drummed the rhythm of English into our German brains. Mutti sent us to the grocery store near Santa Monica Pier to buy the same bread, milk, and cereals that were advertised on TV.

After a steady diet of cowboy shows, such as The Cisco Kid and The Lone Ranger, I came across live broadcasts of baseball games between the Los Angeles Angels and the Hollywood Stars in the Pacific Coast League. Dick Stuart (later nicknamed Dr. Strangeglove), who played for the 1957 Hollywood Stars, had a temper tantrum on live TV. It took me a while to figure out the ins and outs of this national pastime, but once I did, I was hooked. I also became a full-fledged American consumer who enjoyed soft drinks from vending machines that were meant to be drunk straight out of the bottle, a practice that would have been considered rude in the old country. Stacks of comic books were piled on my bed. I looked at an ad that showed a smiling lad with a Daisy BB gun and wondered what it would take to convince my mother to allow me to have one.

Monika and I made regular visits to Estelle's kitchen to taste her freshly baked, crisp sugar cookies that we munched while overlooking Muscle Beach. Estelle influenced my vision of America. She subscribed to the *Los Angeles Times* and talked to me about news items that sparked my interest in politics and current events. She admired Eleanor Roosevelt and had supported Adlai Stevenson. This exposure established my liberal politics for life.

I formed a different kind of relationship with Albert Senior who was not a talkative type. To instill a work ethic, he gave me a job watering the flowerbeds in the Kensington that provided some pocket money. Every day I saw him in the front office minding the store. Behind him was another desk from which his son ran his insurance business.

Gradually, I got to know the soft side of "old Albert." He invited me to his hothouse where he introduced me to his gardening pursuits, perhaps to inspire my flower-watering work. I wanted to please him regardless of his growing disapproval of Mutti who took liberties with social norms. This became obvious when she started to date. When a muscular wrestler came calling at the motel reception area, Albert gave him a disapproving look. This burly gentleman caller took me to a wrestling match where he was the villain who fought the "good guy." When I asked him why he lost, he was silent, obviously no superhero. Afterwards, when I watched professional wrestling matches on television, I understood that they were faked and fixed. I lost interest.

In time, Mutti found a steady boyfriend, Bill Asbury, an amiable fellow from Arkansas. We all got to know his parents, who lived in a bungalow near the JC Penney Department Store parking lot that they managed. Monika and I spent time with them while Mutti and Bill went on dates, and we continued to see them on our own as if we were their grandchildren. We watched cowboy programs while they treated us to heaps of ice milk. Mutti told us that they were Mormons and pointed out the enormous Los Angeles California Temple on Santa Monica Boulevard in West Los Angeles that could be seen from Santa Monica. The Asbury couple were naturally kind people. They knew we were Jewish and never mentioned religion during the many years we knew them as family friends, long after Mutti broke up with Bill. When I was a teenager, Bill's sister, Virginia, invited me to ride bareback on her horse, which took off like a shot after I got on. Unlike Mutti's unsuccessful stunt ride at the circus in Berlin, I managed to stay on.

During our first years in the New World, Monika and I embraced the American enterprising spirt starting with my odd jobs for Albert. We established our soda bottle return business, commandeering a shopping cart from the local grocery store to stash and carry bottles left on the beach. Coke and Pepsi bottles were always good for cash returns, and we quickly learned that the "lesser" brands, such as Nehi, couldn't be redeemed. By noon most any day, we had a shopping cart full of sandy bottles which we took to our local grocer who was "thrilled" to accept our soiled treasure and reclaim the shopping cart that we "borrowed."

From the proceeds, there would be enough money for a burger and shake from Honest John's stall on the pedestrian Speedway at Santa Monica Pier. His full name was John Critoria, a 300-pound wrestler who looked like he could gobble up the little kids who dared approach his burger altar, but we weren't fooled. Seated on stools watching him flip burgers, we got a close look at the tattoos on his arms while we munched.

On occasion, Monika went to the beach on her own. Mutti warned Monika not to go with any strange man and one day, when a photographer took a picture of her, he asked her to accompany him to his apartment so that he could develop the film and give her a copy. She refused, explaining that her mother had forbidden her to go with strangers. In the years to come, Mutti's protective instincts forestalled potential trouble.

On my own, I went to the recreational part of Muscle Beach to play ping-pong and chess with the old men who congregated there under the palms on a regular basis. After taking a gander at the weightlifters, I played ping-pong with an amiable, eccentric fellow who handcrafted exotic paddles with corked surfaces and curved handles, which were supposed to bring extra power and control to the game. I beat him every time with my cheap sandpaper version. I would like to think this was due to my superior skill, not his *noblesse oblige*.

Mutti was a pushover when it came to things we wanted, so long as she could afford them. I got my cap pistols, but she nixed my request to use my saved-up money to buy a Daisy air rifle. By age 11, I had done my share of imaginary military service, much to the chagrin of my pacifist mother. On the sly, I shot a 22-caliber rifle at the shooting game at the Ocean Park Amusement Pier, but other than that I adhered to her admonishment to avoid violence, to know my own strength, and never to hit a girl even in jest.

Gradually, Monika and I became aware of the challenges Mutti faced and the medical treatment she received. A fuller picture emerged over time in her daybooks that included appointments with doctors, dentists, and relatives, as well as details about prescriptions and finances. She noted that on May 3, 1955, her doctor prescribed Thorazine (chlorpromazine), an antipsychotic drug used to treat schizophrenia and manic depression. On July 14 she wrote in German, "Thank you, God, for giving us peace and happiness," followed by the entry at the end of the week, "Pay day 42.05 dollars." On August 11 she noted that she decided to stop taking her Thorazine. That didn't bode well.

Clearly, she didn't make enough money to make ends meet. Lacking American credentials, she was limited to low-paying jobs as a practical nurse in sanitariums. I didn't like seeing her in the white uniform that came to symbolize her unhappiness. Years later, she wrote about her first nursing jobs in America.

> I spent about six years nursing in these sanitariums or rest homes, all of which had fancy names, such as Golden Crest Retirement Homes. I was never addressed by my name. It was always just "Nurse." It was as impersonal as being called, "Hey, you!" But what did I expect? Still, the

impersonal atmosphere of the sanitarium did not bring me to put a "professional" distance between me and my patients. All had the similar two-patient rooms. All these smelled of feces and urine; and the odor remained because patients were not kept clean enough, and Lysol and other disinfectants were insufficiently used to clean the floors. Signifying the shortage of nursing staff and the low pay and respect accorded to nurses, the ever-present odor reminded the nurse who wanted to be a good nurse of the endless struggle to be one. I never remained too long in one place, always giving notice before I was about to be fired for voicing my opinion. I must have worked for at least ten sanitariums within a ten-mile radius.

During 1955, Mutti worked in Berkshire Sanitarium and in 1956, after a hiatus, she was at Crescent Bay Convalescent Sanitarium in Santa Monica where she crossed the professional line when it came to the care of a patient who was completely immobile and needed to be fed.

Mr. James, an elderly gentleman suffered from multiple sclerosis. He was completely helpless but could utter words with great difficulty. I felt compassion for him. He never lost his dignity, and I never lost my patience attending him, regardless the pressure from my nurse in charge. On my day off, I visited Mr. James with Monika to cheer him up. I didn't stay in this sanitarium to see Mr. James through the last stage of his illness. It was too painful for me. Mr. James also didn't want me to stay. I resigned.

Mutti told us that Mr. James' family didn't visit very often, and she believed they resented the attention she gave him because it made them look bad. They accused her of trying to ingratiate herself with him.

Mother's subsequent work history was spotty. In 1957, she was on the nursing staff at Saint John's Hospital in Santa Monica, where she was let go for insubordination for speaking out about patient care practices. For a while she did private nursing and then held various other low-paying, health-related jobs. From 1959 to 1970, she worked as a nurse receptionist in several doctor's offices and afterwards for the Beverly Crest Convalescent Hospital in Beverly Hills.

Mutti came to realize the roadblocks she faced in making a life for herself and her family. Although she valued the personal freedom she found in America, she discovered that its way of life, rooted in individualism, lent itself to the stigmatization and isolation of sick and poor people unable to support themselves. She understood that for single women, especially those with children like herself, marriage was the only viable option for a decent life unless you had a job that paid very well.

There were additional complications. Her low self-esteem, rooted in survivor's guilt, led to unsettling feelings of resentment and entitlement. She still harbored a grudge against Albert whose grumpiness blunted his obvious generosity. Feeling under siege and powerless during her periods of depression, she would joke that what she really wanted was "tea and sympathy," referring to the film with that title starring John Kerr and Deborah Kerr, released in 1956, which involves the affectionate relationship between a sensitive prep school student and the school coach's wife.

11

TRANSPLANTED MISHPACHAH

Mutti craved the warm connection to her family and community that had been her mainstay in Berlin, and which could only be recreated by connecting with her maternal cousins in America. Family members were always present in Mutti's mind, and I sometimes felt she lived in two places, LA and the Berlin of times gone by. Albert and Estelle Stanley, whose ancestors left Poland for America during the 19th century, were sympathetic sponsors but not part of the Berlin group whose bonds were formed through hardship and profound loss.

Although her fluent English expedited communication with Albert, Mutti found no basis for talking about personal or emotional challenges with him, and so their conversations were restricted to here-and-now practical matters. Albert focused on helping our family to adjust and to become self-sufficient. He didn't communicate any understanding of the psychological impact of the Nazi persecutions that shaped our lives. He knew very little about the background of our Silberstein relatives in Berlin; however, there were still the shared Krotoczynski family roots in Poland. Mutti would have loved to hear him talk more about the family's past.

A Southerner by birth, Albert Stanley was born Albert Skalowski in 1880 and grew up in Macon, Georgia. He was the son of Benjamin Skalowski, who was born in Posen, Poland, and Helena Krotoczynski

Skalowski, who was born in Kleczew. Early in his life, Albert's family assumed the anglicized surname, Stanley. Albert studied engineering at Georgia Tech and then married Estelle Michelson, who was born in Cook County, Illinois. Estelle's father came to Illinois directly from Russia and her mother from New York.

According to Mutti, after Albert graduated from Georgia Tech, a job with the Bell Telephone Company brought him to California. At some point after he settled in Santa Monica and went into real estate, he was listed among 14 founders of the Kiwanis Club of Santa Monica, a charitable organization founded in 1922. Albert and Estelle were community-minded members of Beth Shalom, a reform synagogue in Santa Monica. Their sons, Max and Albert, both married Christians and did not practice Judaism.

Her diary entries document regular visits to Estelle that balanced her awkward relationship with Albert. Estelle was kindly disposed and open to forging relationships with us on warm and open terms, but her influence over Mutti's attitude and behavior was limited. On one occasion, Mutti had a quarrel with disapproving Albert and in a fit of anger moved us out to a motel across the street where we stayed for a week. Albert was kind enough to let us move back after she calmed down and apologized.

When in a better frame of mind, Mutti's writings reflected her eventual appreciation of the Stanleys and her connection to them, albeit somewhat reluctantly. She understood that her relatives did what they could to help and that they accepted her, no matter what.

> We went to Estelle's home delivering birthday presents to her, red roses and a big box of candy. Estelle and Albert were happy that we made such a fuss over her birthday, her 84th. I believe we are finally accepted as close family. When we were reminiscing over our ancestors, Albert told me that our great-grandmother lived up to 100 years and he also admitted for the first time that her name was Krotoczynski.

As an antidote to the life her American cousins represented, Mutti conjured a vision of her paternal heritage that was far removed from her years in Germany and England and stood in stark contrast to her new life in California. She revived the cultural disparity between the Silbersteins and the Krotoczynskis. She emblemized her father's Polish origins through imagery that may well have been inspired by paintings of shtetl life by Marc Chagall and by songs she knew by heart from *Fiddler on the Roof*. She wrote about her father and his brother Charlie, who were expected to follow in the footsteps of their late father, Isaac Joseph, an accomplished cantor.

They traveled from village to village, singing in each village. Even the Polish and Russian officers demanded "concerts" given by the little Jewish ghetto boys who had such beautiful voices. When Stephan's teacher offered to send him to Kiev for further study, he said he wanted to go home to live with his mother. Cantor Lebovic said the boy was bringing shame on his Papa's head because he did not want to become a cantor like his father.

In this fanciful account, she tells how the enterprising brothers were targeted by gossips, and quotes their meddlesome chatter as she recalled it from her father's portrayal of the drama.

> 'Have you heard Ruda's eldest son? I always knew it. His head is full of girls instead of the studies. And his brother Charlie is even worse, a real disgrace. He ran away from the cantor. People whisper that he will go to a Russian school.' Stephan spoke Yiddish and Hebrew and broadened his horizons reading books in Polish, Russian, and English. He wanted to go to America where all his half sisters and brothers were. There were 30 boys in Cantor Lebovic's class. Among them was Yankele, the oldest at age 14, who chided Stephan for wanting to leave his Jewish school, 'Do you want to become a goy in America? No cheder, no *schul*? It's easy to become a goy in America, you won't have to wear a yarmulke or tzitzit.'

Whatever the gossips said, Stephan was forced to choose. He wanted to please his mother, Ruda, by continuing his studies to become a cantor, which he did in later life, but also wanted to go to America with his beloved younger brother who was temperamentally unsuited to pursue a religious vocation. Ruda gave in, knowing that there was no future for her sons in pogrom-plagued Poland. At the turn of the century, she arranged their passage to America where they would join their five half-siblings, Rose, Rachel, Abraham, Esther, and Helena, in Macon, Georgia.

According to family lore about their years in America, the two brothers lived with their half-siblings in Georgia and joined them as apprentices in the family store to learn tailoring and the retail business. Stephan, or "Steve" as he was called by his American relatives, adjusted well to his new life. Charlie was a different story. Rachel, the oldest half-sister, had little good to say about Charlie. She also took a dim view of Stephan's desire to become an assimilated Jew. Mutti mimicked what Rachel may have said.

> The older one is fine and polite, but they say he wants to give up everything to be a goy, but this troublesome Charlie, they should have locked him up in the shtetl where he came from.

Although Stephan was really Albert's uncle, they were close in age and got along well. Nevertheless, things took a turn for the worse when one of the half-brothers discovered that Charlie took money from the store till. He threatened to beat Charlie but relented when Charlie agreed to leave for England. Stephan agreed to accompany his brother as he had when they both left Poland.

Stephan (aka Steve) and Charlie lived in London after they left their relatives in Georgia at the turn of the century. They both became British subjects in 1907. In London, both brothers were drapers and tailors. Unlike Stephan, Charlie wanted to assimilate to expand his trade. For that reason, according to his grandson, he changed his surname from Krotoczynski to Josephson (with a nod to his father, Isaac Joseph), not only to avoid spelling problems but also to minimize exposure to antisemitism. The two brothers, who lived under the same roof for several years, had a falling out after Charlie hurriedly married Rebecca Champagne and subsequently, according to Mutti, had eight "unwanted" children with her. While Charlie was struggling to cope with his growing family, Stephan continued working as a tailor. Mutti told a story about how a palace guard came to recruit him to be a tailor for the Prince of Wales, but it is more likely that her father worked for a Saville Row tailor with aristocratic clients.

During this period in England, Stephan's mother and his younger siblings had migrated from Poland to Germany. His legendary career as a tailor to royalty ended when he felt compelled to move to Germany in 1912 to help support and care for his 72-year-old mother, Ruda, who had recently moved from Kleczew to Strasburg with her son, Sally, and two married daughters, Malka Lowenthal and Rosa Heibel.

Mutti didn't tell us much about her paternal aunts, Malka and Rosa, other than to mention their disagreeable presence when she and her parents lived with them in Strasburg for a brief period after being forced to leave Friedland. She talked more about Heinz and James, the two "crazy" musicians and attributed her own "craziness" as well as her interest in music to these two cousins. She never knew that they went on to study music at the University of Hamburg and had long careers as professional musicians.[1]

What a thrill it would have been for Mutti to have known what happened to them. The two brothers fled to Shanghai with their father, Sally Krotoschinski and his wife Nanette Koster. Sally died in Shanghai in 1947. Afterwards, Heinz and James, immigrated to the United States with Nanette, initially settling in Chicago. James moved to the Los Angeles area and died in Laguna Beach in 1984. Neither my mother nor Albert Stanley had any idea that blood relatives from the Krotoczynski line had settled in the United States. One trace of their musical legacy, "The Krotoschinski Polka" performed by Hans Arno Simon, can be found on the Internet.

Mutti's lack of connection to her paternal relatives stood in contrast to the Berlin mishpachah she knew as a child, the aunts and uncles who perished and the cousins who immigrated to America. Her deep emotional connection to these maternal relatives grew from her own memories and countless family stories. One surviving cousin, Fred Wellner, left Berlin in 1938, and his fiancée, the former Lea Schulman, came to New York in 1940 to marry him. They eventually settled permanently in Los Angeles.

Mutti remembered Fred and Lea as a glamorous couple at family gatherings in Berlin during the 1930s. Decades later, this couple was fluent in English and had a family that was in tune with the American way of life. Fred, whom she knew as a self-assured and dashing young man, had become a bald, middle-aged man who was hard working and hard of hearing. While he was razor focused on making a living in the furniture business, his beautiful and charismatic wife pursued a painting career in the bourgeoning art scene in Southern California.

Mutti said that her Berlin cousins were lucky because they managed to get out of Germany before war broke out. What she didn't talk about is that for Fred such luck came at a price. He lost his parents, Salo and Regina Wellner, who died in the Trawniki concentration camp in Poland in 1942.

Our family made regular visits to Fred and Lea and their two sons David and Jamie, via Blue Bus 7 which ran east from Santa Monica to Los Angeles via Pico Boulevard. The Wellners owned a rancher a few blocks from La Cienega Boulevard, south of Pico Boulevard. Their home was decorated in stylish Danish modern and appointed with updated appliances. On one occasion when we stayed over, we enjoyed the novelty of seeing a dad make breakfast when Fred emerged from his study in the morning, a tall thin figure in a checkered woolen bathrobe, ready to try out the new waffle iron on the breakfast table.

Occasionally, we saw the other relatives at family events at the Wellner home, including Lea's parents, Max Schulman and his wife, Judith Hendel Schulman. Max was from a German-speaking community in Romania and Judith was born in Poland where both she and Max lived when they married in 1917. When the Wellners invited us to Passover Seder in 1955 and 1956, there was a lot of talk about the resurrection of Omi Schulman's famous Viennese torte. By popular demand, she would make one for Passover just as she had in the old days. This torte gave us a glimpse of the lost but not forsaken Berlin family life that no one ever talked about.

My second cousins were about my age. David was 11, a year older, and Jamie a year younger. Both wore jeans and t-shirts and sported crew cuts. Since English was mainly used in the Wellner household, I wrongly assumed that the two boys were out of the loop when the adults chattered in their native language. I didn't realize that both understood everyday German, and still do. At that time, my English was still a work in progress, so I didn't have much in common with my cousins; however, there were routine activities that saved the day. After dawdling in their shared bedroom stocked with sports gear and ski equipment, I tagged along with David and Jamie for swims in a neighbor's pool and rounds of miniature golf on La Cienega Boulevard. My connection with them accelerated the process of becoming an American.

I was there when their father announced that he would build an addition at the back of their house to serve as Lea's art studio. On one occasion, I saw her finishing up an exuberant abstract oil painting on a large canvas while listening to classical music, perhaps preparing for one of her solo exhibitions. I liked Lea because she took the trouble to focus on my interests and engaged me in spirited conversation in both English and German. She introduced me to modern art and classical music and described the power and freedom of Abstract Expressionism with the charming authority one might hear in the chichi art galleries on La Cienega Boulevard.

In contrast to his ebullient wife, Fred was serious and task-oriented, intent on doing his best to provide for his family and become integrated into American society. Clearly, he was a well-intentioned person with a keen sense of duty, who commanded respect. Nevertheless, I didn't take to him because he was prone to lecturing without establishing a warm emotional connection, which may have had something to do with his hearing issues. "Dear old Fred means well," Mutti would say, blithely assuming that stoicism was baked into his personality. She didn't mention that Fred, too, had lost his parents and kept to herself whatever feelings of guilt they might have had in common for having left parents behind to die. At that time, I wasn't aware that Fred's parents had helped my mother's financially strapped family before the war.

The Wellners rarely mentioned their years in Germany, and never discussed the circumstances leading up to Kristallnacht that impelled them to leave. To them, bringing up the past was pointless. I never heard any relative talk explicitly about the Holocaust. Mutti also participated in maintaining the wall of silence at family dinners. No haunting memories of life in Berlin were discussed. While Fred tended to be quiet, Lea took center stage alongside my mother bantering about the latest trends and developments like sisters. Mutti admired

Lea. They took to each other, each one attracted to the other's spirited temperament.

Mutti soon sensed tensions in her cousins' marriage due to differences in age and interests. They grew apart and eventually Lea left. They divorced in October 1968. Sadly, she died of cancer a year later. Fred supported Lea financially to the day she died and afterwards carried a torch for her by surrounding himself with her colorful paintings. Although Mutti was very fond of Lea, she reluctantly disapproved of what she did to "poor" Fred. Still, she admired her spunk and took her death hard.

My social contacts with the Wellner family happened mainly during our initial years in America, so my information about them was formed largely by what my mother told me. I saw Jamie several years ago, but we didn't talk much about our family background or Nazi Germany, although we sprinkled a German word or two into our conversation. I got in touch with David recently to learn more about our common family history. In our email exchange, David described the circumstances that forced his parents to flee Berlin and the reason why his paternal grandparents remained behind.

The story my dad told was that he was visited in Berlin by his uncle, who had immigrated to America when he was young. This was at a time when Hitler was coming to power. As my dad put it, his uncle took him and his brother Henry by the ear and brought them to the American embassy for a visa. My dad's parents refused to come, thinking that it would all blow over. When Dad arrived in New York, he got a job at a little men's clothing store, owned by an old Jewish man. I think he said that he worked six or more days a week. Meanwhile, my mom's family escaped from Berlin and found their way to Africa. The story goes that my grandfather, Max Schulman, cleverly melted down some gold he had and cast it into the form of some wrenches. He coated them with dirty grease, wrapped them up, and thereby was able to take his gold with him. My grandmother's brother, Filo Hendel, was a ship captain of some sort and got the family passage to Africa. I don't know which country took them in, but my grandmother, Judith Hendel, told me that this country regarded Germany as an enemy and so she and my mom were allowed to stay in a place of their own. Although my grandfather and his son, Benjamin Schulman, were allowed to work, they had to report to a compound every night since they had been German citizens. They moved to the Belgian Congo where Max had a tire repair shop and Judith made ladies hats. I still have a couple of beautifully made wooden hat forms which Max made for her.

According to the Manifest of Alien Passengers, Lea Schulman immigrated on her own to America. She boarded a ship from Genoa, Italy for the United States in 1940, listing her last residence in the Belgian Congo. There was a story that she had to sleep with the captain because her papers were not in order. David thought that this story may have been apocryphal, told to dramatize the challenges of traveling during wartime. After Lea arrived in Baltimore by ship, she joined Fred Wellner in New York where they married in a civil ceremony. David said that only one or two other people were present. Fred and Lea celebrated afterwards by having lunch at one of the iconic New York automats operated by Horn and Hardart. Meanwhile, Lea's parents and her brother, Benjamin, continued to live in the Belgian Congo. In 1946, the parents left the Congo and arrived in Baltimore, then settled in Los Angeles in 1947. Benjamin remained in the Congo where he met and married a French woman, Mimi. He owned a eucalyptus and tea plantation and had to give it up when he and his wife were forced to leave the Congo. After moving to South Africa, he owned and operated a shoe factory and then an ice cream factory. He and Mimi had three children. Benjamin remained in South Africa and visited his family in America on one or two occasions.

New York City turned out to be a stopping off place for Fred and Lea and their relatives who had fled Berlin. David didn't know all the details about why and when they left New York.

They wanted to go to the west coast because they had friends in L.A. The B'nai B'rith gave them a bus ticket to Sacramento. There my mom worked as a seamstress and Dad had a job as a "skip chaser" for a department store. That meant he was tasked to look for people who hadn't paid their bills to the store. I can't really imagine what that entailed but that's what he did. They finally found their way to LA and hooked up with their various friends. As I recall, Dad got a job selling lamps made of Lucite, which was a big thing after the war. I think he told me that at that point he didn't have a car, and so he took the bus to various stores. Eventually he got a job with Mode furniture, who mainly made the latest couch style, the sleeper.

Fred Wellner's brother, Henry, and his wife, Rita, probably lived in New York for a while after they arrived there in 1940 via Liverpool. They applied for US citizenship in late 1944 while in Kansas City, and moved to California at about the same time Fred and Lea did. Lea applied for citizenship during November 1944 in Los Angeles where she lived with her infant son after relocating from Sacramento to join her parents who arrived in LA in 1947 from the Congo. The 1950 Census shows the Wellners living in Los Angeles. During the 1950s, Fred expanded his work as a salesman despite the challenges of his hearing loss.

> Early on in their life in LA, my dad had an operation to fix his hearing, but it was not successful. I vaguely remember standing in his lap and seeing the stitches behind his ear. He was fitted with a hearing aid, which he wore on his chest while working as a traveling salesman.

While Fred was out of the house, Lea took care of her young children and once they were in school, she had the opportunity to pursue her interest in art.

> My mom may have been influenced by the growing feminist movement and started to branch out. She took some classes at a junior college and began painting. She was tired of being a *hausfrau* and wanted to spread her wings. My dad didn't really like this and so the tension in their relationship grew. I was drawn to my mom's liberal, curious, artistic outlook. She had books on yoga, psychology, and feminism, such as *The Second Sex* by Simone de Beauvoir, and books about artists, such as Paul Klee and Leonardo da Vinci.

In their own way, Fred and Lea made the best of the opportunities in America and avoided dwelling on the past. David didn't learn about the circumstances that impelled his father to leave Berlin until he was older, but even as a child, he saw evidence of the pain Fred carried with him.

> As to my dad's feelings about leaving his parents behind, I remember that every Yom Kippur he would light some candles, put them on fireplace mantel and would silently weep. As a kid I didn't know what to make of that.

Soon after we got to know the Wellners, Mutti's other cousins from Berlin, Fritz and Resi Silberstein, arrived from New York. We called Fritz Silberstein "Freddie" to avoid confusing him with Fred Wellner, with whom he shared the name "Fritz" during their time in Berlin.

Freddie was the son of Paula Schlamm Silberstein and Siegfried Silberstein, who had been the chief benefactor of the Krotoczynski family. Mutti remembers Freddie as a sophisticated young man, who was perhaps more attuned to the cultural trends in Weimar Berlin than his handsome and practical cousin Fred.

Freddie's family fell on hard times after the Nazis confiscated Siegfried's business. Unable to obtain a visa for the United States, he obtained papers for Shanghai and went there in 1939. There is no indication that Freddie ever came across Mutti's cousins, Heinz and James Krotoschinski, during his eight years in Shanghai. Freddie's parents did not leave with him. Siegfried died of heart failure in 1939. Paula died in Auschwitz the following year.

After the war, Freddie emigrated from Shanghai to New York where he married Resi Hanfling, a German-speaking French from Leipzig who had a daughter, Evelyne, from a previous marriage. While there is little information about Resi's family background, we knew that both she and her first husband, whose last name was Feldstein, had been in the French Resistance while their young daughter was sheltered by French Catholic family. Resi's husband was arrested and deported to a concentration camp where he died. After the war, Resi and Evelyne emigrated to the United States, settling in New York where Resi and Freddie's daughter, Marion, was born.

Although we all knew that Resi had been an officer in the French Resistance, I never heard her discuss that period in her life until she was 90 years old when she told me some stories about her sabotage missions against the German occupiers and how she once had to order the execution of an informer. She said that no person should ever be forced to do what she had to do back then.

Resi was an energetic, creative, and independent person. On one occasion in California after she cooked us dinner, we offered to do the dishes as she quickly began to clean them. She looked up and in her high-pitched distinctive German accent she exclaimed, "Oh no! The 'ditches' are nothing to me!" It was clear that many things were no big deal to Resi after what she had experienced!

Freddie never discussed his nine years in Shanghai. Keeping his feelings submerged in his sardonic outlook on life, he sought refuge in his extensive collection of opera recordings and framed photographs of opera stars like Enrico Caruso. To my surprise, he was also devoted to the Los Angeles Dodgers, whose exploits on radio provided white noise for his soul. Freddie recited the latest triumphs and blunders of the LA Dodgers in his thick German accent, and took delight in telling sardonic, some would say, risqué jokes.

No wonder Mutti and Freddie were confidants. Freddie was never judgmental. They formed a lifelong bond based on their shared sense of the absurd. Freddie spent years in poverty as a refugee in Shanghai, so he could relate to how Mutti had to fend for herself as a refugee in England and Germany. They understood that silly Weimar-era licentiousness could soothe their sense of abandonment. She liked him because he was unabashedly "naughty" and not ashamed of his innocent diversions. He would put on an act and tell her that his penchant for cheesecake pictures was a poor substitute for the attention that was not always forthcoming from his loving but no-nonsense wife. We thought that Resi tolerated Freddie's harmless antics but kept him in line in her loving way. They seemed like a close couple and were fond and protective of my mother and very understanding of her mental illness.

The Silbersteins appeared better off than the Wellners supposedly because of the *Wiedergutmachung* [reparations] they received from the German government in restitution for the loss of Freddie's father's nightgown business. Freddie's day job as a bread delivery man could hardly have supported his family's comfortable lifestyle in a nice Jewish neighborhood not far from Beverly Hills. True to her background, Resi took to French furniture and decor including golden mirrors and brocade curtains, glass tables, brass telephones, and a French toy poodle to boot – quite a contrast to the Wellners' Danish modern.

Then there was my mother's gossip about the different lifestyles of the Wellners and the Silbersteins that went way back to the Berlin days. Freddie Silberstein may have had distinct advantages from birth due to his father's position at the Jewish-owned Wertheim department store that gave him the experience and contacts he needed to start his own business selling dressing gowns. Fred Wellner's father also worked at Wertheim in the toy department and made a nice living before the confiscation of Jewish properties and businesses that led up to Kristallnacht on November 9-10, 1938. Without knowing much about their lives, I formed the impression that Freddie was nonchalant, ironic, fatalistic; and that Fred was hardworking, serious, and responsible.

Mutti kept up a faithful correspondence with her Berlin relatives who lived on the East Coast. Grete and Georg Unger lived in New York until their deaths. Elly and Ted Von Holm lived out their older years in New Hampshire as did Irene Von Holn. In 1957, they all came to Los Angeles to attend David's bar mitzvah. This may have been the only US gathering of the whole mishpachah.

Our Berlin-based *mishpachah* in Los Angeles gradually thinned out. Mutti died in 1991. Fred Wellner remained in the Los Angeles area until his retirement and then moved to Grass Valley to be near his son, David, until his death in 1998. Freddie and Resi Silberstein left Los Angeles for Germany for reasons pertaining to their reparations claim that were never explained, and returned to the United States to live in Florida to be where her oldest daughter, Evelyne and her husband had settled. After Freddie's death in 2002, Resi followed her daughter and her husband to Las Vegas where she lived until her death in 2016.

12

UNDER THE ROLLER COASTER

For our Mutti, the Los Angeles area would be her final destination for coming to grips with the her past that would become increasingly shaped through mental illness. Two years after our arrival in America, Mutti had a "nervous breakdown" that involved mania as well as depression. The medical diagnosis, manic depression, came into use during the 1950s to describe this type of illness but it drew from observations traced back to the Ancient Greeks. In the 19th century, the malady was referred to as "dual form insanity" and "circular insanity" and thought to have had a genetic basis. Since "manic depression" described a range of mental illnesses, the term "bipolar disorder" came into use in the 1960s to clarify the diagnosis.

Mutti's first nervous breakdown in America occurred during May 1956 when she stopped taking the Thorazine prescribed by Dr. Whipps, her family doctor. The manic phase followed days of severe depression. Mutti stayed up all night, scrubbed the walls and floors, and shouted obscenities in a distorted voice that mocked the charm that it normally expressed. Mutti talked wildly about what the Nazis did to her parents and accused our cousins of leaving them in Germany to die. She hallucinated her parents, whom she addressed directly, asking for their forgiveness after cursing them. This is the first time I became aware of what had happened to my mother's parents during the Holocaust.

I implored her to stop ranting, but that made things worse. She lashed out at me, tearing up the new Webster's dictionary that Albert and Estelle had given to me on my 11th birthday. I was shocked because under normal circumstances Mutti rarely raised her voice or lost her temper. I clung to the belief that her normal self was still intact despite her mental issues, and that I must have done something wrong to have caused her to be so angry with me, and that somehow it would still be possible to make things better.

Monika and I ran for help, not to the elderly Stanleys, but to Helen and Ray, their employees. This couple, who lived in one of the apartments at the Kensington, tried to comfort and reassure us, but there was little else they could do. The police took Mutti away to be hospitalized and we stayed with Helen and Ray for a few days, expecting to be reunited with our mother once she calmed down, but that didn't happen.

Albert drove Monika and me to the Jewish Family Service headquarters in Vista del Mar in West Los Angeles for interviews and IQ testing. I wondered whether we would be placed in an institution as we were in Germany when our mother became ill. In a few days, a social worker drove us to our new home with a Jewish family in the Hollywood Hills. On the way, she assured us that our mother was in good hands and acted as if nothing bad had happened.

Our new foster family lived in a pleasant Spanish-style stucco rancher on Beachwood Terrace in a hilly neighborhood two miles north of the center of Hollywood. From the kitchen window, several houses were visible through the smog that blanketed the steep decline below. On the surface, our new family exuded the middle-class normalcy and assurance that I saw on sitcoms. The mother, June, wore her blonde hair in a ponytail, as did her daughter, Roberta. June made Monika and me feel at home and served the three of us peanut butter and jelly sandwiches with milk while we basked in the afternoon sunshine that streamed through the kitchen window.

Roberta, a friendly girl my age, introduced us to her girlfriends in the neighborhood. We played Charades which made me realize how much I had to learn about American culture. Tired of playing only with girls, I took off down the steep road for the local playground to play ping-pong and caroms with some neighborhood boys.

All of us were carpooled to a day camp. When it was our turn, June squeezed two additional children into her Nash Rambler. We drove towards the round Capitol Records Building that emerged through the haze, and after a 15-minute drive, arrived at our destination in Griffith Park. The camp offered horseback riding along a trail close to the nearly dry Los Angeles River that provided me and my fellow campers the opportunity to skip stones on whatever water remained in the riverbed. This camp experience provided my first exposure to "boy talk" about girls.

Our foster father, a teacher, whose first name is now irretrievably lost in the dustbin of memory, assigned me to read Jack London's *Call of the Wild*, which I enjoyed, even though I was put off by his didactic tone in telling me about it. He also harped on my eating too fast. His wife tried to get him to back off, but he found odd ways to assert himself. The family liked to play badminton in the backyard which the father insisted on calling "goodminton." I did my best to avoid him.

One night I woke up terrified with the realization that all people die, and that someday, I, too, would die. Since my own mother was unavailable to share this coming-of-age realization, I talked of my feelings about death to June, who was there only by happenstance. I was grateful that she wanted to hear me out, but I still felt despondent and isolated. I never talked to my mother about my feelings on this topic.

While we were in the foster home, Mutti experienced her first involuntary hospitalization in America which she described years later. Monika and I had no idea of what Mutti's hospitalization involved. Her diary for that year noted that we visited her several times. I have no recollection of these visits. There was no guarantee that we would be reunited as a family again.

At the end of the summer, after three months with the Hollywood foster family, our social worker said that we would be placed in another foster home. We didn't understand why. She explained that it had something to do about the father's misgivings about having a boy and girl of the same age sharing the same bathroom. I thought this was idiotic since I had shared a bathroom with my mother and sister all my life without problems. Like the click of the television channel, this congenial arrangement ended. Several years later by chance, I met my former foster sister at UCLA where she was a student. She reintroduced me to her mother who said that she had been sad to see us go and explained that the real reason for giving us up was that she had been in the process of getting a divorce.

Our departure from the Hollywood Hills was in a hurry. We packed our belongings in the morning and our cheerful social worker from Vista del Mar arrived at noon. She drove us in her station wagon to our new foster home in Lakewood, located 30 miles away, south of Los Angeles. Our new Jewish foster family, this one with a Polish name, had a small, light green stucco ranch house in a tract neighborhood built on former lima bean fields in the early 1950s. Located near the northern edge of Long Beach, our new home in Lakewood was worlds apart from the cosmopolitan areas of Santa Monica, West Los Angeles, and Hollywood that for us had become the norm.

This was our first exposure to marginal American middle-class life in Southern California. Alice, the mother, was tall and skinny, with thin lips, and a dyspeptic face pocked with acne scars. She reminded me of Olive Oil with Popeye in tow. We quickly realized that this family took us in only because of the extra money they would receive for it. Alice skimped on everything. We had Cheerios for breakfast served with whole milk for her own two children but instant powdered milk for us. This discriminatory parsimony was a new thing for Monika and me. Even in orphanages, we never felt we were second class.

Alice made no effort to hide her resentfulness at having to take us in. Although I remained polite, I made faces behind her back. Monika didn't like Alice either but got on well with her well-tempered daughter, Liz, who was a year younger than she. I joined the two girls in playing Jacks on the kitchen floor. That lightened things up a bit.

Liz's brother, Paul, was about my age. He was a heavy kid, passive, unathletic, and no good at school. He resembled his bearlike but harmless father, Saul, who took me aside one day and told me in confidence that his son worried about the size of his penis. I couldn't understand why he was telling me this and what he wanted me to do about it. Days later, I rejected Paul's proposal for mutual masturbation after we came back from a Cub Scout meeting.

I shared a bedroom with Paul and slept on the top bunk where I kept a stash of comic books interspersed with my homework. When my head wasn't buried in my collection of comic books, I furtively played tunes by ear on the family's piano with the understanding that piano lessons were not meant to be. My best times were riding my bike in the neighborhood looking for something interesting to see or do, or joining in when I came across a pickup game of baseball or basketball.

Monika and I didn't go to the same school. She went to third grade at Stephen Foster Elementary, also attended by the family's two children. The reason given for enrolling me in a different school, Gompers Elementary, was to avoid academic rivalry with my foster brother. That suited me fine. For me, school was a liberation from personal circumstances. I liked my sixth-grade teacher, Mr. Lightfoot, who went the extra mile by taking our class on a week-long camping expedition to Idyllwild State Park, near the San Jacinto Mountains. We even went on an overnight hike to a mountain lake with a pack mule that lugged our provisions. Mr. Lightfoot believed that education should relate to real life and so had us learn about soil erosion firsthand.

In class, Mr. Lightfoot discussed the Cold War and drew diagrams on the blackboard explaining what would happen to us if the epicenter of an atomic blast were three miles away. Scared and bewildered, I took part in duck and cover drills, careful to shield my eyes from the imaginary blinding flash of the future. By then, I had learned all about the communists and their methods of subversion from the TV series, *I Led Three Lives*. We visited the local Nike missile base, and I wondered what it would be like if we were attacked. I imagined planes falling from the sky with a touch of *Schadenfreude*.

On the weekends, Monika and I went to visit Mutti at the sanitarium in North Hollywood where she was recovering. After leaving the foster home, we walked across a field of dry brush and tumble weeds to a bus stop where we took the express to the LA Bus Terminal. Mutti greeted us upon arrival, and we walked a few blocks past Skid Row and caught a streetcar to North Hollywood where she was being treated. Mutti introduced us to the staff and patients and made a fuss that seemed out of place in the somber clinical surroundings. We went outside to sit and talk. She told us that she made a "miraculous" recovery. We went out to a drug store to order lunch at the counter. I had a burger and shake, and Monika ordered her favorite, tuna sandwich and coke. Then it was time to go.

After our mom was discharged, we continued our weekly visits. We stayed overnight with her at the Kensington and saw Albert and Estelle. One time, we went to McArthur Park where Mutti pointed out the outcasts of society hanging out there and said how sorry she was for them. On November 5, 1956, she bought her first car for $100, a 1946 yellow Buick convertible doomed for the junk yard. She came to pick us up in this jalopy. As she got out extending her arms to greet and hug us, she looked like a flamboyant movie star in her sun dress and scarf whisking us away for a grand weekend outing to Seal Beach, Hollywood Boulevard, and the LA County Museum near the La Brea Tar Pits. Two days later, after Mutti dropped us off, our dyspeptic foster mother made disparaging remarks about her that we readily ignored.

Our trips to the beach in Santa Monica provided respite from the brownish-gray smog that sat over the Los Angeles basin that extended south to Orange County. The sight of the ocean symbolized escape from the endless ribbons of stucco ranch houses and from the dirty palm-studded landscape barely visible from freeway exits and entrances. One day, Mutti's newly found mobility was cut short when she rear-ended another car due to failing brakes on Olympic Boulevard on our way to Santa Monica. After her uninsured car was towed away, we took a bus back to a motel in West Los Angeles where we stayed the night before returning to our foster home.

Several weeks later, Mutti found a new job and went to court to settle the accident, agreeing to pay for the damage in monthly installments. Employed again and on the road again, she went on a campaign to solidify her social connections, filling her diary with lists of the people to be visited or contacted. She noted money borrowed from friends and relatives to be repaid. She made lists of expenditures for every week. She even had a list of her goals in anticipation of getting her children back. On January 1, 1957, there was a written "sky blue" wish list: 1) children home by Easter (from the foster home), 2) get married (happily) in a temple, 3) home, a good, lovely home, 4) have a baby or two, 5) take college courses, 6) be active in school activities of Peter and Monika, 7) write a lot of poems and stories for publication, 8) have a car for me. She added the postscript, "Please, God, love and bless my children and myself, our home and new husband to be."

According to our social worker from Vista del Mar, it was best for Monika and me to remain in the foster home to finish out the school year until June 1957. This also gave Mutti time to rebuild her life. We continued to see her on weekends while she stayed temporarily in the Kensington where Cousin Albert allowed her to remain until she could find an apartment.

As planned, we left the foster home that summer to live with Mother in a green stucco, ten-unit apartment building in West Hollywood, about a mile from Beverly Hills where Mutti worked as a nurse in a sanitarium. Like many kids in those days, I got an afternoon paper route, delivering the *Beverly Hills Citizen News* to apartment dwellers. I knew we needed the money.

In the fall, we enrolled in new schools. I was in the seventh grade at John Burroughs Junior High and Monika was in the fourth at an elementary school whose name we no longer remember. Mine was at Wilshire and North Highland Avenue, within biking distance. I enjoyed biking to school, as Mutti once did when she rode through Berlin to the Mädchenschule in 1937.

Monika and I were home before Mutti returned from work. In her absence, we toasted marshmallows over the stove and overcooked hamburgers for dinner. One day, we decided to surprise her by taking a flash photo as she entered. What we documented was not so much her surprise, but her exhausted look of unhappiness. She looked overweight in the photo, not the beautiful mother of our idealized imagination that had been captured in the few photographs from her youth.

On weekends, we escaped from smoggy Los Angeles, boarding the LA Transit Green Bus on Wilshire Boulevard for Muscle Beach. After we got off at the Santa Monica Pier stop, people could see that Mutti was destined for the beach with her sunglasses, Coppertone suntan lotion, and flip flops. Transformed, she became the complete California woman in her Esther Williams swimsuit. Her colorful bag contained her diary/address book, nail polish, cuticle scissors, emery boards, and a note pad with lists of things to do.

Our time with her involved a concatenation of amusing stories, gleefully told. One of her stories was about Gipsy Gene, a libidinous "free spirit" and "health nut" who ate bananas and according to Mother lived in a tree near Muscle Beach. His carefree life as one of Muscle Beach's Nature Boys group came to an end when he was shot to death by a jealous husband.[1]

On occasion, our fun was mischievously aimed at the oddballs in our midst on the assumption that they didn't understand German. This involved a running commentary in mock Berlin vernacular, such as, *Guck mal den Mann an. Glaub er hat 'n Knall!* (Look at that man, I think he's touched in the head!). Mutti really took to the free-floating "interesting people" that populated Southern California. When spontaneously introducing us to strangers, she peppered her *spiel* with niceties and extravagant compliments, waiting for them to reciprocate in kind, much to my embarrassment. When we encountered people she knew in public, I shuffled impatiently waiting for her grandiosely effusive social display to come to an end. Monika, as I recall, was more patient with these fleeting dramatic social encounters which always drew attention from passersby.

I thought that fishing for the kindness of strangers undermined Mutti's natural charisma. Still, a day didn't go by without her telling us how much she loved and needed us, and thanking us for putting up with her. I began to realize that when she overstepped social boundaries, she was at the mercy of her bipolar condition. I didn't want to reject her, so I learned to compartmentalize my thoughts and minimized my presence at these public adventures of which she was so fond. I was on my way to becoming a loner.

While on my own, I sought out opportunities for pickup basketball, touch football, and baseball. I poured over my comic book collection and shifted my attention to *Mad Magazine* with its satires of consumerism and hypocrisy in modern life. I was also reading newspapers and checked out "real books" from the library, all this in keeping with the great academic success Mutti envisioned for me when she gave me the attaché case in Germany.

Mutti's battle with severe depression diverted her attention from Monika's challenges in school. Instead of focusing on schoolwork, Mutti took Monika under her wing in other ways. She centered on Monika's emotional health, remembering her own experiences growing up lonely as the only child of aging parents. Instead of conventional parenting emphasizing discipline, Mutti provided warm emotional support and believed that having a good time was universal remedy. However, she did have her own way of imposing limits when necessary, as Monika recalled.

Mutti was a lot of fun, but also watched out for me. I remember once we were in a bus station in downtown Los Angeles, I stole a candy bar from a stand while Mutti wasn't looking. When she found out, she said we had to give it back and apologize to the lady. After I did that, she bought the candy and gave it to me without making me feel bad. I never did that again.

When it came to social outings involving Mutti and Monika, I was the third wheel, quiet for the most part, at times morose and bored. Mutti tried to draw me out, attributing my lack of interest to gender and adolescence. Since I didn't take part in the girl activities, the issue of my needing a male role model came up. Mutti contacted the Big Brothers program and to my surprise, a very tall and skinny Big Brother took me to the Coliseum see the Dodgers lose. I felt awkward. We didn't talk much, and he did not come again, much to my relief.

My emotional isolation seemed trivial when more serious problems recurred. Mutti lost her Beverly Hills job and did not explain how she lost it. Since the rent was due, I offered my paper route money for rent, but that fell far short, and so we paid the dreaded visit to the Wellners to "borrow" money to pay the rent.

Mutti was worried and mortified to ask for help. She started to talk again about the desirability of marriage to a nice Jewish man to provide us a stable and happy life; so it was no surprise when Doctor Kay, an internist, showed up in our lives. I had assumed that Fred and Lea introduced Mutti to this newly eligible bachelor since she told us that our relatives wanted to see her married. I later learned that she had worked for him at some point, maybe after she met him. I never got that story straight.

No one ever referred to him by his first name; he was just Dr. Kay, a short, skinny man in his forties who hailed from Detroit. He had a Clark Gable mustache and crew cut. He owned a clinic and drove a late-model black Cadillac. Our relatives encouraged her to give him a chance. When Monika and I were introduced to Dr. Kay, we had our doubts. We thought he was creepy.

Dr. Kay, once divorced, was marriage minded. He was taken by Mutti's good looks and charms. He invited us to his Spanish-style rancher on Olympic Boulevard near Beverly Hills, which was the largest museum for fleas in the LA area. His two huge squat cats, responsible for the flea collection, sat on top of his huge bookcases, which were stacked with medical books and back editions of Esquire that I furtively perused during out visits. He showed me his garage where he was crafting a new bookcase and lectured about the virtues of tongue-and-groove carpentry, and his mastery of it.

After a few months, when it was obvious that he was interested in her, Mutti accepted his offer to move in with him in large part because she couldn't make the rent. There had already been talk about marriage. We met Dr. Kay's amiable tall and heavyset son. His father wanted his "klutzy" son to go to medical school. He never talked about his ex-spouse.

During the period when we lived in Dr. Kay's house, we went to the movies a couple times at Cathay Circle, a movie palace with a looming tower near the intersection of Wilshire and San Vicente. In those days, going to the movies was an elegant experience, complete with ushers in red-trimmed uniforms with brass buttons who used flashlights to guide patrons to their seats. Mutti talked a lot about movies and movie actors. She took us to Hollywood Boulevard to see the names of movie stars embedded in the sidewalk near Grauman's Chinese Theater.

Mutti's relationship with Dr. Kay coincided with her renewed interest in Judaism that had surfaced a year earlier when she arranged for religious instruction for me at Beth Shalom, the reform synagogue in Santa Monica where Albert and Estelle belonged. After a year, I dropped out just before we went to our first foster home, right at the time when it would have been appropriate for me to prepare for my bar mitzvah. Mutti still hoped that despite the time lost and my disinterest in religion, I would agree to take a crash course to prepare for my coming of age.

Dr. Kay arranged to have me tutored in Congregation Sherith Israel, a small Orthodox storefront *schul* on Pico Boulevard near Fairfax under the tutelage of Rabbi Twerski. For reasons that I did not fully understand, Mutti agreed to the Orthodox route that was a departure from the reform Judaism of Beth Shalom. She may have believed choosing Congregation Sherith Israel would have pleased her father whose affiliation with Liberal Judaism did not preclude traditional religious practices, such as the predominant use of Hebrew during services. Perhaps going this route was the only practical path for me to have a timely bar mitzvah. All I had to do was to learn how to read the Hebrew alphabet and be willing to become familiar with certain rituals of the bar mitzvah ceremony.

Mutti was delighted when I agreed to go through the motions of acknowledging my passage to manhood as Jew. Having a bar mitzvah would certainly guarantee that I would be prepared to say kaddish for her father and mother. Given what I knew she went through during the Nazi era, this was the right thing to do.

I agreed to take a crash course from Rabbi Twerski. The only Hebrew words I could read were on kosher food labels. What little I knew about Jewish rituals included saying a few prayers by heart at mealtimes and during Shabbat, Hanukkah, and Passover. I had to laugh because Mutti didn't keep *kosher*. In fact, she made a point of eating rye bread with bacon grease, as we did in Germany after the war, and serving up cheeseburgers with mustard and relish, with great relish. She made fun of Orthodox Jews who employed Shabbos goys to turn on the lights.

Although I had no intention of becoming an observant Jew, I understood that Judaism provided the comfort and reassurance Mutti needed. She liked the simple and pleasant tasks of religious devotion like lighting Sabbath candles and taking a wine sip after the appropriate Hebrew prayer. For her, religious rituals provided the regularity of celestial routine: the sun goes up, and the sun goes down. She lectured us on the virtue of having a routine, which she learned in her British nurses training school, and applied in her harrowing work as a triage nurse during the war, when she gave an extra dose of morphine to suffering patients expected to die. Routine meant absolution from uncertainty. When she counseled Monika and me to have our routines in order, we had visions of bed sheets put on with perfect hospital corners. "The British really knew how to do things right."

The window of time was closing fast on the deadline for my passage to religious manhood. I learned to read Hebrew without the glimmer of comprehension, just enough to prepare me to read passages of the Haftarah from the Book of Prophets. Rabbi Twersky spent a few weeks coaxing me through the Hebrew alphabet. Since Hebrew was Greek to me, I stumbled but bellowed the ancient words so that I could honor my dead grandfather, Stephan Krotoczynski, and someday say kaddish for him at his grave in Berlin.

Rabbi Twersky introduced me to Orthodox rituals. I already knew about the necessity of donning a kippah in synagogue but wearing it all the time was out of the question for me. I made use of the tallit [prayer shawl] once worn by my grandfather that my mother had kept for me, and which has a permanent home in my bedroom chest of drawers to this day. And then there was my introduction to the *tefillin*, which are two small leather boxes with straps, one binding to the head and the other wrapped seven times around the forearm and hand. That was entirely new to me. Right-handed people bind the tefillin around the left, and left-handed people around the right. I could barely get the hang of doing this with either hand.

The day of my religious initiation felt awkward. I had learned enough Hebrew to stumble through the event. Mutti and Monika sat with other women segregated by a curtain hanging from a rod. They stifled laughs when they saw the look on "poor Peter's" face as I stood decked out in bar mitzvah vestments among bearded strangers.

Mutti told me that Dr. Kay had footed the bill for this bar mitzvah that was authentic enough to conjure up her father's religious education in Poland. She added that the majestic and respectable conservative Sinai Temple on Wilshire Boulevard was not for us schnorrers [beggars], but "for rich people." Even the relatively modest Reform Beth Shalom synagogue in Santa Monica wouldn't do because Reform Judaism was "too watered-down" for Mutti, more analogous to mainstream Protestantism. Despite that, Mother still went to Beth Shalom occasionally and kept up with the kind Rabbi Bloch for many years. Her religious devotion was complex but in its own way, ran deep.

I went through all the motions of my sponsored rite of passage. "Thank you for sharing your party with me, Dr. Kay." I wrote facetiously in my bar mitzvah book, documenting the muted gaiety of my coming-of-age celebration at the doctor's house. The standard for this kind of festivity was my cousin David's bar mitzvah celebration held the previous year at the Hillcrest Country Club for which relatives came all the way from the East Coast. Much to my embarrassment, mine paled in comparison. I joked about it and recalled how the obligatory $25 US savings bonds and proverbial fountain pens I received were lampooned in *Mad Magazine*. My awareness of Dr. Kay's role in launching my religious manhood didn't add much luster to the occasion. He tried hard, almost painfully so, to be nice. He attempted to win me over by letting me steer his black Cadillac around one of the large parking lots on Beverly Boulevard near the Farmer's Market. That didn't do the trick. I knew by then that Mutti didn't really like him, and that as far as she was concerned, his days with us were numbered. Yet, I had misgivings about her leading him on so cruelly. There was a shared humiliation in this dishonest situation.

Although Mutti often hoped that someday her prince would come, she also said she didn't want to depend on any man for financial support because she valued her freedom. She wanted true love, not just money. She wanted someone to accept her for who she was, not for someone she could not be. Thus, her engagement to Dr. Kay sputtered to a rapid end as Mutti fought the temptation to improve our lives by marrying him. She knew she wasn't cut out to be a *Hausfrau* for someone she didn't particularly like. In the end she told us that she couldn't go through with it because she wasn't attracted to him and couldn't love him no matter how much he wanted her. Long after Mutti left Dr. Kay, he would continue to hover over our lives, hoping that she would have a change of heart. He was convinced that she needed help, and that as a doctor he could provide the answers to her financial and health problems.

Mother found another job in a sanitarium. We then moved out of Dr. Kay's house and stayed in a motel until we found a cheap unfurnished apartment on Venice Boulevard in Los Angeles, within a mile of our Wellner cousins. This meant we had to change schools for the fourth time in three years. I transferred from John Burroughs Junior High to Louis Pasteur Junior High School, which was by coincidence also attended by my cousin, David. As in my previous junior high, I was assigned a locker and had to learn another combination. Monika doesn't remember the name of the second elementary school she attended that school year.

I had mixed feelings about my junior high. Each day began in homeroom reciting the Pledge of Allegiance. Then we listened to crackly announcements on the intercom. Much of the education in class was busywork. Teachers shouted and blew whistles while I moved along with the flow of bodies in the corridors. I didn't mind the routine. The film noir grimness of the factory-like architecture, much of it brick and asphalt, provided a gritty reality devoid of sentimentality. That suited me fine, as long as I could buy a sticky bun during recess.

I didn't see my cousin David much. He was a year ahead of me and I thought he avoided me for that reason. The situation was awkward for me as it must have been for him. We had nothing in common other than the obligatory family ties that focused on Mutti's problems.

School offered a few pleasant diversions. My art teacher, a friendly young woman, praised my watercolors. She also discussed in class her encounter with space people who stepped out of an unidentified flying object while she was driving on an isolated road in the Valley. I listened intently to this far-fetched story she told with a sincerity that I didn't want to explain away. I came to my senses during my next class, metal shop, where I learned to use the blow torch and drill press without injuring myself. My two shop projects, a walnut bowl and a black metal table lamp wound up in our living room. I didn't complete work on an aluminum archery bow because someone stole it from the class storage bin.

I looked forward to my gym class, which was run by a muscular ex-Marine, who kept accurate records of our push-ups, 50-yard dashes, and the pole climbs that I almost managed hand-over-hand despite my extra weight from eating sticky buns. I liked the square-jawed gym teacher because he took his work seriously. I realized I had to get in shape when I had a run-in with Jay, the school bully.

Jay taunted me by calling me a fat boy and dared me "to do something about it" after he pushed me around during recess. And so I did. I took a hefty swing at him, and we rolled on the ground as Jay's ring cut my eyebrow. Our fight attracted a crowd and got both of us suspended for three days, a perverse form of punishment, especially for kids who didn't like school. For the rest of the year, I mapped alternate routes for walking home from school to avoid Jay's gang that he said would get me, but that threat did not materialize. No one else bothered me from that point on. I learned the value of standing up to bullies.

Although I was bored with my regular classes in math, English, and social studies, the school routine took my mind off problems at home. With "borrowed" money from relatives to supplement Mutti's meager earnings, we found a semi-furnished apartment that had only beds, a table with chairs, and a fridge. As things were, I didn't want any of my potential school friends to find out how we lived and so kept them away from our apartment. Not long after I took notice of "no money down" ads on television for cheap couches and end tables, Cousin Fred Wellner gave us a used old-fashioned, navy-blue velvet couch which stood out in our stripped-down "mid-century barren" living room with its popcorn ceiling. As an exercise in wishful thinking, I scouted out rentals for vacant apartments that might be affordable, such as one in a four-unit Spanish-style apartment house on Western Boulevard, a charmer with built-in bookcases and plenty of sunlight in the living room and kitchen.

Mutti wanted me to have braces for my teeth to further enhance my chances for future success. Since we couldn't afford to do this privately, she had me go to the free orthodontist clinic at the University of Southern California. I was excused from school and took the Pico Boulevard trolley into Central LA to have my braces installed and adjusted. I dreaded these outings because car sickness made me bilious once the trolley got rolling. On one occasion I had to get off to vomit.

In early 1959, with Dr. Kay out of orbit, another comet emerged, the fair-haired Bill Wintersole, who was nine years and two days younger than Mutti, a Prince Charming without a Cadillac or a bank roll. Originally from Ohio, Bill was handsome, talented, and at that time, an aspiring actor who studied at UCLA and worked as a disk jockey at a classical music station. In later years, he became established in Hollywood as a successful character actor with numerous movie credits, television appearances, and commercials. For a long while, Bill was part of the family conversation, but hardly part of the family. When she broke off with him years later, Mutti alluded to vague character flaws on his part that made it impossible to continue their relationship. Unlike the other ships that passed in the night, Bill was to become one of our mother's life-long friends, the only former beau to cheer her up with phone calls and outings to dinner, long after the allure was gone. In 1974, my wife and I saw Bill in Ron Milner's play, *What the Wine Sellers Buy* at the Zellerbach Theater in Philadelphia where he introduced us to Ezra Stone, the actor and director, famous for playing a character named Henry Aldrich on the radio for years. Bill was Mutti's only past admirer present at her funeral in 1991.

When I was 14, I was more concerned about the fate of the Dodgers than the fate of Mutti's relationship with Bill. While my head was lost in baseball, Mutti lost hers when our rent was overdue yet again. No doubt, our relatives had become exhausted by our perpetual penury. Cousin Fred pressed a five-dollar bill in my hand as he took me into his study and tried to tell me all about my responsibilities, as if I didn't know. It seemed that he wanted to put boundaries on his future involvement in what was looking like a forever problem.

After our finances bottomed out, we gave up our apartment on Venice Boulevard and moved into an even cheaper place, on top of a dilapidated store front on 5412 1/2 Pico Boulevard near busy Hauser Boulevard. Here one could hear the street cars of thwarted desire clank and clatter below. Mutti said that this place would be temporary until there would be enough money to get something decent.

Although chronically short of money, Mutti still wanted to do something for our education. She subscribed to the *Los Angeles Times* and said she would buy the *Encyclopedia Americana* when we had more money, which she did but without producing the next payment due. It was repossessed.

The *Los Angeles Times* still arrived on our doorstep. I followed the news about the emerging US Space Program and found an escape in reading about baseball, seeking solace in the daily box scores provided by the sports section and avidly listening to radio broadcasts of games on the radio. I became an entrenched Dodger fan and gave up my erstwhile favorite, the Milwaukee Braves, when the Dodgers abandoned Brooklyn for Los Angeles in 1958.

One a sweltering summer day, I listened to the Braves play the Pirates on the radio. It was May 26, 1959, when Harvey Haddix pitched 12 perfect innings for the Pirates before losing the game to the Braves. Although I favored neither team, that outcome didn't do justice in the greater scheme of things, so out of frustration, I put my fist through the paper-thin wall in our living room without feeling a thing. I was numbed by the realization that baseball and other pastimes no longer provided a diversion from our humiliating circumstances. Mutti, too mired in depression to be bothered by my outburst, didn't say anything. I lost hope for a normal family life.

A few days before the end of the school year, I was called into the principal's office and told to return home because my mother had been hospitalized. The Jewish Family Service sent another cheerful social worker who had picked up Monika from school on the way. She reassured us that Mutti was in good hands at the mental hospital and that our belongings would be stored at the Kensington. After telling us that we were going to another foster home not too far away, she helped us pack our belongings in grocery boxes that we carried downstairs to her station wagon. We then headed to Norwalk, a suburb south of Los Angeles in the direction of Disneyland via the Santa Ana Freeway. She told us about the Samuelson family, including parents, two children, and a cocker spaniel. She mentioned that we could visit our mother at Norwalk State Hospital after she was better. By then, we knew the drill.

13

ANOTHER FOSTER HOME

Norwalk was 35 miles south of Los Angeles, only seven miles away from our previous foster home in Lakewood. Again, we would live in the hinterlands, away from our beloved Santa Monica. The Samuelson family lived in a housing tract in one of several ranch houses on a colorless street without trees, part of a grid pattern that included churches, schools, strip malls, and shopping centers. Here and there were empty lots of desert brush from which one could see cars whizzing by along the Santa Ana Freeway, barely visible through the smog shrouding the sun. This recently built neighborhood was less established than the one in Lakewood.

Our new foster mother, Beverly, welcomed us while the family's snippy black cocker spaniel scooted back and forth as we carried our belongings into the house. There was a garage with a basketball hoop facing the street, and a dichondra lawn that didn't require mowing. Like many others on the street, this house had a rose-colored stucco exterior. Inside, it resembled the typical development homes displayed in advertisements with a prominent television, modern appliances, slipcovers, and wall-to-wall carpets. It was modest but complete.

I took to Beverley, but not so much to the family's cocker spaniel which reminded me of the East Berlin dog responsible for the scar on my forearm. As usual, Monika mixed right in with the family, whereas I was at first more reserved, albeit polite. I was several years older than the family's son, and so he and I had little in common.

The Samuelsons were secular Jews who never talked about religion. Beverly told us about life "back East" where her family owned a small grocery store in Brooklyn that couldn't compete with a new A&P supermarket in the neighborhood. They had come to California a few years before we arrived to build a new life.

Beverly made us the standard peanut butter and jelly sandwiches on demand; however, it didn't take us long to find out that this generous family struggled financially. Our foster father, Sidney, was a salesman with a history of heart trouble whose station wagon was full of rug samples. On his way to work one day, he saw me standing alone waiting for the school bus and asked me later why I didn't mix in more with other kids. I shrugged like any teenager would.

Beverly retained her cheerfulness while her husband seemed despondent and defeated after he returned from his work as a traveling salesman. He had health problems and often didn't feel well. Once while snooping, I accidentally saw an open chest of drawers in his bedroom with snapshots of stark-naked, dark-skinned women from one of the Pacific islands, which must have been taken during World War II when he was a soldier. This seemed a strange and sad display. I wondered why he would leave these photos laying around to be discovered by others like his kids or wife, but I didn't mention this to anybody. I felt like an intruder.

The Samuelson home was about a 15-minute bike ride from Norwalk State Hospital. With Beverly's permission and encouragement, I visited Mutti at this large institution on spacious grounds with mature trees. I saw her being escorted by a nurse to the visitor's reception area, just hours after she had received a shock treatment. She looked tired and depressed. Her once clarion voice was weak, and her speech slurred. Instead of her usual colorful outfits, she wore drab institutional garb which communicated to the world, "I am less than nothing."

A few weeks later, her demeanor had improved. She assured me that she would get better. More weeks passed and she regained some of her upbeat, enthusiastic old self. She introduced me to some of her fellow inmates and told me how popular she was with them and with the nurses whom she described in detail. She smoked a lot and either bummed cigarettes or gave them away.

Mutti noticed that I felt ill at ease. This prompted her to lighten things up. She gave a positive slant to her hospitalization experience, telling amusing stories about group therapy and doctors who didn't have a clue about what was happening with the patients. Although I listened attentively to what she said, I felt guilty because I wanted to escape on my bike to resume my routine. Mutti later wrote about the darker aspects of Norwalk State Hospital, which she didn't mention to me at the time. I did not fully comprehend her fear of hospitalization and of going mad until many years later when she wrote about the humiliating and frightening shock treatments she endured.

The stigma of mental illness hovered over our family. I didn't want to discuss Mutti's latest hospitalization. It seemed to me that Cousin Albert regarded her mental illness as a character flaw within her power to overcome. Others, like our cousin Fred, believed that her condition was the result of her difficult life during and after the Holocaust. He repeatedly reminded Monika and me to be "good children" to stand by our mother no matter what, and urged us not to make matters worse by our inevitable selfishness. Resi and Freddie simply accepted our mother's problems without judging her or us. "We're all a little crazy," they said to lighten things up.

Being away from her in the Norwalk foster home provided me the opportunity to unload the emotional baggage presented by my mother's mental illness by focusing on my daily activities during and after school. At that time, I was in the eighth grade and Monika in the fifth. I took the school bus to Centennial Junior High and Monika walked to Bellflower Elementary School. For me, schoolwork was repetitive and often pointless. I received good grades without much effort because of the undemanding and repetitive curriculum. The low point was when one of my teachers lost control of her class. The students moved desks to play soccer with a board eraser while I looked the other way in disgust. Bored, I looked for diversions after school, riding my bike looking for pick-up baseball games and joining up to play in the local Pony League.

I mostly kept to myself, but struck up a friendship with Ira. He was a nerdy Jewish kid in the neighborhood whom I met at school where his lack of popularity didn't bother him or me. He was smart and nonjudgmental. After school, we played chess and sometimes talked about what we wanted to do in the future.

To expand my social horizon, I joined the Boy Scouts, mainly to go camping. I earned my First Class rank by learning the Morse Code, but the coveted camp trip was cut short by the inability of the scout master to deal with a downpour. So, I quit.

Then came the news that Mother would be transferred from Norwalk State Hospital to a clinic in downtown Los Angeles where she could complete her recovery, find a job, and live on her own. Monika and I saw our mother on most weekends by taking a bus to downtown Los Angeles where we joined her for outings in the area, one time for lunch at the famous Schwab's Pharmacy on Sunset. One weekend she cancelled a visit, and so we spent Saturday shopping for tires for the Samuelsons' station wagon.

Towards the end of our stay with the Samuelsons, Monika was hospitalized for a tonsillectomy. Mutti sent me a postcard explaining that she couldn't come because she had been in Palo Alto. She had a new boyfriend, a graduate student at Stanford, who wrote for the *Stanford Chaparral*, the third oldest continually published humor magazine in the world. To my chagrin, the much maligned and spurned Dr. Kay dutifully showed up at the hospital to visit Monika after the operation. Mutti's absence was a serious breach that undermined the belief that her love for us was unconditional. After I wrote her an angry letter, she left Palo Alto immediately to make amends. The boyfriend faded away. Mutti no longer talked about him and said she wanted us to have a fresh start. I had faint hopes for her turning over a new leaf.

I had to accept that Mutti's chronic mental illness had reshaped her role and limited her capacity as a parent. Long gone was the mother who told us fairy tales and spoke German in dulcet tones to soothe and reassure us. Although I never doubted her sincerity and expressions of love and affection, I began to doubt her capacity to achieve a stable life for herself and us.

However, my nagging doubts were put on hold when it was time for us to be reunited as a family. We packed our belongings and said goodbye to Beverly who waved us off as we headed for Santa Monica. I was sad to leave our kind foster mother who understood our situation so well. Things began to look up when Mutti found a furnished two-bedroom apartment in Santa Monica in a ten-unit yellow stucco building near Seventh and Broadway within walking distance of the beach and the Santa Monica Pier. It was great to be back and to see Mutti being her old self again. I cast aside my apprehension about the future for the time being.

We bought a used television set and settled right in. Mutti took the green bus up Wilshire Boulevard to Beverly Hills where she landed a job as a nurse-receptionist for Doctor Edell, whose patients included movie stars. The Santa Monica Library was around the corner from where we lived. Ralph's supermarket was on Third and Wilshire with Sears and JCPenny also nearby.

Monica attended sixth grade at Madison Elementary School, the same school she attended as a first grader. I became a ninth grader at Lincoln Junior High School that drew from the upscale part of Santa Monica. The quality of this school was much higher than the junior highs I attended in Los Angeles and Norwalk. It had well-maintained buildings and even an Olympic-size swimming pool. For a while, our lives seemed to be on track.

During 1960, our fifth year in America, Mutti turned 38 while Monika and I were firmly in the adolescent phase. I teased her about her Elvis and Fabian crushes and made fun of the posters of the pop idols she hung on the bedroom wall. That didn't go over so well. Neither Mutti nor Monika knew what to make of my moodiness. I excused myself from their girls' outings and spent time away from our apartment, feeling increasingly crowded out by the din of television, pop music on the radio, the visual clutter of knickknacks, and the vile smell of cigarettes. I had little patience for the girl talk that drew mother and daughter close. Mutti talked about "sweet Monika" to point out the difference in our temperaments. "You never really liked to sit on anyone's lap when you were a kid," she told me several times. "You are independent and aloof, just like your father." By comparing me to my ever-absent father, she rationalized the growing distance between her and me.

Our mother could be reasonable and reassuring and we could talk to her without reservation, but I knew better than to be candid about my challenges, which were eclipsed by the brewing emotional turmoil of her own. Looking directly into our eyes, she used her musical voice to charm the cobra of our lingering misgivings concerning her mental health. Monika and I wanted to accept the little lies of wishful thinking that gave us hope for a better future. Mutti counted on our loyalty when she used the phrase "sticking together through thick and thin" that she picked up in England. She wasn't much for imposing no-nonsense parenting on us and instead offered herself as a "fun-loving" mom to show us how life ought to be lived. For us, there were no visible strings of responsibility that parents use to guide their children toward productive lives. Rather than being a mere parent, she wanted to be a confidante, a co-conspirator, a light-hearted mischief maker who brought magic and mystery to our lives, outshining all those who were dull victims of unfairness, like some of our more stable and practical relatives.

"Your mother knows how to live!" she would tell us half-jokingly, urging us to appreciate the finer things in life that the denizens of the humdrum world were incapable of enjoying. "All they are interested in is money, big houses, and cars." Although this sentiment was transparent and overblown, it played well in our marginal circumstances.

To make up for her shortcomings as a conventional parent, Mutti set out to expose us to the arts and literature. She bought tiny paperbacks called "minis" that were published by ABC Tudor Publishing, including volumes about Rembrandt, Van Gogh, Picasso, Matisse, and Russian icons. I still have them on my bookshelves. Monika and I were quite open to her culture outings that included art at the LA County Museum where we would also stop by the La Brea Tar Pits and the Farmers Market. Our favorite luncheon spot, Zucky's, the landmark delicatessen on Wilshire Boulevard was established in 1954, the same year we arrived in Santa Monica.

Mutti introduced me to *Catcher in the Rye, an* apropos choice for my adolescent moodiness. She encouraged me to make use of the Santa Monica Public Library on Santa Monica Boulevard where I could browse and check out books in quiet solitude under the friendly gaze of the librarian.

On my rusty but trusty bike, I delivered the *LA Times* in the morning and the *Santa Monica Evening Outlook* in the afternoon. Santa Monica was a wonderful place to explore by bike, from the Pacific Palisades to the Santa Monica Pier, all the way down to Venice on the cement-paved pedestrian Speedway stretching from Santa Monica Pier to Venice Beach a few miles south.

Our mom kept us up to date about her latest job as nurse/receptionist in Beverly Hills where she had "the honor" to give vitamin injections in the bum to celebrity patients including the composer, Igor Stravinsky and his understudy Robert Kraft, the singer Peggy Lee, and Ray Moyer, the Oscar-winning set decorator for the movie, Cleopatra. They all responded well to her integumental intrusion, including Stravinsky who invited our family to an art opening to see his wife Vera's paintings. One night, Robert Kraft came over to our apartment for dinner.

Mutti's intoxicating circle of connections from her job of jabbing cultural icons expanded when Cousin Lea drew her into the social whirl of the local art community. Lea, ever the self-assured diva, was the perfect guide to the colorful, edgy LA scene in the 60s.

Lea introduced Mutti to Vito Paulekas, a bohemian sculptor who was based in North Hollywood, several years before he gained notoriety in California's "freak scene." He and his young wife, Szou, ran a ceramics studio frequented by celebrities. His students included Mickey Rooney and Jonathan Winters, and Beverly Hills ladies out for bohemian kicks. Vito symbolized freedom and creativity and was a breath of fresh air, according to Mutti. She accepted his invitation to join his ceramics class, and occasionally took Monika and me along to the studio "for our education." We went during the daytime when the studio's "anything goes" ambiance was relatively tame. Vito was kid-friendly and gregarious, but I riveted my attention on the cookies that he laid out for his students.

Mutti quickly became part of Vito's circle of friends, which included the artist, Paul Wiesenfeld, and Harvard-educated Thomas Teal, later an editor and a noted translator of Swedish literature. At one of the sessions at the studio, Mutti overheard Vito's friend, Eddie, mention the name, Denis Horne, while describing a recent trip to Rome. Her ears perked up when she learned that Eddie's girlfriend would be going back to Rome. She drafted a letter "to the old man" to be hand-delivered to Denis, complete with family photos taken by Eddie's girlfriend. Some weeks later, the response came with a preamble of mixed messages about his feelings.

Dear Mary,

I was amazed and delighted to hear from Eddie (what a mad coincidence was that!) that you were in Los Angeles and that his girlfriend duly delivered your letter with photographs of you and Peter. At last, I have a few minutes to scribble even fewer thoughts (idiotically too few) to give you an idea of all that has happened to me since those faraway Oxford days. But very soon I hope to come to America and to see you and Peter. Build no false hopes on this, my dear! I am as impossibly unmarriageable as ever! I made one serious attempt at it after you left Oxford and it failed miserably. I am now resigned to my fate, as a man ill-adapted for the norms of life, unable sometimes to conceal my envy and hope of normality, when I see people getting happily (?) married and (apparently?) settling down, but for the most part content with life as it is. So I imagine are you, judging from your photograph. Well, you are very pretty still, Mary! Even, I think, better looking than in the Oxford days and just as youthful! Amazing! How do you do it? I am full of admiration for your pluck and determination as I can well imagine what struggles you have had. And if you think that it is easy for me to say this, I must tell you something of my life after Oxford – a story of work, disappointment, illness, and now, I hope, of success.

I was perplexed by my father's letter, unsure of what to expect from him since he promised next to nothing, and as Mother said, he couldn't even do that properly. She explained that he was well-meaning but unreliable, just trying to run away from himself," a description that fit several of the men she brought into her life. She didn't think he would come to the United States, but alluded to the possibility that someday I would meet him. His letter continued with an account of the troubles that led him to be an expat in Italy, a mysterious saga that put him center stage.

It is a long story, and impossible to tell in a few words. I will give just a thumbnail sketch. I had some (artistic) success in the theater (three plays produced in rather snobbish theaters), then a nervous breakdown which was the most terrible period of my life, and which I never wish to remember. Then, on doctor's orders, I decided to leave England and go to Spain or Italy. But fate stepped in. I was introduced by an Oxford friend at the British Film Institute to the Italian director who wanted to make a film in collaboration with an English writer (this was 1953). I wrote the film and co-directed it. It won an award at Cannes Festival of films. Since then, it has been shown all over the world. The British Film Institute is rich in prestige and as this film was showing in Cannes (April 1956) I was sleeping on my suitcase, but literally. I had no bed, only an empty room. However, because of the film's artistic success, I received several offers from producers to write films. One of these, *The Teddy Boys*, was to be financed by the Film Finance Corporation of Great Britain. We started production and spent 2,000 Pounds of the NFFC/National Film Finance Corporation) money and then the film was stopped by the British Censor (A.T.L Watkins) who said it was likely to cause disturbances in the cinemas, a bitter blow because it was a first feature film. The producers blamed me and demanded a new script for nothing. They paid the large sum of 200 Pounds for the first script. I wrote another, but it was also thrown out, and I was completely discredited in the eyes of the producers and back just where I was in 1953 when with 30 Pounds in my pocket I was leaving for Spain. Then another miracle – a friend of somebody who had seen the prize film, called *Together*, wrote to me from Rome, asking me if I would write a film about youth in Italy. They made no other offer, except to pay my passage. I went. Well, I have written, directed and produced the film, entirely paid for by an Irish American priest in the Vatican. It was a success. Probably a big success. They want to send it to Venice this year, and they also want to win the Italian government prize. And they want, of course, to discard me now that they have the film.

So here I am, with a battery of lawyers and the bitterness of ten years of struggle, fighting the Vatican (who have huge power in Italy) to reap some of the rewards of the film. I have not a leg to stand on, as I have no written contract, but I have grabbed all the negatives and I am sitting on them, until I get one. Wish me luck!

Although Mother showed little interest in my father's battle with cinematic windmills, she was flattered by the part of his letter describing his quest to look her up in Berlin not realizing we had left Germany. He went to Berlin with a friend and spent the night in an East Sector train station where he found the East Germans "pleasant and quite drunk!" His letter betrayed guilt for failing to step up as a provider. He was convinced that financial security was all that she desired and felt compelled to make empty promises that were tied to the unlikelihood of his financial success.

My dear Mary, you know me well enough. If I do make out financially, you shall be the first person to receive a portion of my success. I have no interest in being rich, only in being able to enjoy the simplicities of life. I don't know whether Peter knows I am his Pa, but if so, give him my love, and tell him I think he looks swell! And does a credit to his Ma! Is he good at school? He looks pretty intelligent to me. I understand from Eddie you are nursing in Los Angeles. I have a fond respect for nurses. So don't give it up. I know the life is hard. Don't be surprised if you don't hear from me for months, but I am surely going to turn up shortly. I hope with money! Maybe, I hope, we can send Peter to college. Meanwhile, Mary, don't upset yourself for those happy-sad days at Oxford. You were always yourself and you still are – full of optimism and an enormous zest for life. I like and admire that as always and send you and Peter my best. Care wishes and hopes. Denis.

For a brief period, there was talk of my assuming the name, Horne, as if that would strengthen my connection with Denis, but there was no consistent follow-up by him and hence no motivation to assume his name. Heinz Wiesner, for all his failings, had once wanted to be a father to me and so I had some rationale to continue using the Wiesner family name I had in common with my mother and sister.

A few years later, Lea traveled to Rome where she looked up my father. She was excited to learn that Denis and I had mannerisms and traits in common. While this revelation spurred interest in the nature-nurture debate, Lea's full description merely reinforced what Mutti told me all along about what I had in common with my father, not all of it flattering.

In subsequent years, we received occasional letters from him about the vainglorious "bitch goddess of success" that eluded him. One time he sent us $50 and given the dollar-lira exchange rate then, this must have made a dent in his budget. I wasn't sure what to make of this "father" who made no sustained effort to claim me as his own. The reality of this tenuous situation sank in and added a layer of indifference to the way I felt about him.

On June 24, 1960, Monika's 12th birthday, Mother and Monika became US citizens. I was too old to be part of the automatic mother-child citizenship package and so I remained a British subject. It took an additional 20 years for me to take that final step, years after I married, and long after I had set aside my bitter feelings about America's undeclared war in Vietnam.

US Citizenship didn't change Mutti's real allegiance to being a citizen of the world and a champion of all those she met who were free spirits. We had a parade of visitors, outsiders who were fascinated by our mother's ebullience. Although she was often apologetic and sheepish about throwing caution to the winds, she asserted her right to flings with happiness to maintain her mental health. Tempted to walk on the wild side, she often tiptoed over without jumping in too deep. She no longer pined away openly for a marriage-minded prince and a comfortable way of life. She had entered the land of adventure where the momentary magic of an evening outweighed the promise of a lifetime of humdrum devotion. She made a diary entry addressed to us to justify the vagaries of her social life.

My dear children,

I am trying to live a life of my own, without neglecting you, or without wanting to neglect you. Every person who is a thinking and "worthwhile" person, needs satisfaction created for himself or herself, to survive, to function, and not to become frustrated. When I am not frustrated, I will be able to be a happy person, and a good person, a mother to live and to be with.

I was chagrined every time I heard about a new beau on the horizon. One such was Eugene, a shy, slender-featured Frenchman in his late twenties, whom Mutti championed as "magnifique" and invited him over for dinner. He rode a ten-speed bike in European competitions and offered to sell it to me for very little because he was leaving town. I had misgivings about such a deal because it smacked of quid pro quo, but my reservations were trumped by the generosity of his offer.

I rode this competition bike all over Southern California, and after my 16th birthday, I informed Mutti about my plans to go on a solo bike trip north on Highway One to San Francisco using the money I earned from my paper routes. Mutti was apprehensive but powerless to do anything about it. Given the parenting vacuum at home, I felt justified in doing whatever I wanted, within reason. Packing a sleeping bag and money, I rode up Highway One and on the third day while passing through Carmel damaged the bike's rear wheel by hitting a rut. The wheel wobbled without mercy, and I barely made it to Monterrey. I shipped the bike home in a large box from a bicycle shop and continued to San Francisco by bus where I stayed in a YMCA and then returned to LA via Greyhound.

This trip that was meant to symbolize my declaration of independence was in the end inconsequential. Nothing changed afterwards. I was still ashamed of my mother's mental problems and avoided bringing friends to our barely furnished apartment. Yet, no matter how alienated I felt at times, I was sympathetic and supportive when Mutti and I talked and kept my interior life concealed from her.

While I was out and about, Monika spent a lot of time with her mother. Although they were more like best friends, there were moments of Mutti's protective shield of motherhood. One of Monika's favorite stories concerns an incident in which Mutti's maternal instincts were co-mingled with her brash humor. After Monika told her about the antics of a flasher downstairs in their apartment building, she knocked on his door and told him, "I understand that you are parading without your pants in full view of my daughter when she passes by your window. If you don't pull down the blinds, I'll come downstairs and cut it off." From that point on, the man closed the blinds. Monika and Mutti had a good laugh and went out to have fun while "Peter did his thing." We had come to use the 1960's catch phrase "doing your thing," as shorthand for the unique coping skills each of us needed for getting through the day. .

For several months, our lives still seemed to be on track, but just as before our money problems gnawed through. Mutti was depressed and joked about being on "Queen for a Day," a popular mawkish daytime television show on which the contestants who blabbed the best sob stories won washers and dryers to alleviate their lot through laundered redemption. Only half-joking, she applied in vain to become a contestant. Meanwhile, we continued to use the local laundromat.

Mother said she needed a break. At the end of the summer of 1960, she proposed a family trip north to scenic Big Sur and Monterrey. We took off in our two-tone green '48 Pontiac, a heavy, lumbering, straight-eight gas guzzler that was affordable because gas was still cheap. We got to Monterrey only to find out that gas cost twice as much there, so we barely had enough money left for the remaining trip. We spent two nights in sleeping bags at a campground at Big Sur, where Monika and I walked among the tall pines with a flashlight left over from my Boy Scout days. Driving back on Highway 1 late in the afternoon, we were thrilled to see the stunning scenery of stone-studded cliffs that gave way to an ocean resplendent in blues, greens, and reds. We stopped by a beach to collect pieces of driftwood as souvenirs and then drove into the night passing through hilly stretches approaching San Louis Obispo, then along the desolate coastline past Santa Barbara. Tired and with miles to go, we looked for a place to pull over and found ourselves confronted with barbed-wire fences and private-property signs. After we found an open spot away from the road, we settled down to sleep in our car. We woke up when a man with a shotgun brandishing a flashlight approached our car and ordered us to get off his land. We got the message that this land was not meant for us and went our way. Dead tired and left with only pocket change, we stopped in Ventura for just enough gas to get back to Santa Monica by morning. Our first and only car trip was documented by a photo of

Monika posed on the hood of our beloved two-toned Pontiac. From that point on, we abandoned the wilds of rural California for local drives around scenic Malibu and Topanga Canyon.

The day after we returned to our apartment, Mother went back to work, but a few weeks later things finally fell apart. Her one-year stint as nurse-receptionist in Beverly Hills came to an end. Instead of explaining to us why she was fired, she launched into a diatribe against the "greedy" doctor who paid her the standard low wages while getting rich. Dismayed, Monika and I wondered what would happen next.

Mutti quickly found a stopgap job as a waitress at the Lio-Da-Mar, a bowling alley on Fifth and Wilshire, a few blocks from where we lived. We were embarrassed to see her in a red-striped outfit that seemed a mockery of her nursing uniform, but we didn't mind the unexpected pleasure of being served decent hamburgers, fries, and malted milk shakes "on the house." Although the burgers and shakes tasted good, we worried about living hand-to-mouth with the old specter of rent looming large. Then, Mutti fell into a deep depression.

14

CAMARILLO

The manic phase began with crying fits. Whatever we did to try calm Mutti down only made her angry. "There is no way for you kids to understand." She smoked and paced about in the kitchen, refused to get sleep all night, and left the apartment early in the morning while we were asleep.

We found out what happened to her when the police called our Silberstein cousins, who were her emergency contacts. It turned out she caused a ruckus at her favorite lunch place, Zucky's Delicatessen, where she cursed her fellow Jews for not wanting to hear her story. In a matter of minutes, the police arrived and whisked her away to the psych ward at Saint John's Hospital so that the patrons could eat their pastramis in peace. By the time we found out, she had been transferred to Camarillo State Hospital, 50 miles north of Santa Monica.

After our mother's hospitalization, we gave up the apartment. Monika stayed with Resi and Freddie, and Albert let me come to stay at the Kensington where I worked as a laborer on the renovation of his hotel until I started high school. I was teamed up with two men employed by Albert to clear rubble and was pleased to hear them say good things about "the old man."

After Mutti underwent a series of shock treatments, Resi and Freddie took us to Camarillo for a visit. A nurse brought Mother to the visiting area and said in a cheery voice, "Mary, we have some people here to see you." Finally, she gave a muted response with a blank look. I was disheartened to see her so diminished.

The next time, I took a Greyhound bus to visit my mother on my own. On the way up to Oxnard on the Pacific Coast Highway, the bus driver bent the rules by letting me off at the Camarillo exit ramp. I was in training for the high school cross country team; so instead of hitching a ride, I decided to run to the hospital. For nearly an hour, I jogged along alfalfa fields, surrounded by hills that caught the last glimmer of dusk. I was taken by the beauty of the landscape and its dark shadows, momentarily forgetting my personal circumstances. Being on the road alone on foot gave me a sense of freedom. No one knew where I was. No one cared what I did. Running put me in charge and let my thoughts be guided by what I saw.

I showed up all sweaty at the courtyard of a cluster of Spanish-style buildings with red roof tiles and went to the same reception area as before. This time, Mutti stepped forward on her own to greet me a bit more like her former self, although her speech was still slurred from medications. The friendly nurse told me how much everybody liked Mom, who was by then more talkative and up to her normal theatrics as she introduced me to patients and staff. When I was alone with her, she said her case was special and that all she needed was common decency and loving care from the people around her. When visiting hours were over, I hitched a ride with a hospital employee who dropped me off in Oxnard where I caught the bus back to Santa Monica.

Mutti later wrote about this hospitalization in optimistic terms that overlooked the darker aspects of her depression following the initial shock treatments. What she wrote reminded me of the fatherly Dr. Noah Praetorius, played by Cary Grant in *People Will Talk,* who had infinite time to treat and woo his beautiful, but difficult patient. In her writings, Mother described a scene that could have been straight from the silver screen.

I was visited by a young clergyman who used to visit the ward. He found out I was from Germany and obtained permission for me to help him translate from German to English for work on his doctorate. I had a great time. Although I was high, this didn't interfere with my knowledge of German. Unfortunately, the young clergyman wasn't always around, and I misbehaved myself right onto the shock treatment table. And that was the end of my happy hours spent translating. When I saw the clergyman again after the EST, I must have aroused his pity, since I had fallen into a state of depression. He said, "I'd rather see you high."

Within weeks, Mutti's depression finally lifted. "I am ready to fly the coop." She stressed the goodwill she had built up with her doctor and nurses by being a helpful patient. She was popular with the other patients who elected her as the head of the patients' council. In another month, Mutti said that she would be discharged "cum laude" to be reunited with her kids. She talked about getting out of Camarillo and making things up to us. On the day of her release, Monika and I were in school. We expected to start our normal life with Mutti again, but then the unexpected happened. Monika and I were with Mutti at the Kensington when the police came by to take her away. She didn't put up a fuss when I reassured her that I would call Resi and Fred to get her released. We later found out that Dr. Kay had called the police, using his power and influence as a medical doctor to have her hospitalized at Camarillo again. Perhaps this was done out of spite, or out of fear that she was still not well, or in the crazy hope of winning her back. What was clear to me was that the civil rights of mental patients were in limbo, even after discharge.

Thanks to the intervention of our cousins, Mutti was quickly evaluated and released again from Camarillo. With help from her social worker, Mutti found a pleasant and affordable one-bedroom apartment in an old Victorian-style house in Ocean Park, on what was then Washington Boulevard. Unbeknown to us, this house was once the home of the Thomas H. Dudley, who had been the mayor of Santa Mónica at the beginning of the 20th century. We lived on the second floor from where we could hear the gentle thud of ocean waves a few blocks away. I had my own "room" in a semi-finished space carved out of the attic where I spent hours alone reading and typing papers for school. I tried my hand at writing a play after reading Eugene O'Neill's *Long Day's Journey into Night*.

Our mother became a full-time welfare mom on disability for the first time, and we got by thanks to food stamps and additional help from relatives until she could find work. Her social worker encouraged her to get further training in the medical field so that she could qualify for better paying jobs. Things looked good but we dreaded the inevitability of another mental breakdown and repeated hospitalizations.

Even with life back on an even keel, Mother's financial and mental health issues were still center stage while school matters took a back seat. Monika was in the sixth grade and back at Madison Elementary, the same school we attended after arriving in America. She was an average student who behaved well in class, but for her school represented a hostile environment. She felt lost in the shuffle except when it came to one teacher, an Afro-American musician, who was popular with all his students. On the days when Monika remained in his class while the other students had off to attend weekly religion classes, he engaged her in conversation and built her self-esteem. He talked to her about music and encouraged her to share her own interests. She did well in his class.

From 1960 to 1963, Monika and I didn't have to switch schools. Monika went on to John Adams Junior High School from seventh to ninth grade. I attended Santa Monica High School, known as Samohi, all the way through to graduation. We were making friends and led separate social lives except for the times we spent with Mother.

When she began junior high, Monika confronted the hassle of rushing from one class to the next, taught by various teachers who barely had time to get to know their students. Her school drew from lower middle-class as well as disadvantaged households. The ethnically and racially diverse student groups did not always get along well with each other.

Monika recalled being bullied. While on her way to class carrying her books, she was knocked to the ground by a gang of Black girls. One of them was Zelda, the same girl Monika had befriended in first grade. Zelda recognized Monika and told her friends to leave her alone, and they did. Monika later said, "It's good to have friends," to explain why she ran with a streetwise crowd.

Neither Monika nor I talked much about school at home. Monika said she didn't like school and that she only did what she had to do to get passing grades. There was never any talk about favorite teachers or extra-curricular activities. She mentioned friends at school, but I rarely met them. Because of our age and sex difference, our social lives didn't cross paths much.

Placed in the accelerated program at Santa Monica High, I focused on selecting courses and set goals for grades and activities that would look good on college and scholarship applications. I wanted to join the tennis team but was discouraged by the coach. I got the hint that tennis was reserved for kids who were known to have had lessons, so I didn't try out. Instead, I joined the cross-country running team that simply required egalitarian sweat and willingness to train. Because of my interest in politics, I also joined the Samohi Debate Team.

Many of the school activities were run by the *soches* [socialites] who were in my accelerated college-prep courses. I joked about their preference for khakis and fuzzy sweaters. A few of my fellow scholars commuted to school from Malibu by bus or in their cars. Among them were a few "red diaper babies" who were predisposed to champion liberal ideas. I made friends with those who didn't judge me because of my modest family circumstances.

I compartmentalized my family concerns while indulging in rebellious high school fun. My classmates and I enjoyed spirited critiques of the teachers who fell in and out of favor depending on our success with them. There were mindless assemblies in the outdoor Greek Theater to drum up school spirit for the Vikings, Samohi's football team. I attended only one football game in the three years and that was on a dare from my friends.

Folk music was in vogue. Among my fellow students was the talented and affable Ry Cooder, who became a well-known musician and song writer. As a member of our folk music club, he dazzled us with his technique for finger-bustin' blues on his guitar and mandolin. At the end of my junior year, I ran for president of the student council as a lark. My opponent was the very amiable Frank Nishamura, who was among my circle of friends. Because of his Japanese and my German background, we called it "the Battle of the Axis." My platform included abolishing the school's football team and focusing attention on the school's dropout problem. After I lost the campaign as expected, my campaign staff conducted a survey as a class project for probability and statistics indicating that the freshman class had been overwhelmingly opposed to my radical agenda.

Our band of activists struck again when Dr. Fred Schwarz, head of the Christian Anti-Communist Crusade, lectured at a school assembly that all students were required to attend. With prior coordination, several of us walked out to protest Schwarz's one-sided, politically tinged presentation. We scored one for free speech with no repercussions from the school administration.

The most interesting events were outside of school. I went with Samohi friends to hear Martin Luther King Jr. give a powerful speech at the Santa Monica Civic Auditorium that deepened our interest in the Civil Rights Movement. For my Social Studies class I wrote papers with political themes, including one debunking the libertarian author, Ayn Rand. The right-wing John Birch Society was anathema to me and my friends. We speculated facetiously about what genetic and environmental factors might explain why some people are liberal and others conservative.

Meanwhile, my various jobs kept me in money. I worked as a cashier in the school cafeteria in exchange for lunch. After school, I delivered telegrams on my ten-speed racer, some to Hollywood notables including Peter Lawford and Daryl Zanuck. Others were dunning notices for people who answered their doors in work uniforms, like the message addressed to one Dave Birdshitt, a burly six-foot-eight cook at a restaurant on Wilshire Boulevard. I could hardly keep a straight face when I mentioned his name while handing him the Western Union envelope in the restaurant kitchen. I also had jobs tending gardens for "ritzy" homes in the Pacific Palisades, including one owned by a rabbi whose name I recognized in the paper when he was convicted of child molesting after my time as his paper boy.

I carved out a social life removed from family life. There were parties in Malibu, grunion hunting behind beach-front homes, a bike trip to

San Diego to attend a Unitarian teen get together, and impromptu car trips to San Francisco and Portland. I got into a bit of trouble in cahoots with a best friend while attempting to heist several boards of lumber from a construction site to build a bookcase. We were caught red-handed by cops with their weapons drawn, but our school covered it up because we were both honor students. You can imagine what would have happened if we were poor and Black or Hispanic.

Meanwhile Monika, who was by then in the eighth grade at John Adams Junior High, spent time with her friends and did not say much about the boys who were starting to notice her. She was into pop music and adept at remembering all the lyrics, something that I found difficult to do. She spent more time doing this with Mutti than I did.

For both Monika and me, family time became tied to our mother's non-conformist social scene. While the going was good, there was never a dull moment. We marveled at the infectious laugh with which Mutti peppered her stories at the countless parties and gatherings she hosted or attended. Monika loved that her mom had the ability to engage and involve people of all kinds, to make them feel important and wanted. We both marveled at her ability to draw people out to tell their stories. She listened to people and remembered what they said.

15

MUTTI'S BEATNIK REFUGE

Ever so gregarious, our mom never forgot to keep tabs on her non-conformist buddies in Venice or her more sedate friends and relatives in Santa Monica. Her daybook held records of dinners, musical events, parties, and trips to the beach mingled with entries regarding personal and family matters. There were entries about our report cards. One note read: "Monika dissatisfied, almost depressed – school, life, everything." Her solution for raising Monika's spirits was to involve her in her own social whirl as a diversion.

Now when Mutti showed Monika and me off to her Venice friends, they would tell us what a wonderful mother "Maria" was, using this new version of her given name. Mutti introduced us to the Beat Scene without allowing us to partake in drug and alcohol abuse which she, too, steadfastly avoided since she didn't need any accelerant for her manic depression. Her Marlboro cigarettes and an occasional glass of wine sufficed as her vices. Although she never allowed any of her male friends to stay overnight, we were still privy to accounts of failed off-site romances told as cautionary tales about the pitfalls of adult life.

Mother's colorful Venice friends and their merry conversation provided a diversion from the downers of mental illness, unemployment, and low social status. They showed up for spaghetti dinners served on a red-and-white checkered tablecloth topped with a

Mateus wine bottle used as a candle holder. One visitor, a tall Belgium ethnographer, Jean-Pierre Hallet (1927-2004), had a missing hand that I thought wound up in a crocodile but later learned was lost in a dynamiting accident. A dynamic storyteller, Jean-Pierre talked about his commitment to wild animals and befriending the Pygmies in the Congo. In his French accent, he described plans to develop a zoo in Southern California that would allow animals to roam freely while visitors were encaged. Mother later told me that she dropped him because he had an eye for Monika. Monika confirmed that Mutti was watchful when it came to men and their proclivities.

Although I grew to accept her relationships with men, I felt uncomfortable about strangers invading our family privacy. Although I enjoyed meeting her friends on a casual basis, I spent more time away from home. Mutti joked that my refusal to go out with her and Monika to the movies was an attempt to assert my male identity.

The parade of Mother's friends included Ross Lavroff, a self-assured, vodka-drinking Russian in his early thirties, fluent in English with only a hint of a Russian accent. He was stocky with a strong, square face and straight, black hair. His family were Ukrainian Russians from Kiev. In 1950, he and his sister settled in Rochester, New York with her American husband after fleeing from Soviet repression. Ross was 14 years old when he arrived in America and became a US citizen in 1955. He went to the University of Rochester and served in the US Army.

Ross and his friends told tall stories about travels to Big Sur, Mexico, Alaska, and New York. One of them, Gary, was a bald, muscular tile setter with a little Hitler mustache who hailed from Portland, Oregon. He drove a Ford stick shift and fancied himself a macho writer like Jack London and Ernest Hemingway because he was in the Merchant Marines and did a stint in the Alaskan fisheries. Marginally educated but not without native ability, Gary would occasionally produce one or two pages of fluid prose poetry that he said were inspired by Dylan Thomas. He didn't talk about his wife and three kids stashed in Torrance.

Then there was Ross's other friend, Jack, a slightly built, gentle and diffident individual whose mother came from Poland. Jack was semi-fluent in Polish and had met Ross while both were at the Army's

Language School in Monterrey, California. They occasionally bantered in a Slavic hodge-podge.

Jack loved Walt Whitman and gave Mother a copy of *Leaves of Grass* which she appreciated. I am not sure she was aware of Whitman's influence on Beat poetry, especially the poems of Allen Ginsberg, whose "Howl" became the Beat Generation's collective cry of anguish and protest against the conformist 1950s. Mutti was touched by Ginsberg's poem, "Kaddish" about his mother's struggle with severe chronic psychotic illness which was much graver than her own.

Ross had gravitated to Venice to enjoy the casual and freewheeling lifestyle of the Beats and wound up managing a run-down apartment house within a stone's throw of the Gas House, a dilapidated, neo-classic Beat hangout and showcase for the arts near Venice Beach that was immortalized by Lawrence Lipton in *The Holy Barbarians*. Ross maintained a blasé attitude towards the characters in the Venice "scene" that had become a magnet for tourists and hangers-on. The Gas House was an architectural remnant of real estate development in the 1920s when "Venetian" canals and neo-classical buildings were put in place to attract visitors and potential residents to an ersatz version of the Old World. In the early 1960s, tourists could pop a dollar into the "tip jar" at the Gas House and see a painted vintage bathtub, hear poetry, and view paintings while taking in the aroma of fresh oil paint. Patrons could even have their trash cans painted for free should they happen to have brought them. The Gas House was famous for flooding the neighborhood with the loud, sweaty rhythms of bongos played by Beat drummers. Dismayed Venice neighbors preferred the real Caribbean bongo players who performed at a quieter distance for crowds on the Speedway at Venice Beach.

And then there was the Venice West Café. Mutti got to know John and Anna Haag, who ran this coffee shop and art center from 1962 to 1966 where underground poets gave readings and held court. John Haag was a soft-spoken Harvard man who grew up in New York and had set out to become a Beat poet. His temperamental Italian wife, Anna Haag née Ricci, was an immigrant who didn't exactly see eye-to-eye with the crasser aspects of the American way of life. At first, they rented a small space and called it the Venice Music and Arts Center, then in 1962 they bought the Venice West Café that had been opened in 1957 by revered

Beat poet, Stuart Perkoff. Little did the Haags know when they came to Venice in the 1960s that they would become part of local history.[1]

Ross, in his beguiling way, gave us the lowdown on the aspiring poets, artists, druggies, hangers-on, and femme fatales who hung out at the Venice West, but he seemed to think that my attention ought to be focused elsewhere on more wholesome pursuits, starting with soccer and must-read books. He taught me how to kick properly on a lawn in Venice Beach near the Gas House and took me to soccer matches between teams representing Russian, Polish, Ukrainian and other Eastern European nationalities. He introduced me to anti-communist literature, including *Darkness at Noon,_Out of the Night*, and *1984*. These books about the legacy of totalitarianism appealed to the Libertarian outlook that was influential among the Beats. Through Ross, I met the tall 400-pound "Big Daddy" Eric Nord, who ran the Gas House. Ross took a patronizing view of Nord and the unsavory aspects of the Beat scene and appointed himself as its only responsible member qualified to observe the rascals while having fun along with them.

The beatniks provided plenty opportunities for Mother to take center stage which she took with a wink that she knew it was all for a lark. She wore capri pants and black sweaters and kept her hair long. Mother was happiest in the Venice social whirl where, unlike in middle-class social circles, her wit, creativity and knowledge were more important than her lack of money and a college degree. The denizens of Venice on the Pacific found her exotic, enthusiastic, and full of life. She was intellectually sharp, never boring. I didn't mind her relationship with Ross whom I liked a lot. He treated her well as far as I could tell, but there was no permanence, according to what she wrote down at that time to tamp down her emotional volatility and to manage her expectations.

> I must stop melting in stupid feminine desire to please. By smothering others with overwhelming attention, I overlooked their real desires and wishes, giving them little room to breathe and to reciprocate. I don't intend to make any drastic changes, but I want to tone down to medium nice to give men a chance to do more for me. If Ross goes to Mexico with Jack to have a ball, drink and fiesta, I don't know what to say or do. Once he said if he had an affair (sex) with someone, he

would tell me to gain experience and to improve our relationship (?!), but what if I had an affair (sex) with someone else? I wonder how he would like it. As far as his pure sex routine is concerned, it has room to improve.

Eventually, Mother's relationship with Ross faded in 1962. I don't recall any precipitating event that ended it. They exchanged letters and best wishes for a long time after Ross left for Seattle that year. By then, Eric "Big Daddy" Nord had left the Gas House for North Beach in San Francisco and was rumored to have wound up in Hawaii.

When Ross and his friends left Venice for Seattle at the end of 1962, Mutti lost interest in the counterculture. She dismissed the worst of beatnik art and poetry as evidence of disturbed souls to be judged with gentle condescension. Despite her tendency to lionize newly discovered friends, she was not taken in by the grungy pretentiousness of the Beat leftovers, who, if nothing else, violated her sense of hygiene. She felt sorry for the addicts, pointing them out to me in her repeat warning to avoid drugs.

Despite her avowed bravado, Mutti wasn't made for the hard-bitten fallout from temporary, uncommitted relationships between men and women. In her diaries, she analyzed her lovers and described the tortuous path of committing to love in the face of male indifference and sexual exploitation. She understood the politics of love but lacked the mysterious and unachievable sophistication to navigate its perils. Now, almost 40 years old and set in her ways, she was convinced that a mature, stable relationship of give-and-take was out of reach.

After living in Seattle with his friends for a while, Ross moved to New York on the Lower East Side. My mother kept in touch with him during that period. Monika and I visited him once in New York and I saw him several times while I was in graduate school in Philadelphia. At that time, he was living in Washington, DC working for the US State Department aa a translator. He had married and quickly divorced a Spanish language professor because he didn't think he was suited for married life. Finally, he moved back to retire in his beloved Seattle where he lived on a houseboat on Lake Washington.

In 1992, a year after Mutti died, I visited Ross in Seattle on his houseboat. He had aged and was in poor health but proud of his accomplishments. He showed me pictures of himself with Eisenhower and other world leaders when he was a simultaneous Russian translator for NBC and various governmental agencies, including the US State Department and NASA. He served as an interpreter to Presidents Ford, Carter, and George H. W. Bush.

We went drinking in the Blue Moon Café near the University of Washington where he introduced me to his friends, including a reputed Native American princess. He caught me up on his ongoing freelance work for the US State Department hosting visitors from the Soviet Union.

Ross, whose worldview was honed during the Cold War, was excited about the impending breakup of the Soviet Union, telling me, "Peter, you won't believe the proposals that are floating around the Kremlin, a hell of a lot more capitalistic than what we have in this country." Around the time of my visit, he was diagnosed with a heart condition that eventually led to his death on March 31, 2001. In his obituary, he is remembered as the interpreter for the historic 1975 Apollo-Soyuz docking.

During the years after Ross left Venice in 1962, Mother's affairs of the heart continued to lead nowhere, despite all her good intentions. Still, she revived the narrative that she was holding out for true love and respect in a mature relationship. She didn't want a sugar daddy and didn't appear to be victimized by the men who mysteriously entered and left our lives. When there was trouble, she beat them to the punch, dropping relationships as soon as she realized they were on the wane.

She was sure that her difficult relationships with men, even younger ones, did not undercut her love for Monika and me. We believed her when she said that men were not as important to her as her kids. She had no intention to seek a life apart from Monika and me.

> Life is great. I must make life great with the children, include them directly. Five years will fly by, and we might no longer be close. Life will always be great, but I want to include Peter and Monika actively.

After Mutti broke up with Ross, she had already befriended the much younger Paul Wiesenfeld, an artist she had met at Vito's studio. Paul was a zany graduate art student at UCLA. Monika and I liked him because he was a lot of fun, more like a kid. We didn't think of him as Mutti's boyfriend until much later when Mutti modeled for him on the sly and later confirmed my suspicion that their friendship had turned into a May-September affair. I was dismayed but did not bring my feelings out into the open. It didn't help matters that I found out by coincidence that Paul was the older brother of a friend of mine.

I don't know about Mother's impact on Paul. He disappeared from our lives after they broke up. It was easy to look him up later because he became a noted artist. I found out that he moved to Germany, married a German woman, and fathered two children who also became recognized artists. He achieved recognition as an accomplished realist painter, influenced by the Dutch artist Johannes Vermeer, whom he admired early in his career when I knew him. I was sad to find out that he died in 1990 from cancer in Munich at the age of 48. Among Paul's earlier works are portraits of Mutti.

I became aware of my growing separation from my mother. As the dynamics of our small family changed, there were also visible changes in Santa Monica that eroded our sense of place. During the 1960s, rapid real estate development began to change our city. Cousin Albert updated the Kensington Motel by renovating the entrance way with a modernist stucco facade to hide the old-fashioned bungalows inside. The venerable Henshey's Department Store, where Estelle bought me my first suit, also received a disfiguring facelift in 1962. On top of that was the decision of the city to replace my beloved Spanish Revival library, built in 1927, with a larger modernist monstrosity. Third Street became the Third Street Promenade in 1965, a pedestrian mall that became a haven for teenagers, shoppers, and panhandlers

Real estate values also rose in dilapidated Venice. The historic Gas House was torn down in 1962 and became a parking lot for the tourists who came to Venice Beach to get a whiff of the ersatz bohemia that remained. All that was left was a nearby plaque to mark the spot of the cultural panoply that was Venice.

Mother's mental issues smoldered below the simmer of her diminishing social scene and the changes taking place in her life. Monika and I had internalized the ups and downs of the moods that inevitably led to her breakdowns, so we built a fragile buffer of denial instead of hope to keep anticipation at bay. All the while, as if on a tornado watch on a calm day, we were on the lookout for the oft-repeated spiraling stories about her life and her unwarranted criticism of friends and relatives who didn't do enough for her. When she claimed to be completely sane, we realized what lay ahead.

In the wake of Mother's ebbing social whirl, the long-expected breakdown finally arrived. Up all night, she wrote her thoughts down furiously in oversized letters, using up stacks of lined, three-hole paper. She scribbled in her diary on the pages remaining for the year and jotted down lists of friends to be written and phoned, and then came up with yet another "shit list" of those who put her off or tried to counsel her to seek help. She spent hours going through her papers and documents, denouncing those "sons of bitches" who had killed her parents and were now trying to tell her what to do. "They don't know your mother!" she proclaimed.

Mutti ranted about what the Nazis did to her mother. She announced that her father, a Polish Jew, was the finest person alive and that no one was "fit to walk the ground he walked on." She made pronouncements which became increasingly slurred the more she was deprived of sleep. "Did you know that your mother is a millionaire, a great lady? I am rich and I am going for a trip around the world." It was useless to call our relatives for help. What could they do? "Convince your mother to see a doctor." Good luck!

Just having received my driver's license, I talked Mutti into a ride to the LA County Hospital, hoping to get help without involving the police. When we arrived, we were directed to the LA County General Psych Ward where, much to my surprise, Mutti signed herself in without a fuss. She had a frightened look when the medical staff escorted her to the ward. Later, she was transferred to a mental health clinic where she recovered quickly and was released. We dodged the bullet of yet another lengthy hospitalization and yet another foster home.

Within weeks she was home, and things went back to normal. Starting at the end of 1960, Mutti managed to stay well enough to avoid hospitalization for almost two years straight. I pursued my studies and social life. Monika did her best to hang on in junior high. She made the rounds with Mutti to friends and relatives. Occasionally I went along. Mother took pride in my academic progress in high school and decided that she would finally "compete with her son" by pursuing a college degree herself. I wasn't sure what to make of this rivalry. At the beginning of my senior year in high school in the fall of 1962, we took a French class together at Santa Monica City College. We rode to class on my unreliable Lambretta scooter. Sitting next to each other in class, we attracted the attention of the mock-stern, Mr. Belozubov, who gently chided Mother in flamboyant French for not knowing her irregular verbs. I felt good about this shared lighthearted episode in our lives, but also had my reservations because I questioned the wisdom of including her in my social life.

Up for mischief, Mutti wanted to know if she could learn to drive my scooter. To communicate my justified reluctance, I joked about a billboard ad showing a driver's education school that claimed to have trained a horse to drive. The ad featured a horse at the wheel with its rear end in prominence. This impertinence earned me an angry slap across the face, the only time that I recall her ever raising her hand against me. The adage "turnabout is fair play" applied here.

This calm period in our lives ended early in 1963 when Mother's mental condition imploded again. She had crying fits and denied that she was going nuts and scrubbed the floors as if that would make her troubles go away. After days of no sleep, her mania increased. This time, no ruse or cajoling on my part worked. My pro forma call to Resi and Freddie produced no new ideas. Monika and I took turns staying up with her while she ranted and raged until one morning, it was clear that we had no choice but to call the police and her social worker. She was out of control, stark naked, her arms flailing about. I tried to restrain her, to convince her to put on some clothes. She finally paused, looked at me, and then tore off the window curtain, wrapped it around herself like a toga and exclaimed defiantly, "So finally I have my dignity!" The police came to take her away, without incident.

Relieved but upset, we didn't know where she would be taken, whether she was safe, or what would happen next. We wondered what would happen to us, especially underage Monika, who feared she would end up in a foster home again. Since I was close to 18, I convinced the social worker to allow us to remain in our apartment. In lieu of a foster family, she suggested hiring a live-in housekeeper, an affable Dutch-Indonesian woman whom she knew, who cooked us the spiciest dishes we had ever tasted. She was to keep an eye on things until Mother returned.

This cozy arrangement ended when Monika and her friends were picked up by the police for riding in a car after curfew. Monika was placed in a foster home in Culver City with a kindly African American couple who were Seventh Day Adventists. This move to Culver City meant she also had to change schools in the middle of ninth grade. Monika knew the drill of how to adapt once again and developed a friendly relationship with Emma, her new foster mother.

Now on my own, I could not afford to pay the upcoming rent for our apartment, but I found a cheaper one to share with Ross's friend, Gary, who had just left his wife. We moved into a cheap semi-furnished apartment on 2860 Exposition Boulevard in an industrial area about a mile from the Santa Monica Airport, where I could temporarily stay and store Mother's belongings. Since Gary and I didn't have money to turn on the utilities, we burned kerosene for cooking that turned the ceiling black with soot. He ended up selling some of my mother's furniture without consulting me or sharing the proceeds. I had to find work.

I dropped three classes I didn't need for graduation, got weekend work with Monika's foster parents as a roofer's helper, and took a part-time job as a clerk in the biostatistics lab run by a friend's father at UCLA. In the May of that year, Mutti was discharged from Norwalk State Hospital shortly before my graduation from Samohi. Monika remained in her foster home while Mutti stayed again with Freddie and Resi at their home La Cienega Heights. As she had done previously, she worked out a recovery plan with her social worker.

Released again, still very depressed, I received a letter that I was to report to a social mental welfare office. There I was greeted by a

smartly dressed, petite lady, Mrs. Lasker, who told me that she was
going to be my psychiatric social worker. I sat in front of her, limp, no
attention span, incapable of communication. But I did have the feeling
she was sincere, and she knew a lot about me, based on my file which
followed me wherever I went. In answer to many of her questions, my
answers often were, "I don't know." I really didn't know anything. But
when she mentioned Peter and Monika, I cried bitterly and wouldn't
speak any more for the rest of the interview. Mrs. Lasker wanted to see
me once a week, and a doctor supplied the medication to help lift the
depression. Thank God, he didn't send me back to the hospital, back
to EST to shock me out of my depression. I shall always be deeply
grateful to Mrs. L. for this and many other human acts that followed. I
don't know how many weeks I went to see her, but I do remember her
kindness and patience. She even took me out for lunch. Each visit to
Mrs. L's office ended in tears and she usually made me a cup of coffee
hoping that it would cheer me up a little. It didn't cheer me up, but I
felt that she cared, the first person in the American psychiatric system
who cared about me. Finally, after many weeks I started to talk a little,
I told her that I hated my parents, which, of course, was accompanied
by body-shaking tears. Mrs. L. asked me why I hated them. At first, I
didn't know. After a while I gave her insignificant reasons. It was too
painful for me to remember. I was incapable to admit that I loved my
parents with all my heart and that I felt I had deserted them in 1939,
and I felt like a coward having avoided Auschwitz and that I had no
right to live. I was incapable of any enlightened thoughts despite the
encouragement I received from her. The time was not ripe, or did I
decide I hadn't suffered enough?

By July with money coming in from disability, Mutti no longer needed
to stay with Freddie and Resi. Monika joined her after she found an
apartment on top of a garage on Highland Avenue in Santa Monica.
Her school records were transferred from Culver City Junior High to
Santa Monica High School. After they settled in, I moved in for the
remainder of the summer. For several weeks our little family was
under the same roof. It would take additional time to get things back
on a somewhat even keel.

Monika and I found temporary work with UCLA Food Services that
hosted banquets for alumni donors. We had a few carefree weeks

together commuting to UCLA on my scooter. When our work stint was completed, we participated in a food fight that would have made John Belushi proud.

When I left for Berkeley to start my freshman year in college, Mutti said she was happy to see me go and wished me well. I was too preoccupied with arrangements to think about how Mutti and Monika would cope after I left. I rode my scooter 400 miles to Berkeley to arrange housing and find a job to supplement my scholarship, then shipped my belonging to my new place, a room in a small house rented through University Housing Services. I found temporary work hashing and painting for a fraternity. One week into the job, an older co-worker introduced me to Tijuana Gold imported from Brazil. This was nasty, powerful stuff that sent me around the bend and added another dimension to the distance of 400 miles between me and the problems at home.

While away at an institution of higher learning, I was less aware of Mother's never-ending "experiential education" in California's mental health system. My attention was caught years later when I read what she wrote about her forced hospitalizations.

16

NOTES FROM THE LOONY BIN

Mother had been hospitalized three times in California's state-run mental hospitals – Norwalk in 1958, Camarillo in 1960 and Norwalk again in late 1963. She had also been treated periodically in various psychiatric clinics and hospitals in the Los Angeles area that accepted mental patients, including Resthaven, Gateways, and Culver City Memorial Hospital where she landed four times. In conversations and later in her writings, she referred to mental hospitals humorously as loony bins, nut houses, and funny farms, particularly two of California's largest mental hospitals located in Norwalk and Camarillo where she received anti-psychotic drugs as well as numerous shock treatments to neutralize her mania.

> I had so many manic-depressive psychotic episodes, almost every year since 1958, at times even twice a year. If you asked me about any particular year, I could give the location and name of where I was hospitalized and how many ESTs I received. I received 48 in all. I can relive in minute detail what happened. My first visit to a state institution remains a blank, except for the terror. That is when I received too many ECTs without Pentothal.

Still an emerging therapy when it was widely used in the United States during the 1950s, Electroconvulsive Therapy (ECT) was developed in

Italy during the 1930s. During ECT, small electric currents are passed through the brain to trigger seizures that were often effective in treating mental illnesses, such as severe depression and bipolar disorder as well as other forms of psychosis and catatonia. In most cases, ECTs provided a temporary benefit but no lasting cure. After ECTs were introduced in America, they were sometimes applied punitively against the patient's will, often without proper anesthesia, to pacify manic behavior as portrayed in Ken Kesey's novel, *One Flew over the Coocoo's Nest*. Although its widespread use has diminished since the 1960s, there have been significant improvements in the methodology for its effective application. Since those days, mental health research has refined the diagnosis of bipolar disorder and methods for treating it, as reflected in recent definitions of bipolar disorder, by the US National Institute of Mental Health.[1]

In addition to ECT, Mutti's doctors prescribed chlorpromazine marketed as Thorazine, which was a pioneering drug widely used to treat the symptoms of mental illness. Developed in 1951, it was used during the 1950s and 1960s to quell agitated patients diagnosed with schizophrenia and manic depression. Until she was put on lithium in the 1980s, Mother was on Thorazine and other medications to stabilize her moods and prevent the manic episodes of her bipolar disorder that on occasion had been misdiagnosed as schizophrenia. Mutti noted the variation in the quality of the care she received.

In America, only a movie star or wealthy person can have a breakdown and recuperate in a fancy private room in a private hospital. But if a poor penniless person like me collapses, the diagnosis is mental illness, not nervous breakdown, regardless of the cause. Inevitably, there is a trip to the mental institution where shock treatments and endless pills are the only cure. My nervous breakdown symptoms in West Berlin were no different than those in America, but in Germany I was treated for a nervous breakdown – no ECT, no insulin shock treatment, no massive medication. I was treated by a psychiatrist on pleasant grounds. There were no locked doors, no bars on my windows, and I recovered quickly. After one visit to a state mental hospital in America, a person is marked for life. Once you are told that you suffer from a psychiatric illness, you have a tough time getting over it, as though you were told that you have terminal cancer.

No matter how much you want to recover, you will always slip back.
There is always the fear of the return visit. You can't shake the stigma.

Mutti understood that mental hospital inmates lose the right to determine the course of their own treatment. During the 1960s, psychiatrists saw little need to get a patient's permission before administering ECT.[2] Whenever Mutti was back to her normal self again, she tried to understand the underlying causes of her mental illness, including the Holocaust-related trauma and survivor's guilt that surfaced during her breakdowns. But she also realized that many people with memories of horrific experiences manage to muddle through. This led her to blame herself and the weaknesses that could be traced back to behavior issues during her childhood years. She also understood that the artifice of self-blame could demonstrate to her doctors her will to recover, so long as it didn't become obsessive.

Although she took pride in taking full responsibility for her problems in order to get well, she still recognized that her personal anguish was what became known during the late 1970s as post-traumatic stress disorder. She instinctively knew that her life experiences had affected her psychological well-being. She also noted the side effects of anti-psychotic drugs as well as lithium, which caused weight gain and affected mental acuity.

Mutti was convinced that in the complex mélange of causes for her mental problems, there was a significant biological basis for her illness that was even greater than the impact of her life experiences and upbringing. Even before she was told that her lithium levels affected her mental state, she attributed the onset of her mania to biochemical forces that she couldn't control. She described the onset of mania as an out-of-control locomotive that no amount of self-coaching could stop.

Like so many of her generation, she had no way of evading the influence of Sigmund Freud whose theories had permeated her worldview, but she was not inclined to blame her parents à la Freud since that would have dishonored them. She believed they did their best to raise a difficult child under challenging circumstances. Although she was aware of Freudian theory and explicated it with a sharp sense of humor, she was never under the care of a Freudian psychologist. One obvious reason is that there was no way she could have afforded to pay for the hours it would take to help her untangle her past rooted in the Holocaust, and so she tried to do that on her own. She spent a lot of time pondering the probable causes of her mental illness.

Many experts say that mental illness has a specific cause, often pointing to one's childhood and parents. I find it difficult to say when "it" started or why. I certainly don't blame my parents; may they rest in peace. They couldn't have loved me more. For years, I didn't want to believe that my mother died in a concentration camp. I kept thinking that she had escaped and would eventually show up here in America. Perhaps it all started in England when I felt that I should have stayed behind with my parents to share their fate. I must have suppressed my anxieties during my youth when I felt favorable towards life. I loved to dance and had fun as much as any healthy person Then there was the stress which kept accumulating during my postwar adventure in Berlin and the new way of life in America, which was no picnic. Then there were the boyfriends without serious intentions and abortions which presented stress without compare. And then there was the constant lack of money.

Mutti certainly was aware of the vagaries of patient care and talked about the influence of Freudianism on the group therapy that she considered a laughable, useless, bureaucratic exercise. But she never felt prepared for the institutional cruelty she experienced when being hospitalized against her will. What follows is her lengthy account of what happened in 1959 when she was brought before a judge.

It was always difficult to get me into mental institutions because of the fear of receiving shock treatments. There was always a kindly friend or relative who managed to trick me into going. Where was the doctor? He must have ordered all those pills by proxy. And I was told that there would be a trial for me. What had I done? What crime did I commit? Oh yes, I wetted my pants for several days. I was even to have a lawyer to defend me. Defend me from what? I soon found out. I was taken into a large room which did appear like a court room. There was the judge in center front and opposite him rows of seats for the spectators. Among them were Peterle and Minkalein and two cousins.

As I found out, my so-called "sanity" was on trial. They were trying to find out whether I was insane. Whatever I could make out of what the judge was saying, I had the feeling that this trial was certainly not in my favor. I tried to tell my lawyer that he should try and say something favorable about me, but he constantly told me to be still. At the end, the judge decided that it would not be "safe" for me and other people for me to be without hospital supervision and that I was to be sent to Norwalk, a state mental hospital south of Los Angeles. I rose to my feet, both arms high up in the air, third finger erect, shouting, "f-you, your honor, and thank you for your f-ing justice!" That same day I was riding a big bus with bars on the windows, the same bus used for prisoners, to the hospital which was to give me supervision.

My sister and I were not allowed to visit our mother while she underwent preparation for ECT. It would be years until we knew the whole story about what happened. The guilt our mother felt for having "abandoned" her parents to their fate was transferred to my sister and me as we did little more than watch and look away while she underwent the trauma and humiliation of being a mental hospital inmate whose rights were forcibly abrogated. We were the lucky ones living in relative peace and quiet, relieved that the medical establishment took on the care of our troubled mother. That peace came at the price of realizing we were complicit in what seemed like our mother's humiliating martyrdom. We were powerless to stop it but also unwilling to try anyway. I felt guilty, shocked, and dismayed when I read the account of her ordeal after she died.

My ward had 150 women crammed together. Four nurses and one doctor. The supervision was like herding animals. At mealtime, two nurses shouted for everybody to line up and the herding began. Once patients finally lined up as ordered, the march and shuffle to the mess hall began. Then another waiting period. Each patient was handed a food tray, and afterwards the same routine was repeated for returning to the ward. This happened three times a day. Once the doors were locked behind me, my behavior always took a turn for the worse. I became so wild that the maximum of all treatments was applied. On one occasion, I was put into an empty room which had a tiny thick glass window high up in the door. I must have spent at least three days in this room, screaming all kinds of slogans and profanities until my voice gave out. I caused so much commotion that I was put into restraints with leather straps and iron rings. I managed to free myself and then it took six people (supposedly nurses) to get me onto a table and hold me down for an emergency ECT, one with Pentothal and one without. In those days, it was usually without. The ECTs interfered with breathing. I could breathe in, but not out, a petrifying fact, and I thought I was going to die. I felt and saw a flash in my head, which produced a click, and then I was out. This "great" treatment continued until I was totally depressed and incapacitated. Then there were the hallucinations. I thought I had died a physical death and entered a higher sphere, but still in the form of a human being, rejoicing because Peter and Monika were with me, and I found parents by my side. In another hallucination, I thought I was "mother of all life" here to save the world. These hallucinations were repeated during several illnesses. At first, they frightened me, but later I accepted them. Screaming that I must go to the toilet did not seem to move anybody, and I had to urinate down my pants (I remember they were bright blue) until they were drenched. I had a blanket thrown into the room. They thought I might become exhausted soon, but I didn't. Occasionally, the door opened, and two nurses entered with a handful of pills I took under protest. I became more and more frightened, thinking I was going insane. The wood strips around the room seemed to be disappearing and reappearing. In the end, I lost touch with reality and couldn't figure out where I was and how I got there and which country I was in. Finally, the nurses took me out of this empty room which looked like a kennel, took off my wet clothes and put some odd-looking things on me. Oh yes, I had calmed down. I simply had no more energy left. All the pills they had me swallow took effect. They not only calmed me down, but made me feel seasick, the ground swaying so that I could not walk properly. I walked with my hands extended in fear of falling, but none of the nursing staff seemed to care. One of the three wards was for the noisy and restless patients, and, of course, I was among these. Each ward has 50 beds, barely enough room to get in. Earlier I had received knitting material and I remember wandering up and down these rows of beds, knitting all night long in the dark. Although there was a strange feeling of kinship among the patients, the mood was one of hostility and resentfulness which often ended in a fistfight. For even minor indications of misbehavior, patients were put into solitary confinement in an empty room with a bare bed. I was once put into solitary because a nurse decided I had dressed improperly, putting on a long skirt to wear at a dance. The nurse ordered me to take the skirt off, but I refused. A screaming argument drew all four nurses, grabbing me by arms and legs, dragging me along the corridor into one of the empty rooms. I was struggling and screaming, "I am J.C. They are putting me on the cross," until I was pushed and kicked into that room. Confinement lasted a couple of hours, and I screamed profanities on top of my lungs. I removed the mattress of the bed and used the spring frame as a trampoline until my toes got caught and I doubled over with pain. I stayed in this position, now screaming in pain, until the nurses decided I had enough punishment. A few days after this incident I was on the shock treatment table again, without ever seeing a doctor. But he, the invisible, ordered an EKG, which was always done prior to ECT, a protection to doctor and patient, so they shouldn't have a corpse on the table. A series of eight treatments got me close to a vegetative stage, a deep depression. Now I was allowed to leave the hospital. They had broken my spirit, but nobody in the "hospital of supervision" was interested in why I was upset in the first place.

17

PICKING UP THE PIECES

Monika and I had become inured "bipolar brats." Monika often said, "Mutti went through a lot." And so did we. We racked up five years of "learning experiences" in orphanages and foster homes, and coped with forced change the best we could. Monika went to seven elementary schools, including the one in Germany, plus two junior highs. I attended three elementary schools in Germany and two more in the United States, plus four junior high schools. Yet, despite the discontinuity of our lives, we still bought into the idea of being a fortunate family as long as Mutti managed to stay well enough to shower us with her customary heartfelt love and affection. We grew to understand the fragility of her recoveries and the cyclical dynamics of her mental illness that we came to expect.

When she was discharged from Norwalk State Hospital in 1963, her main task was to maintain a positive attitude for a successful recovery. Her support system was in place, a network of boosters, mainly women providing mutual aid and friendship. Mutti found an apartment and entered a training program for a job as a medical assistant. Monika returned to live with her after spending six months in the foster home. The loyal Mrs. Lasker was the go-to social worker who helped her navigate her recovery and rehabilitation.

This was also the year I moved to Berkeley to start college and Monika started Santa Monica High School where she knew no one. Since I was gone, Monika had to bear the brunt of Mother's recovery while facing academic problems on her own at school. She fell behind in her work and sought little help from her teachers who were busy serving many other students in crowded classes.

Mutti worried about Monika's social isolation at school, but I don't know whether she was fully aware of how much Monika fell behind in her studies. She tended to focus on Monika's psychological well-being and tried "to get her out of her shell." Frequently absent from school, Monika spent extended periods alone at home while her mother was busy with the training program.

Mutti's parents actively managed their daughter's education under dire circumstances. One would expect that under somewhat more normal circumstances, she would focus on the education of her own daughter, but that didn't happen even though she had written in her 1957 daybook, "Be active in school activities of Peter and Monika." In retrospect, Monika said that Mutti didn't expect her to do well in school because she was a girl, but that seemed odd for someone who had stressed the importance of education for herself. No doubt, mental health issues diminished her capacity for the practical aspects of parenting to encourage success in school. To make matters, Monika's ocial studies teacher tried to motivate her by telling her about what a good student her brother had been. This well-meant but ill-advised approach certainly didn't motivate Monika.

Mother's continuous praise for me as the scholar of the family probably alienated Monika even more. I was put off when she called me her "prodigal son," a jab that may have been intended to make me feel guilty for leaving home. In an odd way, she derailed my sense of entitlement when she bragged about her team of dedicated people, such as friends named Bertha and Bill, who were strangers to me but there for her in my absence. She said she didn't want me to worry too much about her and that my success in college was all that mattered. That still left Monika out in the cold when it came to her schooling that went by the wayside. To this day, I feel guilty for not having stayed closer to home to help Monika, although I am not sure what I could have done.

When I left for Berkeley, Mutti was doing as well as could be expected. She sent me letters, including one with a five-dollar bill and a cheery note telling me to have some fun and go to a movie, which I did. She never mentioned Monika's problems in school, and I never talked about my money problems during my chaotic first year at Berkeley. When I came for a visit after the end of the first semester, I found out that Monika had dropped out of high school and that Mutti was in no shape to persuade her to go back. I was appalled because I had expected that Monika would muddle through in school without Mutti's help, since she was intelligent, even-tempered, well-adjusted, and never complained. I didn't fully understand that high school just couldn't be an escape for Monika as it had been for me. Her disaffection with school coincided with the return of Mutti's stark depression and wild mood swings that lasted through the night. Her mother's bipolar disorder eclipsed Monika's formal education altogether.

Although Monika understood the involuntary aspects of Mutti's illness, she felt betrayed by the volatility of Mutti's charisma and good will and regarded her bizarre behavior and rants against the world as the return of her "evil twin." When Mutti's depression worsened again during that first year I was away at college, Monika couldn't reach me because I didn't have a phone. Cousin Resi advised Monika to contact Mrs. Lasker, who referred Mutti to a mental health clinic in West Los Angeles. At 15, Monika had to be the responsible adult in charge of ensuring that her mother would receive the care she needed. Going to school was impossible and irrelevant to her while life at home was in crisis mode.

Since they did not have a car, Monica took Mutti to a psychiatric clinic by bus. After the intake evaluation, Mutti had a shock treatment and several hours afterwards a nurse led her through double doors into a large space adjacent to the treatment area. Monika, who had been waiting for her, was dismayed to see her mother emerge completely disoriented. Barely able to recognize her daughter, she didn't look like herself and didn't know where she was. The nurse assured Monika that her mother would be all right and then took Mutti's arm to walk her in circles around the room. A while later Monika took over this task.

After discharge, Monika took her disoriented mother home by bus. A few days later, Mutti's friend Bertha, who had a car, helped her move into a boarding home where she could receive follow-up care at the clinic. No longer in school, Monika was left alone in an apartment she couldn't afford and was forced to move out because the rent was unpaid. One option was to go to a foster home and re-enroll in high school. The other was to become independent and find a job to support herself. She chose the latter option. However, at 16 she was underage to qualify for a full-time job. To get around this, she lied about her age when she applied for a job at McCarthy's Drug store. With her Social Security card in hand, she claimed to be 19 years old, and the manager hired her as a cashier. She arranged with Cousin Albert to have Mutti's belongings stored at the Kensington and then moved in with a friend. Monika's newfound life in the workaday world provided her with a connection to people that she hadn't had at home or at school.

From 1964 on, Monika lived mostly apart from Mutti, but stayed in touch with her. She worked at McCarthy's for about a year, then moved in with friends in Los Angeles where she found other retail jobs, and later moved back to Santa Monica after finding work at another McCarthy's drugstore in Westwood. Since she did not have access to a car, taking buses became a way of life. She faithfully visited Estelle at the Kensington with Mutti and sometimes on her own. When Estelle took Monika out for lunch, she insisted on treating her to something fun like a new hairdo. For all of us, and especially for Monika, Estelle was a beacon of gentility, stability and normalcy. Her kindness and generosity meant a lot. I don't know if Estelle knew that Monika had dropped out of high school.

Monika described the rough years on her own as "character building" without dwelling on the episodes she would rather forget. Monika developed coping skills by emphasizing the positive. "I got to see a lot," she would later joke referring to the parties, outings, and events they attended like the Monterrey Pop Festival. Along the way, she earned a high school equivalency diploma. On one occasion, she moved back temporarily with Mutti to help her recover after a mental breakdown.

While Monika started to establish a life on her own after she left school, I completed my freshman year in the bosom of university life.

We kept in touch during my visits to Santa Monica and she visited me in Berkeley. In our own way, each of us tried to separate our new lives from our mother. That was easier for me to do since I was away from home involved in my studies.

During the summer of 1964, I worked on a research project funded by the California State Health Department and spent eight weeks in Kern County collecting data in anticipation of Robert Kennedy's factfinding trip about inaccessibility of healthcare for Mexican American and Mexican farm laborers, including participants in the Bracero Program. Finally, I had a chance to apply the three years of Spanish I took in high school to interview farmworkers and their families regarding health services and was shocked to see the kind of extreme poverty in America that our family never experienced, even during the postwar years in Berlin. The survey team included Caesar Chavez's wife, Helen, who invited us to a picnic of the United Farmworkers Union at Chavez's house where we met her soon-to-be-famous husband.

After completing the project in early August, I took off for a two-week bus trip to Mexico with a school friend, Daryl, who had the poor judgment to be high on Bella Donna and the bad luck to be arrested for causing a ruckus when the Mexican border police boarded our bus to check the identification of all passengers aboard. Relying again on my school Spanish, I offered to join my friend, but the police ordered me to remain on the bus, which was headed for the next stop, Guaymas, from where I telephoned his parents about what had happened. By the time they bailed out their son, I was in Mexico City making the rounds with some Mexican kids my age. Then I went by bus to the Great Pyramid of Cholula, also known as Tlachihualtepetl and afterwards to Taxco to buy souvenirs, including silver jewelry for Mutti and Monica.

I returned to Berkeley that fall with a new Mexican blanket to start my sophomore year and to find work fast to make up for having lost my scholarship from Levi-Strauss that was earmarked for living expenses. This happened because I got a "D" in Calculus during my freshman year. My difficulty with integrals and differentials, not to mention my inability to comprehend the Korean professor's spoken English, cemented my intention to major in history after I was invited to join the History Honors Program because of my good grades in the humanities.

My federally funded work-study job at the Department of Mathematics provided me with rent money as well as access to a Xerox copier, which came in handy for making decent copies of my cut-and-paste history papers typed on my standard Underwood. Later that year I found gardening work and then bought an old Chevy convertible so I could deliver the *San Francisco Chronicle* in the Oakland Hills. By semester break, I had enough money to fly home from Oakland to LA on Southwest instead of taking the bus or hitching a ride.

During Thanksgiving dinner, Mother and Monika teased me for being a nerdy and impractical "genius," a label that didn't really match the facts. I gave them the gist of the Berkeley scene without dwelling too much on my initial academic setbacks. Drawing from her experience with fellow mental patients who were burnt out from drug abuse, Mutti warned me again not to fall prey to the drug culture that had surfaced in Berkeley. I heeded her advice for the most part.

Politics became my drug of choice. I joined SLATE, a leftist political organization on campus that promoted civil liberties and civil rights on and off campus, ran candidates for student office, and published the *Cal Reporter*. Later, I also became involved in advocacy and fundraising for the United Farm Workers and the Free Speech Movement (FSM) that sprang from SLATE. In reaction to the growth of student activism on campus, William F. Knowland, publisher of the *Oakland Tribune* and former US Senator from California, as well Joseph Alioto, Mayor of San Francisco, pressured the Berkeley administration to prohibit on-campus political advocacy and fundraising by students. As a result, the university cracked down on student activities in reaction to the widespread involvement of Berkeley students in picketing organizations and businesses that discriminated against African Americans. Students picketed high-profile targets including the Sheraton Plaza Hotel, Lucky's Supermarkets, and the *Oakland Tribune* for their hiring practices, as well as university fraternities for not accepting Black members.

The Free Speech controversy began on September 10, 1964, in response to the University's prohibition of on-campus student political activities.

The leaders of the newly formed FSM filed petitions, threatened legal actions, held vigils and organized demonstrations. They met repeatedly with university officials and gained the support of the Faculty Senate. On October 2, Jack Weinberg, a graduate student, was arrested for distributing leaflets for the Congress of Racial Equality (CORE). Hundreds of students responded by surrounding the police car holding him. By late afternoon, the number of students swelled into thousands. Student activist Mario Savio and others fired up the crowd by speaking from atop the car's roof while the police and demonstration leaders conferred to prevent violence. FSM leaders later passed the hat for funds to repair the resulting damage to the police car.

At a December 2 rally, I heard Mario Savio, by then a key FSM leader, give a speech in front of Sproul Hall which housed the university administration. Savio called out the now famous words, "Put your bodies on the gears!" to urge students and faculty to stage a sit-in at Sproul Hall as part of a strike against the University's autocratic "machine." Savio was hailed as a gifted orator in a *San Francisco Chronicle* headline. With some reluctance, I joined the Sproul Hall occupation where students remained overnight to protest as well as to study for finals. We demanded the restoration of our right to conduct political activities, including on-campus fundraising and advocacy. Before entering the building, I drew the three large initials, FSM, on three big posters that were placed in the windows above the entrance of Sproul Hall to provide visibility for the occupation. The next day, mass arrests began after students ignored police orders to vacate the building. Most of us were escorted out. Some engaged in passive resistance and were dragged out. A revolving fleet of yellow busses transferred about 800 demonstrators to a facility adjacent to San Rita County Jail, one of three jails receiving arrested students, where we were fed peanut butter sandwiches before the FSM lawyers bailed us out. I had expected much harsher treatment. Weeks later, there was a stormy trial and calls from organizers for students to show defiance. I didn't go to court and ended up paying $50 for trespassing, a misdemeanor. Resisting arrest carried about a $150 dollar. Some of the leaders received higher fines or jail sentences. After months of negotiation, the Free Speech Movement held its first legal rally on the steps of Sproul Hall at noon on January 4, 1965.[1]

The period after the Sproul Hall sit-ins radicalized campus life. Although civil rights actions continued, the rhetoric on campus increasingly focused on fighting "the system" and its suppression of individual liberty pertaining to sexual behavior and drug use, in addition to freedom of speech. Mission creep and wedge issues vitiated the core ideology underlying the civil rights struggle and the fight to stop the exploitation of workers by the "ruling class." In some cases, truth became a casualty amidst the conflict. The *Berkeley Barb* ran an article about a young man carried out of Sproul Hall as the "victim of police brutality." What really happened was that this man had an epileptic fit. Some of us demonstrators notified the police who brought a stretcher to carry him out. In that case, the officers were only doing their job. Freedom of the press is complicated.

With the expansion of the Vietnam War in 1965, Berkeley students protested American imperialism. Civil rights and free speech issues were redefined and expanded with the rise of the Black Power, Women's Liberation, and Sexual Revolution movements. When activists conflated politics with lifestyle issues, the advocacy for free speech in politics competed with the emerging hippy culture espousing free love, psychedelic drugs, and lifestyle changes that opposed conventional ideas of work, education, property and law enforcement.

Back on the home front, Mutti really took to the anarchistic flavors of both the free speech and hippie movements. She loved the flower children and their flower power. Unlike many parents who were aghast when their sons and daughters made the front pages, her rebellious spirit identified with the kids. After I described to her my involvement in the Free Speech Movement, Mutti wanted to see the activism firsthand. She visited me in Berkeley several months after the students occupied Sproul Hall and joined a CORE picket protesting employers who discriminated against Blacks, who were still called Negroes then. On the picket line, one of my friends led the chant, "What do we want?" The crowd responded appropriately, "Freedom." And then he shouted out again, "What kind of freedom?" The crowd was silent. We had ourselves a good laugh.

In late 1965, Mutti had another mental breakdown but was sufficiently compos mentis to admit herself. This time, she no longer had to repeat the horrors she experienced at Norwalk State Hospital.

> I went for help to a local hospital which had a psychiatric unit. I talked to a psychiatric social worker, but don't remember what was said. I even saw the psychiatrist. Guess what? Eight more ECTs. But this time they showed me mercy (it was a Catholic hospital). I was put into a private room, and the doctor gave me Pentothal prior to the shock. When I woke up, I was greeted by a nun who brought me a tray with coffee and toast. It was mercy. And I recovered! In fact, I always recovered in due time. I was my old bouncing, high-spirited, life-acknowledging self again, until the next stress situation would pull me down. I found myself a job again. I was functioning. Yet, I carried the stigma of having been mentally ill, afraid that sooner or later the illness would strike again. Nobody knew why I got ill or why I recovered.

Mother's improved access to stable medical and social services contributed to longer periods of normalcy. In her diary, she referred humorously to her doctors, Lunsky and Weinstock, as the "Lithium Brothers." Indeed, lithium was effective in decreasing the severity and length of her bipolar downtime, so long as she kept up the drug regimen. The doctor routinely monitored her lithium levels and advised her to avoid alcohol and to drink coffee in moderation. The undesirable side effects, such as weight gain continued to plague her despite her efforts to regulate her died and exercise.

Mutti was told that she had to be "a good girl" to stay well and that medical treatment was effective so long as she followed the doctor's orders, something that she often repeated to herself in the presence of others. Keeping up her medications was the priority.

To support her efforts to stay well, her doctor introduced her to Recovery, a self-help organization that helped ex-mental patients to stay well by following the writings of Dr. Abraham A. Low, a neuropsychiatrist who founded Recovery in 1937 and preached commonsense moderation in all things, and all things in moderation.[2] Dr. Low taught his students to avoid thoughts of "exceptionality" and to place troublesome people in a safe "outer environment" so that they wouldn't cause the patient further anxiety. Mutti put to use her mother's favorite term, *Die Goldene Mittestraße* [the golden middle road], to avoid the roller coaster of manic depression through moderation in all things.

Mutti attended weekly Recovery meetings with other ex-patients. There were even insipid songs to reinforce Doctor Low's wisdom, such as "Just Be Average" which was sung to words of "Ol' Man River," and went like this: "Just be average. I hope I'm average and not exceptional or perfectional. Just be average and keep on going along. I've no ambition for top position. I simply follow my disposition to Dr. Low. Just be average and keep on going along." Given her negative opinion about group therapy, I was surprised that she was amenable to attending these Recovery meetings.

Ah, what a pill to swallow for a perennial flower child like our mother! Yet, she maintained that "Recovery tricks" helped her to control her bipolar disorder. She handed me Dr. Low's book to deepen my understanding of the Recovery philosophy, particularly the concept of self-endorsement. Endorsing is one of the things you do to congratulate yourself for not falling prey to the sins of "exceptionality" convinced that you are on a mission from God to do your thing. You are supposed to endorse yourself when you stay on the straight and narrow human plane.

But Recovery only worked up to a point when Mother became depressed and dwelled on her problems. She described the trajectory of her feelings on January 29, 1966.

> I was lonely and felt detached from society all my life. I kept endless diaries helping myself along with my poor memory and empty days. I never gave up. When I was a teenager, I felt superior and protective towards my parents. I don't think I loved them, particularly my father. There were periods in my life when I managed to function, but I always collapsed after there was a little strain. Now I am facing total collapse and I lost contact with everything. This feels like it is the end. I am only 43 and my physical life may last another 20 years. The thought of 20 years of suffering mentally and eventually physically is beyond my comprehension. I am scared to death.

Although doubtful about sure cures, Mutti enshrined Doctor Low's wisdom even though she did not practice it to the letter. When it suited her, Dr. Low and her medical accoutrements, including her prescribed medications, were cast aside in her crusade for mental freedom. Once Mother's wild horse was out of the barn, the rationality of Dr. Low's program flew out the window. Yet for a significant period, Recovery gave her a social life with people who understood mental challenges. Mutti shared her Recovery friends' stories with us, and we met some of them at her apartment including her pal, Mike Schuster. He was a husky Jewish guy, a friendly but assertive, take-charge type, hardly your typical insecure ex-mental patient. Most other Recovery friends were more evidently needy in their quest for affirmation and support.

While life was verging on calm during my sophomore year, Monika visited me once in Berkeley and I managed to finance a regular pattern of visits home to see her and Mutti. I became more acquainted with the Recovery pals and saw more of her old circle of acquaintances and long-term friends like Bertha who seemed to be there for her even when their names were temporarily added to Mother's famous "shit list" during her downward spirals.

Mother had become friends with Linda and Al whom she met while working at UCLA Food Services. Linda was an accomplished artist doing graduate work at UCLA and Al was a PhD candidate in sociolinguistics. Al and Linda became life-long friends of our family. Intelligent and good-humored, they brought the best out in Mother. It was fun to hear Mutti try out her English accent on Linda, who had come to the United States from England as a young adult. She called Al "the Dristan Kid" because his bouts with hay fever kept him reaching for that over-the-counter drug.

Some friends were active in civil rights. Gene, an affable African American fellow who belonged to CORE, said he had gone to Selma as a Freedom Fighter. Through him, Mutti met Ned Glass, a noted Hollywood character actor in his late sixties who supported civil rights and other liberal causes. He invited Mother and me to his tastefully furnished house with built-in bookcases and photos of his show biz appearances. Mutti said Ned Glass wanted to meet me, which I took to mean that she wanted to introduce me to him. This was a Jewish Mother thing to do. She wanted to see how he might help to get my career started, since I had a budding interest in film. When I met him, I didn't have much to say. I did nothing to impress him and couldn't bring myself to talk about my interests and ambitions that were in flux. I wasn't ready for it. I didn't even bother to convey to him my left-leaning but lukewarm interest in politics. Although I appreciated Mother's efforts to connect me, I wasn't interested in promoting myself. Mother was disappointed and surprised at my unwillingness to leverage her tribal connection.[3]

Mother's friendship with the affable Gene blossomed into an affair. He would stop by on his hefty Harley motorcycle while Monika and I would smile and nod to acknowledge that Mother was doing her thing whether we liked it or not. Gene's being African American gave her a sense of daring. She may have wanted to test our liberal beliefs and may have been using his Blackness to express her disaffection with mainstream values. In 1965, she wrote about her attraction to him.

> I am full of the idea that nobody will humiliate me anymore and I walk around with my head up in the air very high, so nobody can touch me anymore, and then I see you, and I feel like a little girl. You are in my bloodstream and in my thoughts, even in the middle of the night when I turn over in between dreams. But you keep a distance which I don't like. I want you to become all me, and I don't even know why I have chosen you of all the many people in the world. You don't even belong to my people I can speak to, like I can speak to myself. You are a different world and yet I feel all those wonderful things when I look at you.

Mother went on joyrides with Gene in 1965 as well as to civil rights protests at the Federal Building in downtown Los Angeles and CORE strategy meetings at Freedom House. After their whirlwind protest tour, they went to Arizona to meet his parents. Nevertheless, it didn't take long for her to see some questionable motives underlying Gene's freedom fighting and declarations of love. Mother said that Gene was a wannabe who spoke of love with promises like, "I want to settle down, stop running, and give up partying for you." But he turned out to be a con man who took her and a few white liberals for a ride. Ned Glass became disgusted with him for mishandling CORE finances. Mother ended the relationship and expressed "bourgeois" sentiments in her diary:

> Ja, ja, ja, I got myself a real-life psychopath, oh boy! Talk with Amelia and Miss Forestall [her counselor]. Psychopaths are the most pleasant company anyone can wish for, but you pay for it, $100 so far. I wonder if my ship will ever come in! I would love to overlook so much and overcome so much, if all his behavior would have just been a little deformation of character, but a full-fledged psychopath?! No respect for other people's property!

Mother sounded like the establishment when she was the one who had been taken in. She wasn't surprised that her dreamboat ran aground. As several times before, she was ready to move on.

> Strangely enough, I am not so-called heart broken. Now I am confronted with a person who practically wants to own me, but who does not know how to own himself. Nobody has the right to own or possess anybody. Two people who want to share certain things in life and who want to be successful in doing so must remain a graceful distance from each other, and humbly respect the life and actions of their so-called beloved partner. People should be together like two graceful swans, and not grab, demand, shout, and dictate.

Mutti identified with the Civil Rights struggle that provided a mixed metaphor for her own struggles and brought back memories of racist persecution in Nazi Germany. Although she sympathized with the problems of Blacks and Hispanics, she was slyly condescending when they didn't live up to her middle-class expectations of how they should fight their battles. She was incensed when she, not "the man" was ripped off by someone using equal rights as an excuse. Not forgetting that her own parents pointed out the otherness of "gypsies" in describing her own dark looks, she gave a lot of thought to the omni-present racial bias in America that permeated mainstream ideas regardless of politics and class. "I am a citizen of the world," she said indicating her awareness that the human nature of every race and nationality is fraught with frailties that troubled her.

While my mother was coping with the conundrums of caste and class, I was living off-campus, entangled in my student cocoon, riding on the fringes of the white privilege that Stokely Carmichael derided via KPFA Pacifica Radio in Berkeley. I was absorbed by my new life as an undergraduate, but that changed in the spring semester of 1966 when I transferred from Berkeley to University of California, Los Angeles (UCLA) to pursue my interest in theatrical and documentary films. I planned to take courses in the film department for a double major in history and theater arts, with the idea of eventually working in the entertainment industry. I also thought that moving to LA would enable me stay with my mother, maybe help her out. Her place in Santa Monica was within commuting distance to UCLA and also close enough to a part-time job I got tutoring children at an elementary school in Culver City.

This arrangement didn't last more than a week. Mother stopped her medications cold turkey to free up her manic demons. The more I tried to reason with her to take her meds, the angrier she became. She didn't want me to meddle and so in a rage, she demanded that I leave, and so I did. I felt guilty but relieved.

Within a day, I found a room to rent in an elderly couple's house in Venice. This lasted for several weeks until the landlord burst into my room at four o'clock in the morning, demanding his rent which was one day late. I paid up and moved out despite his wife's apologies. By then I had better prospects for another rental. The mother of one of my high school friends knew about a house for rent in Culver City that was owned by the Unitarian Church where she was a member. I closed the deal and moved into the house in Culver City with a fellow film student at UCLA and two other students he knew through school.

Although I expected the worst after my blow-out with Mutti, she managed to avoid another breakdown. She credited her new social worker and counselor, Miss Forestall, who had replaced Mrs. Lasker as her go-to person. She also spoke highly of her doctor, resumed her meds, and reengaged with her Recovery group. This piece of good news provided me the opportunity to focus on my own life. I worked on my film projects and took in the excitement of the bourgeoning counterculture in Los Angeles, exemplified by a "happening" staged in Culver City near where we lived.

My new living situation with three roommates presented a new set of challenges. One roommate, an escapee from white-bread America, pursued his trade of peddling the drugs he acquired while serving as a Peace Corps volunteer in the Dominican Republic. The second, a Jewish medical student, used his connections at the UCLA Medical Center to get the third of my roommates admitted to the hospital when he got strung out on a concoction of LSD and Methedrine. This poor fellow, after listening to a record by Mimi and Richard Fariña, climbed up a huge pine tree outside the second-floor window and threatened suicide before we coaxed him down. His story was that he was traumatized by the suicide of his father, who had managed a copper mine in Chile during a violent strike. With all these goings on, I knew that trouble lay ahead.

After completing the spring semester, I found summer work as a counselor at a Jewish day camp. I taught swimming and drove a group of kids to and from their homes in Beverly Hills in my old Plymouth station wagon. I was surprised that parents would entrust me with their children. I continuing to live with my three roommates that summer. Much of my time was spent on campus learning the basics of film production and delving into the history of cinema.

In the beginning of August, I got a concussion from an ice skating accident that landed me in the Emergency Ward at Culver City Memorial. When I regained consciousness, I told the hospital staff that I was a student with medical coverage, so I was transferred to the UCLA Medical Center where I stayed for about a week under observation. Mutti did not rise to the occasion, just as she had not when Monika had her tonsillectomy. I saw her a week after my release. She didn't explain her absence and I didn't ask.

Meanwhile, my roommate situation deteriorated when the tree-top suicide watch switched to a crime scene watch. I panicked when two armed thugs came to the house to complete a Meth deal with my drug-dealing roommate. Since I didn't want to be entangled with drugs and guns, I moved out and discretely advised the Unitarian Church to terminate the rental agreement that was in my name.

That fall, I returned to Berkeley after the renewal of my Levi-Strauss scholarship. For one reason, I didn't want to continue living in Los

Angeles as a helpless bystander where my future would continue to be intertwined with the unmanageable problems of my mother. But there were other reasons. Although I enjoyed film studies at UCLA, I realized that I didn't have the right stuff to succeed in the entertainment industry. I was unwilling to hustle opportunities in an industry dominated by nepotism and cronyism. I was more of a documentary film type, interested in content but not savvy when it came to breaking into the industry. I decided that I would be better off with an undergraduate history degree, with a focus on American studies, and then to see what would come next.

I finished my senior year at Berkeley having written a senior thesis on Madam Blavatsky, the co-founder of the Theosophical Society.[4] Not sure whether I was cut out for an academic career, I nevertheless decided to apply for graduate school so I could keep my draft deferment.

Much to my surprise, I was accepted by Stanford University and the University of Pennsylvania and chose Penn because it offered a generous fellowship and provided me with the opportunity to redefine my life elsewhere while on a student deferment. I was worn out by the turmoil at Berkeley and had decided not to live in Southern California. My mother had mixed feelings about my decision but didn't object.

18

THE NOSTALGIA OF DISPLACEMENT

Mother and Monika drove up from Los Angeles to attend my graduation from Berkeley in May 1967. While we walked up Bancroft Avenue and followed the crowds to the Greek amphitheater overlooking the sun-splattered splendor of San Francisco Bay, Mother noted with approval that I wore jeans underneath my cap and gown. Harry R. Wellman, who came out of retirement to serve as Acting President, was slated to give our commencement address.[1] During the ceremony, several of my classmates passed around joints to commemorate this rite of passage, which provided the opportunity for a contact high while listening inattentively to the words of inspiration uttered by the lineup of notables. After the event, Mother took possession of my graduation certificate that bore the signature of Governor Reagan, whom she called "Uncle Ronnie." I was fine with that since I had no intention to frame and display the governor's name.

Graduation day underscored our growing physical separation from Mother. Monika was living on her own. I was going to Philadelphia of all places, thousands of miles away to attend the Annenberg School at the University of Pennsylvania. I told Monika about my plans to go to Europe for several weeks that summer and invited her to come along. For both Monika and me, this would be an opportunity to reconnect with the past by visiting our respective long-lost fathers in Berlin and Rome.

This rite of passage, to see my father in Rome for the first time since I was a toddler in England, was to be my last hurrah before going to graduate school. Also, Monika and I would be reunited with her German father and our German family in Berlin. Since I would already be back East before the trip, we planned to meet in New York to catch our charter flight to Paris.

I left Berkeley for Philadelphia on a rideshare with an ex-landlady who was going east to visit her mother in Camden, New Jersey. We took a detour to Minneapolis to visit her friend, Bishop James Pike, an influential progressive activist who was the fifth Episcopal bishop of California from 1958-1966. When I met this legendary figure in 1967, he was a senior fellow at a liberal think tank and an adjunct professor at University of Berkeley School of Law. Enmeshed in controversy, he seemed troubled and talked almost nonstop. Two years later, he died alone in the Judean Desert in Israel while his companion forged ahead to find water after their car got stuck in a rut. Pike had wanted to travel where Jesus had gone into the wilderness to fast and meditate but had packed only two Cokes for the ride.[2]

Before my ex-landlady dropped me off in West Philadelphia, she talked in off-putting, euphemistic language about how much the racial composition of Philadelphia's population had changed. This marked the end of a clearly weird trip.

A couple of weeks later, Monika came by bus to New York where we met at Ross Lavroff's place on the Lower East Side who gave us a quick tour of the local hippie scene. Then we took off for Paris. The plan was to head for Berlin to see Monika's father for the first time since 1954, and then on to my father in Rome, who last saw me in 1947. Although Denis and I had exchanged those few letters in a flurry of correspondence about my mother, we would meet like complete strangers since he only knew me as a baby and toddler.

In anticipation of my visit after graduation, he sent a letter to my mother that fell short of a straightforward "congratulations!" When I read it, I wasn't sure what to make of his casual invitation for me to visit him in Rome.

Dear Mary,

I was pleased to hear Peter is taking his BA. But neither you nor he have said exactly what he has qualified in. I just hope it isn't English Literature. Most degrees are no goddam use anyway – everybody's got one. However, I do congratulate you on your wonderful tenacity and family feeling. You should be the honored guest of General Dayan. How about writing to him, giving a brief description of your battles and how you won them? I am slowly but steadily going down the drain – the gurgle of drink reminds me of the slimy reality. I keep telling myself I am going to pull out with a bang someday, but I guess it's too late. Cancer will get me if this lousy Italian climate (all extremes like the Italians) doesn't. However, I am not by any means depressed. The world still interests me, but more to sharpen my teeth on than as my oyster. That's for Peter – what will he do with it? I hate writing letter. You're lucky to get as much as this. Yes, I intend to come over when I get enough cash together. Heartfelt wishes, Denis.

P.S. I live by translating. Money is always tight, but I can put Peter up for a time if he comes.

The flight to Paris turned out to be an all-night party. Our perky Air France stewardesses passed around champagne bottles and joined in. The night we arrived, Monika and I stayed in a seedy hotel on the Left Bank. The next day we walked up to the Gare du Nord and back again to see the sights on the Champs-Élysées. I took a gleeful photo of Monika with the Eifel Tower in the background carefully aligned to look like it rested on top of her head. We made the museum rounds on foot, getting a glimpse of the Mona Lisa at the Louvre, where again we bumped into our Air France stewardesses who waved to us as they descended the museum steps. That night, we drank Pernod while "debating" America's involvement in Vietnam with two insouciant Frenchmen and a Moroccan who wanted to try out their English.

After three days in Paris, we took a train to Brussels to see Mother's childhood friend, Jenny Stanesco, who escaped to Belgium in 1938. She bore a faint resemblance to the Jenny we had seen in the photo with Mother taken when they were 14-year-old students at the Jewish Girls School. The young Jenny, fair and full faced, would have passed for a German girl.

Jenny took us to see *Manneken Pis* and other sites in Brussels and then on a daytrip to Ostend where we spent the afternoon in a seaside café. Jenny's face darkened when we alluded somewhat callously to the impact of our mother's mental illness on us. We met Jenny's lesbian partner and wished Mutti could have been there, too.

Jenny didn't talk much about her days in Nazi Berlin; however, she mentioned her wartime experiences in Belgium saying she was grateful that the "good people" around her kept her Jewish identity quiet. Now she was a café violinist, still a bit sad that she never had an opportunity to realize her serious musical ambitions.

After staying for two nights, we took a morning train from Brussels to Berlin that went through East Germany. At the border, the Transportpolizei [the name for the transit police of East Germany] checked our passports, mine British and Monika's American. It had been 13 years since we departed as children from Berlin. Now we were back, with vague memories of rubble and ruins, to witness how much Berlin had been rebuilt and how the concrete wall divided East from West.

My rusty German was then put to use. We found our way to Monika's father and his second wife, Pippi, whose West Berlin apartment was so near the elevated S-Bahn that their dishes clattered every time a train went by. We stayed with Heinz's sister, Dorchen, and her affable African-born husband in their nearby basement apartment. She was still the affectionate, good-hearted person I remembered when she taught me German. We drank beer and went on an outing to Hitler's bunker and picnicked at Wannsee, the famous lake within sight of the villa where the Nazis plotted the Final Solution.

Needing a break from family, Monika and I went for an outing on our own. We looked up some German students whom we had met at UCLA on the assumption that they would be as friendly as they were in LA when they invited me to visit them. After our arrival at their communal residence, they whisked us off to have coffee at a lakeside café on Krumme Lanke, a lake near Grunewald, to forestall any discussion of our staying with them. Over refreshments, we discussed politics. Our stiff German hosts, who lived comfortably in West Berlin, spoke in glowing terms about East Germany while we nodded dutifully, but when I pointed out that the basis of their own prosperity benefited from the largesse of capitalism, the conversation cooled. Meanwhile, I received hard stares from two older ladies who must have taken me for a Turk because of my coloring. For all I knew, these women might have appeared in a Nazi newsreel as young women in a crowd, cheering and waving their arms as Hitler passed by in a motorcade. Monika and I excused ourselves from this social encounter, much to the relief of all involved. We had a good laugh and returned to the Wiesner household.

On the next day, I went to East Berlin on my own, confident that my British passport guaranteed my return. Monika was reluctant to go with me and stayed with her father's family. At Checkpoint Charlie, I exchanged my Deutschmarks for East German currency at the one-to-one exchange rate, enough to cover lunch and minor purchases that day. Drab East Berlin was far from rebuilt; There were empty lots with hints of rubble and little evidence of reconstruction.

As expected, East Berlin was a food desert. It was impossible to get a real cup of coffee or a decent lunch at the museum café. All they served was insipid soup and a vile hickory coffee substitute. I used my awkward German to start a conversation with a young man who worked in the museum bookstore. I asked him what life was like in East Berlin. He was polite but reluctant to say much, perhaps because for all he knew, I worked for the Stasi. I didn't press him and paid a pittance for a book by Bertolt Brecht.

Weeks later, I left Berlin to see my father in Rome while Monika stayed in West Berlin to spend more time with her father and then decided to visit friends in Hamburg when it became painfully clear that Heinz's struggle with alcoholism had taken its toll. We agreed to meet in London at the end of our separate journeys. I took an overnight train to Rome that arrived while it was still dark. I passed the wee hours walking among ancient ruins at Largo Argentina, where stray cats roamed freely because of Rome's no-kill laws. Later, I learned that Julius Caesar was assassinated in the Curia of the Theater of Pompei, close to where the feral cats meandered.

By late morning, I found my father's address in Trastevere. My rudimentary Italian came in handy when an elderly woman greeted me at the door and gave me his new address and telephone number. I wandered around Rome for a while and finally reached Denis by phone in the afternoon.

We met in the middle of Piazza Navona at the Fountain of the Four Rivers, topped by the Obelisk of Domitian. Our initial encounter was awkward. I couldn't tell if he was by nature reserved or simply English. We went to his place where I first met his thin, black-haired Italian wife, Fausta, who understood English but could speak only in broken sentences.

Fausta seemed remote and uneasy but made the effort to welcome me. Their flat was on the outskirts of Rome near a rail line, where the windows jittered as the trains zoomed by. How very odd that my father had the rattling railway setting in common with Monika's father. I wasn't sure what to call him until he said that he preferred to be called Denis, spelled with one "n."

By evening, the initial awkwardness diminished. Denis talked about his life in Rome and how he met Fausta while living on Via Margutta on the fringe of the expat community. He scraped together a living doing translation work and writing, as well as teaching and journalism, while his wife made a living as a classically trained artist. Although Denis had a lot to say from a foreigner's point of view about life in Italy and the Italian character, he didn't ask me much about my family's reinvented life in America.

Denis talked at length about the history of Italy and the long-standing love-hate relationship between Brits and Italians to explain the Italian attitudes that made life in Italy difficult for him. He attributed the rise of Italian fascism during the 1920s to the kind of provincialism and xenophobia he observed during his expat years in Italy.

Denis admired the aesthetics of Italian culture, but he derided the corruption and incompetence of contemporary Italian politics and the widespread malpractice of its civil servants, especially in managing auto traffic and postal service. He showed me reams of newspaper pages draped over racks that had informed his research about Italian politics for a book he was writing about the Italian centennial. Already I blithely assumed that Italy, like so many other Latin countries, is valued more for its culture and food than for its politics and civil service.

My father's eccentric lifestyle seemed exotic at first, until I realized the extent to which his career prospects were limited as an expat. He admitted that he had an uncanny ability to be his own worst enemy. When he joked that he wrote out of revenge, I wondered what made him pick on the Italians rather than on the British who didn't live up to his ideals either.

Like Mother, Denis was a good storyteller, and wine was his catalyst. He praised the health benefits of broccoli. He took me to see the sights in Rome, from the charming piazzas to the architectural remnants of fascism, translating and explaining the protest graffiti sprayed on ancient walls along the way. We went to the Porta Portese, Rome's largest flea market on the edge of Trastevere, and on the way there he gossiped about the people he knew in the expat community, one of them an artist friend who reputedly drew ugly caricatures of himself. Later, I met several of his fellow English expats, a few seemingly on death's door, at an excellent performance of *Blithe Spirits* on an oppressively humid night. Afterwards, Denis told stories about Richard Burton whom he knew from Oxford and later met up with in Rome. He admired Burton but thought Liz Taylor was a cow. Denis knew Federico Fellini, and out of pride had refused a cameo part in his acclaimed surrealist, comedy-drama film, *8 1/2*. He preferred his earlier films about Italian small-town life, such as *Il Vitelloni*.

My father's Volkswagen had been in the 1966 Florence flood before he bought and restored it. We drove it around in the mountains surrounding Rome in search of picturesque orchards with cheap wine cellars that Denis said didn't match the quality of Italy's exports. One day, Fausta accompanied us on an excursion to the 13th-century town, Civita di Bagnoregio, also called *"la città che muore"* [the dying city], perched on a small mountain surrounded by a chasm spanned by a modern bridge. Every year, bits of the mountain fall off, taking along pieces of the town. My father loved the place because he thought it served as a metaphor for Italy, and for his own life.

Denis was a judge for the film program at the Spoleto Festival dei Due Mondi and knew many film directors and actors. He actively promoted the work of Joseph Losey, the American film director who had studied with Berthold Brecht and was celebrated for his work in England and Europe after he was blacklisted in the United States. Although he hobnobbed with famous people in the arts, Denis was stubbornly independent and seemingly loathe to exploit his connections in Italy and England to advance his career. When I asked him to talk more about his once-promising work in England as a Shakespearean actor and filmmaker, he launched into a diatribe against the acclaimed film director Lindsay Anderson for hijacking the film, *Together*, which was based on Denis's own short story, "The Blue Marble," that he adapted for the screen.

Together was a Special Award Winner for experimental film at Cannes. The magazine, *Sight and Sound*, deemed *Together*, "A poet's film... its mood is strange and delicate; its conception, daring; its method secret, intuitive, visionary..." Contemporary Films, the oldest Independent Distribution Company in the UK, described it as "a haunting and poetic study of two deaf-mutes imprisoned by silence and solitude in London's drab East End... A neorealist film poem of rare intensity infused with deep emotion and melancholy."

Denis told me that he was solely responsible for directing and managing the project, including all arrangements and finances, and recruitment of local non-actors as performers. Lorenza Mazzetti, Denis's lover at that time, was the co-producer and co-director responsible for casting the main leads, who were friends she knew through the Slade School of Fine Arts where she was a student. She had a connection at the British Film Institute that funded this project which ran out of money after most of the shooting was completed. Denis left London at that point for personal and financial reasons. He broke up with Lorenza and left England for Italy on the promise of work there on another film. During Denis's absence, Mazzetti teamed up with Lindsay Anderson, a film director and critic. They completed editing *Together* without Denis's involvement and omitted his name as director in the credits. At that time, Anderson was one of the producers of documentaries funded by the British Film Institute to portray the everyday lives of the working class. He hit on the idea of promoting all of them, along with *Together*, under the rubric of "Free Cinema" because of the candid portrayal of ordinary people.

According to Denis, Anderson hijacked *Together*, the only fiction film among the documentaries.

I took an interest in Denis's battle with Anderson, which he documented in an article, "The Free Cinema Hoax," that was published in the April 1961 edition of *Film Journal*, an Australian publication. Denis debunked Free Cinema and opined on how the opportunistic Lindsay Anderson used *Together* to promote his own career.

Clearly, the two men didn't like each other. According to Denis, Anderson's snobbery was nurtured at the public school, Cheltenham College, and then at Oxford, where both he and Denis had known each other as students. The basis of Anderson's professional mendacity was his contempt for Denis having been a conscientious objector during the war, whereas Anderson had served in WWII in the British Army and as a cryptographer for the Intelligence Corps. Denis accused Anderson and his spurned ex-lover, Lorenza Mazzetti, of minimizing his creative role in the production of *Together* and neglecting to credit him. Denis disagreed vehemently with the artistic decisions Anderson made during the final editing of the film, particularly the inconsistent use of sound effects and a jazz score that gave the film an artsy feel that gave short shrift to the silent world of the protagonists and the film's portrayal of proletarian grittiness.

I asked my father why he was still crying over spilled milk and calling Anderson out, ten years after the fact, instead of focusing his energy on new projects. He said that I was not the only one who wondered about that. An elderly titled lady, also an expat, who took an interest in Denis told him, "You can't expect to get anywhere by insulting people."

My expressed willingness to be pragmatic about striving for success prompted my father's forgiveness, if not condescending approval. "I'm glad to see that you are not deterred by things the way I am," was his conceit.

After my two-week visit in Rome, Monica and I reconnected in England where we visited mother's friend, Constance, her fellow nurse in training days at Savernake hospital. Since Constance was out of town when we arrived, her 90-year-old mother was the host. She took us on a vigorous hike to pick mushrooms that became the featured part of our dinner. The next day, we caught our flight from London. Monika returned to California, and I went to start graduate school in Philadelphia.

Mother suggested that I reach out to our East Coast cousins, Ted and Elly, to pay my respects and acknowledge the financial help they extended to Mutti over the years. At first, I hesitated because I hardly knew them and didn't want them to think I was looking for a handout for myself. Still, it felt like the right thing to do, and I was interested in getting to know them. So off I went.

Ted picked me up at the bus terminal in Keene, which was about 20 minutes by car from their home in Winchester, a small town with a population of about 4,000. On the way he talked about how, in the 1950s, they had fixed up the dilapidated property that became their home. Soon we pulled up to a charming white farmhouse on 40 acres that extended beyond a red barn that functioned as a garage for two Mercedes Benzes and a red Triumph. Ted and Elly had improved the house with a screened-in porch, enlarged living room, and updated kitchen and bathrooms. Upstairs was a sauna that was out of commission. Outside was a landscaped goldfish pond and Elly's vegetable garden.

The day after I came, I helped Ted hoist his large American flag up a tall pole. In reaction to my quizzical look, he explained the importance of blending in with the locals. When he said that they joined the local Protestant Church, I naturally assumed it was because Ted and Elly didn't want to be taken for Jewish. They already had taken steps when leaving Germany to assume Elly's Aryan maiden name, Von Holn, instead of Ted's family name, Leib. They further changed the spelling of this name to Van Holm to appear Dutch. Van Holm was also the name of Ted's business in nearby Brattleboro, Vermont.

Ted was proud of his goldfish pond that was visible through the picture window in the kitchen. He joked that Elly's vegetable garden cost a fortune in seeds and maintenance and that it would have been a lot easier to buy all their produce at Kulick's Market. Elly praised this modest supermarket with the superlatives, prima and *fabelhaft* [fabulous], for carrying her favorite sausages. Dinner was served on a large table on the screened-in porch within sight of the garden. In the yard was a large tree under which Ted's ashes would one day be buried. They never had children, but they fussed like parents over their dogs, a succession of boxers all called "Tony." Tony II zigzagged through the meadow while we took an after-dinner stroll on the property to explore its pathway through the pines.

I enjoyed Ted's company, especially his sardonic sense of humor that deflected memories from his past. I admired his tenacity in rebuilding his life after losing everything in Germany. When Elly talked about family life in Berlin, she focused on personalities without alluding to any negative stories or descriptions of what life was like under the Nazis. The main focus on their storied past was reflected in their home, which harkened to their way of life in Berlin before and during the Weimar Republic. I was struck by the absence of Judaica in the Van Holm's home that was otherwise dominated by curiosities and souvenirs from their world travels, including a painting of the Madonna and a stuffed monkey brought back from Latin America. Ted's library included German classics and art history books published before and during the Weimar era, and also recent works in English, related to history, science, and politics. He was proud of his creative streak as an amateur painter, photographer, and sculptor whose metal sculptures and artwork were exhibited in a local museum as well as in his home.

Ted was an only child with a strong will. He told the story about how his indulgent parents even tolerated his prank of flooding the floor of an outbuilding at their home to create a skating rink. Most of the talk centered around Ted's mother, who was always called Mausi, a strong-willed matron by all accounts, who inherited the family's wealth after Ted's father died. Elly showed me the family silver, including a ladle used to serve soup to so many of Ted's family members that it had needed mending and had an extra patch of silver added on the bottom.

Eventually, Ted did talk about the "crazy times" of the Nazi era and how he and Elly were forced to leave Berlin after his family's paint business was confiscated. They had hoped to have Elly's mother and sister join them somewhere safe outside of Germany once they were reestablished. The outbreak of war changed that calculus. Unlike the other Silberstein cousins, Ted and Elly did not lose immediate family members during the Holocaust. Elly's sister, Irene, her brother, Kurt Konrad, and their mother, Martha, survived the war years in Berlin because their looks matched their non-Jewish Von Holn surname. The women worked as milliners and were fortunate that no one turned them over to the authorities.

Ted and Elly decided that going to Italy would provide some safety, but soon after they arrived, they realized that Italy wasn't safe for Jews either and looked for the best available opportunity to find a haven. Ted's credentials as a chemist worked in his favor. He succeeded in obtaining emigration visas to Ecuador through military contacts interested in having him start a paint factory in Ecuador. After arriving in Quito, Ted and Elly bought a house and lived a comfortable life with plenty of household help. Ted showed a photo of Elly in jodhpurs posing with a horse in front of their charming home in the Andes. After the war, they invited Elly's mother and sister, who had survived the war in Berlin, to join them in Ecuador. Elly's mother, Martha, accepted their offer in 1948.

Although life had been good for Elly and Ted in Ecuador during the war years, Elly found it hard to adjust to the thin air at Quito's high altitude and suffered health problems because of her thyroid condition. Consequently, the three Von Holns obtained emigration visas to the United States and chose to settle in New Hampshire where the climate approximated that of Berlin. Irene joined them there in 1950.

Once in Winchester, Ted set up a small paint factory just across the river in Brattleboro, Vermont. This venture provided sufficient income for a prosperous life in New Hampshire, vacations, and travel to Europe to revive social connections with Elly's brother and friends.

During the 1970s and 1980s, long after I left Berkeley for Philadelphia, my wife, Linda and I went to New Hampshire several times to visit Ted and Elly with our two sons. We also went to see Cousin Irene at her apartment in Brooklyn where she had settled. She always served goodies, including her favorite Entenmann's coffee cake. She saved absolutely everything, even string and wrapping paper, which had been in short supply in Berlin during the war. Upon our leaving, she was happy to bestow upon us whatever knickknacks we might want from her vast collection.

My sister's family also visited Elly, Ted, and Irene. On her own, Monika came from California to visit Elly a few times after Ted's death in 1982. These visits provided her with an insight into our family's past free from the prism of our mother's experience as a disadvantaged refugee struggling with mental illness. Elly's practical, stereotypically German sense of order and control, a source of amusement for us all, helped her run her home as an elderly woman as she marshalled the support of several caregivers.

19

CAN'T GO HOME AGAIN

My choice for graduate school on the East Coast was partially decided by accident because my acceptance letter from Stanford was delayed in the mail, but I didn't regret my hurried decision to accept the full fellowship from the University of Pennsylvania. When I left Berkeley for Philadelphia, I placed the full breadth of America's continental land mass between me and my mother's empty nest. However, this did not get me off the hook. Mother bombarded me with letters, as she had when I traveled to Europe. There was no escape. I was up against the most assiduous letter writer in the world. With my father, it was a different story. In the ensuing years, there were one or two letters per year from him, often with the promise that success was just around the corner and that he would someday come to America to visit. I didn't believe that he would ever come, and he never did.

During Christmas break of my first year in Philadelphia, Mother came to visit, thanks to Cousin Fred Wellner, who gave her the fare money and encouraged her also to visit her Van Holm cousins in New Hampshire. I expressed my misgivings about her impending arrival to my roommate, Howie Baum, a PhD student at Penn whom I had known at Berkeley. He took issue with my apparent lack of filial piety with respect to my Jewish mother. Several days after she arrived, Howie took it upon himself to take Mother to Beth Sholom, a temple designed by Frank Lloyd Wright in Elkins Park, a Philadelphia suburb.

Mother let me know how much she appreciated Howie because he was "a nice, Jewish boy who knows how to treat a mother."

I shrugged off whatever guilt feelings I could muster to redeem myself the way I preferred. In an effort to bring her into my world, I took her to meet Sol Worth, my professor and advisor at the Annenberg School. He was known for his work as an anthropologist studying Navajo culture and making films about indigenous people. Bearded Sol reminded Mother of Chaim Topol, who starred in the 1967 production of *The Fiddler on the Roof*. I also took her to the Philadelphia Mummer's New Year's Day parade in freezing weather on the assumption that "everyone loves a parade."

That following night, we walked back to the apartment and tromped through fresh-fallen snow that had scared away traffic. We had the streets of Philadelphia to ourselves and laughed against the stillness and whiteness all around us, delighting in the crunching sounds of our footsteps that left a distinctive trail in the wake of our shoeprints. For the moment, there was no history except for our footprints. This was the indescribable happiness of the moment.

Two weeks after her arrival, Mother went to visit Irene in New York and then Ted and Elly in New Hampshire. She didn't say how the trip went except for a few cracks about Elly's penchant for giving advice. Afterwards she returned to Santa Monica, glad to be home in her apartment on 421 Marine Street. This was a small two-bedroom place in a three-unit, single-story apartment house on a hill, several blocks from the Santa Monica beach in the community of Ocean Park. On one side, her neighbors were a Mexican family with a friendly dog and two small, shy children and on the other, a young couple with left-wing political views.

Mutti said she was in seventh heaven when I came from Philadelphia in 1970 to visit at Christmas. During that visit I met her politically active neighbors, Ruth Galanter and David Freeman, at a Christmas party. In keeping with her idea of the real spirit of Christmas, Mutti shaped dollar bills into ornaments and hung them from a Christmas tree to the delight of all the guests. Ruth and David got a big kick out of my rebellious mother. As a proud denizen of what was often called "The People's Republic of Santa Monica," Mutti appreciated Ruth and

David for their progressive views on social and environmental issues that reflected the spirit of the People's Party founded in 1971. She helped them hand out buttons and campaign flyers for Dr. Benjamin Spock who was the People's Party candidate for President. Later, Ruth served on the LA City Council from 1987 to 2003 as a tireless advocate for slow-growth urban planning and responsible environmental policies. She was a leader in achieving improvements that saved the Venice canals that our mom loved so much.

In 1987, while on the LA City Council, Ruth was severely injured in a brutal knifing in 1987 by an intruder who nearly killed her in her own apartment. She recovered to resume her career in public service. After Mother's death in 1991, Ruth passed an LA City Council resolution in tribute to her memory.

Political activism did not deter Mutti from keeping up her diary to document the overnight stays with Cousin Resi, dutiful visits to Albert and Estelle, outings with Bertha and her affable taxi-driver friend Bill, and going to the beach. There were entries for paying bills, keeping appointments with social workers and psychiatrists, paying $5 to go to a Recovery party.

Mutti's diary listed folk dancing at UCLA as well as a group session at Synanon, a drug and alcohol rehab center founded by Charles E. "Chuck" Dederich, Sr., who invited interested members of the public to observe the Synanon Game, a unique program of therapy which employed peer pressure and confrontation. Mutti dropped in on Synanon when it was housed in Club Casa Del Mar, a former beachside hotel, which was within a stone's throw of the Kensington. Started in a small storefront location, Synanon was acclaimed at first and then vilified and engulfed in controversy as its therapies became abusive. Mutti was struck by the deeply troubled people she saw there and told how she managed to keep them at an arm's length for fear of getting involved in the "wacky" Synanon community. She wrote me about her other friends and adventures.

> All is well on the Western Front. Today I went to the Venice Canal Festival. A very colorful scene – decorated houses and the usual artistic displays in arts and crafts and leather, etc., and a band, and dogs with flowers in their collars and children with flowers painted on

their faces. It was quite different from the Labor Day "Kiss-in," where people appeared "to care" more (whatever that means). I went there with the GLF (Gay Liberation Front) with Gene and Monty and eight or so other GLF people. Prior to this, six of us had breakfast in Marina del Rey and had lots of fun with the waitress who couldn't quite figure out the scene, since not all of them "looked the part." All she could figure out was that three people had blue eyes and the other three brown eyes.

Gene and Monty were a biracial, gay couple who drew Mutti in with their liberating indifference to any conventional ideas on love, marriage, sexual orientation, class distinctions, or racial identity. Friends like Gene and Monty helped her take a break from her European-Jewish angst. But, despite all the diversions offered by her circle of diverse friends, her attention invariably wandered back to the Old World of her youth.

Her correspondence with friends from the past provided a counterpoint to freewheeling life in sunny California. There was occasional news from Constance in England and always regular updates from Jenny who still lived in Belgium with her lesbian partner. I don't know if Jenny knew of Mutti's vocal support of gay rights.

More extensive was Mutti's correspondence with her former music teacher. She learned that Rudi's children, Peter and Monika, left their home in England to establish lives physically and emotionally distant from their parents and their German Jewish roots. Rudi's son became an English professor in Canada. His daughter became a parole officer in Wales, a far cry from the romantic cultural landscape Rudi might have idealized for her. Given her awareness of Rudi's open mindedness in religious and cultural matters, Mutti felt free to write to him in 1983 sharing her mixed feelings about her German cultural roots. Rudi responded in a letter reminiscent of the one he sent to her in 1951 extolling the virtues of those aspects of German culture which are timeless and immune from the coarser elements of its Volk.

My dear Kunigunde,

I am always amazed to see that you still harbor our time in Berlin in your heart. And yet, I am not surprised. In June, you wrote about your ambiguous attitude toward German culture – not an easy thing to resolve. I share your feelings. In all my work with choirs over the past decades, I have cultivated the heritage of German music and its compelling appeal. Yet, when I go back to my homeland, as happens several times a year, I am occasionally struck with horror. There are some lovely people there, as there are in other parts of the world, but the widespread rudeness and ill will (pushing, shoving, slamming doors in the face, horrible officials, etc. etc.) makes it harder for me to ply my gondola across the canal again. Wagner once wrote to Liszt: "Believe me, we have no fatherland. Since I am a German, I carry my Germanness with me." Exactly! What we found German at that time was the beautiful landscape, the romanticism in literature, painting, and music, and, yes, also the enthrallment of our youth. This idea is difficult to reconcile with the impression of Germans that we see today, whose parents and grandparents pushed millions of children of God off the face of the earth to untimely deaths. Let us, then, restrict the love of Germany to the true one, to the one within us.

Rudi's "love of Germany" was the love of its culture that exists apart from the abyss of the Holocaust. Mother's nostalgia, rooted in the romanticism of her youth, drew her to Rudi and the emotional conundrum that defined their friendship. However, unlike Rudi, she didn't find as smooth a pathway to the Germany within. She wanted to travel to the real Europe to visit him and other friends from her youth.

The fact that Monika and I had traveled to Europe in 1967 to see our respective fathers, cemented Mother's travel plans to visit England, and her nursing school friend, Constance. Afterwards, she would go to Brussels to see Jenny. She even floated the idea of a reunion with my father in England or Mallorca. I don't know what possessed her to try to see him again. She took him literally when he had written about wanting to redress the past, but whatever she thought he had in mind dissolved instantly once she floated the reunion idea. In August 1969, he wrote that limited finances prevented him from traveling from Italy to England or Mallorca to meet her. He didn't mention that he was respecting the feelings of his Roman partner and future wife Fausta, who would not have welcomed Mutti's return into Denis's life.

Dear Mary,

I left here about two weeks ago with the intention of going to Sienna for a week to stay at the same place Peter came too when he was here. Then I intended to go on to London. But as you can see, I am back here. In Sienna, I had the bad luck to crash into another car which was wrecked. My own was not out of action but the lights didn't work. You can guess the rest. Nobody was badly hurt but there was a lot of trouble because the other man was not insured, and so I had to pay for all the damage to my car (this is very common in Italy where the insurance companies charge such high rates that only very rich drivers are insured). The occupants of the other car were both unemployed workers from the industrial region of Bologna. I had to take them home, nearly 200 miles – just my luck again. This is the first-ever accident in my car driving life and it had to happen now! Well, there it is. I have neither the time (must be back here for September) nor the money to come to England now. I particularly wanted to go to the British Film Institute to see why they have failed to keep an agreement to keep me informed about any money which may be due on the film, *Together*. It is several years since I heard from them. If you can go and see them yourself, you can keep any money you succeed in getting out of them for yourself. I suppose they will say there is nothing, but this is impossible. The film is in every cineclub in the United States. Anyway, I enclose a note of introduction, just in case you care to try. I do hope you enjoy yourself in England, France and Spain. I really expect to get to America next year. I am translating two or three books and I may get the chore of placing them with US publishers. I certainly hope Peter will succeed in getting off the draft. Anything justifies refusing to go to Vietnam. I personally think all military activities are criminal. If I can help, let me know. But I'm sure you know how to take care of this situation – you have had worse ones to deal with. Keep me informed, particularly about the British Film Institute, and tell me what you think of Britain. I haven't been there for ten years and have an idea I shouldn't enjoy it. Best Love and every good wish, Denis.

Denis was circumspect, but not altogether candid in expressing his sensible but self-serving misgivings about seeing her again.

Dear Peter,

Knowing my near-pathological aversion to family matters, you will not expect me to say much, as I never do, about your mother. But I have to say that her threat to take off again for Europe where she asserts her real roots are, or her roots really are, does worry me quite a lot. After all, she is quite capable of doing it. She seems to be perfectly aware that it would be crazy to do so, and frankly admits that she does not count her blessings which she then lists as "good health, beautiful sea, work, handsome son and grandson (this was not the order) etc." I don't know what this sudden excess of nostalgia for filthy old Europe is due to. I could guess but would probably be wrong. Besides, when she was in Europe, that is to say in Oxford, England, I remember that she had the same bouts of nostalgic depression. But maybe she did not consider England was part of Europe. Now that I come to think about it, I share her opinion. I feel my roots are somewhere in Europe, but not in England, certainly not. I never really understood the full repulsiveness of the English outlook before coming to Italy and seeing English TV films on the Italian video.

Mother never talked about the letter my father sent her. I can only assume that she "got the message" given the empty promises in previous letters, his final gesture was snarky. While she held out the romantic hope that he would change his mind, his absurd and insulting suggestion that she go to the British Film Institute to ask for money surely rankled her. He had no idea that adding insult to injury would lay the groundwork for her later revenge to fulfill the proverbial, "Hell hath no fury like a woman scorned."

Mother announced her definite plan to travel to Europe, no matter what. There was no opportunity to encourage or discourage her. She took a flight to Dublin and stayed there overnight before making a connection to London, which ended up being her final stop. Years later, Mother blamed the failure to complete the trip on poor planning, but the actual reason had to do with emotions released after a visit to her friend Constance from her nurses training days.

In 1969, I left for England and later Belgium, first to see Constance and Rudi in England, and afterwards to Belgium to see Jenny, then on to Mallorca. These were my plans, all on about $1,500. I wanted to go alone. When I arrived in Ireland, I realized that my trip was poorly planned. 1) I did not have enough money, 2) I took the wrong clothing, I froze because of wrong footwear, not even an umbrella (I bought one in London), 3) I took one enormous suitcase that I could barely carry. After my arrival in London, I planned to visit my friend Constance in Saffron Walden, Essex. I remember the frustration of making a simple phone call at Liverpool Street Station to let Constance know that I was on my way. My "exceptionality" would not permit me to ask for help to place a call to Essex. Somehow, I managed. Being with Constance was unforgettable. She lived in a beautiful house, chestnut trees in front, garden in the back, tomatoes, and vegetables. There was her husband, John, two sons and a little girl. And her old mother, whom I used to call "Mutter" Nina when I stayed with them in Wales during the war. I tried to adopt her as a substitute mother, but it didn't work out on my part. To me, the entire household seemed a great togetherness. I stayed with them for about five days. On my last day, the entire family gave me a concert downstairs in the drawing room. Constance played piano and John sang Schubert and medieval madrigals. One boy played oboe, the other cello, and so did Constance. Even Mutter Mina allowed us to persuade her to play piano (she played well). I tried to turn pages, but what did I really do? I fought tears from beginning to end and couldn't stop shaking inside and outside. Everyone was so kind and sweet to me! I felt I didn't deserve it. I felt as an outsider. I felt envious. I could not accept the fact that Constance and her mother truly cared for me. My departure was like running away, running away from people who loved me?!

The visit with Constance hit a nerve. Constance lived the fulfilled life she once had envisioned for herself.

So I went to London. I wanted to be with people who didn't care. And they didn't. People who didn't know me. I was running out of money, and I canceled my trip to Belgium to Jenny. I was afraid the same thing would happen with Jenny, only worse, as it happened in Essex with Constance only a week ago. I continued in London with an empty feeling, not even being able to admit guilt or regret. I rented an empty house way out of London without proper transportation on a street where Pakistanis lived, so I couldn't converse with them. The total physical confusion I created in this house was unbelievable, including ripping two phones out of the wall. I finally managed to call the police station. Two men arrived and helped me pack and sort all the things I had thrown around. They treated me as though I was a human being, and I did accept their help. They took me to the local police station and after clearing my identify, they packed me off with just one policeman who drove the car and I sat right next to him. We went to Napsbury Hospital where I was able to relax. My stay at this British hospital, an institution for the mentally ill, holds many fond memories for me.

Mother was admitted to Napsbury Hospital near St. Albans, north of London. The sympathetic doctor at the hospital sent a letter to me explaining what had happened.

I do not think that you need bother too much about this breakdown. It is difficult to deal with a long flight, and then all the excitement of meeting people and coming to familiar places. I think that she had many plans and intentions competing with one another, and she found it more and more difficult to organize all the things she wanted to do. I understand also that she has been anxious about the possibility of your being drafted, and these together were too much. This does not make it more or less likely that she will break down again in the future, as the whole circumstance was an abnormal one, and she seems very well in touch again now.

A week later, the hospital notified me about her discharge and relayed information about her return flight. I picked her up at JFK Airport and she stayed with me for a few days in Philadelphia before heading back to Santa Monica. Mother talked about her disastrous adventure as a "learning experience," and I didn't press her to explain. Instead of talking about what went wrong, she gave a rave review of her stay at the hospital, praising the doctor and the nursing staff for their compassion that contributed to her rapid recovery. Mother returned to Santa Monica to resume her old life, to prove that there was still "some life in the old girl."

The year after Mother's derailed trip to England, I took time off from graduate school to work on documentary films with four other students, three of them British, from the Annenberg School at the

University of Pennsylvania. We received funding from the Philadelphia Redevelopment Authority to produce a program about the challenges faced in Tioga-Nicetown in North Philadelphia, one of the most impoverished sectors in the city. This project led to additional film projects on environmental issues under auspices of the Philadelphia 1970 Earth Day Committee. One of these, *Circuit Earth*, was shown at the Kennedy Center as well as at the Aspen Conference on Environment and Technology. Another film, *Tinicum,* documented the activists who fought to preserve a wetland marsh near Philadelphia Airport that was later named John Heinz National Wildlife Refuge.

My documentary film activities put me on the path to visiting my father again. I wrote Denis that our *Tinicum* was accepted by the Festival dei Populi in Florence, and that I could visit him in Rome as well. After I arrived in Rome, Denis and I drove to Florence in his flood-rescued VW. He stayed in Florence to help with the translation of the transcript from English into Italian for simultaneous interpretation during the screening. This was welcome help from my father, who had seen many American films and knew colloquial Yankee English. He also provided a less welcome critique of what he called the "clunky camera work" our film used to record various "talking heads." Our film group had sought to employ informal, candid, close-up interviews on site to provide a platform for academics and community activists who advocated saving the marsh. Maybe we ended up with too much talk and not enough see. To be sure, our approach differed from the visually poetic style of documentary production that appealed to Denis. His documentary heroes included Robert Flaherty, best known for *Nanook of the North* and *The Louisiana Story*. With her artist's eye, Denis's wife agreed with him that our film lacked visual style. Can't say I totally agreed.

Denis also warned me not to be intimidated or deterred in my own artistic vision by any intellectual snobbery my three British collaborators might deploy to defend their approach. He was clearly harkening back to his unsatisfactory collaboration on *Together* with Lindsay Anderson. Despite Denis's less-than-rave review and suspicions about my collaborators, I was grateful for his help, but was put off by the dogmatic aspects of his criticism and his unwillingness to consider an approach to documentary filmmaking in which the spoken word plays a leading role in interpreting complex subject matter.

After the festival, Denis returned to Rome. I spent a few extra days in Florence to see Renaissance masters at the Uffizi, then took a train back to Rome with a Florence teapot under my arm, a gift for my father and Fausta. I stayed for another week in Rome to sell a copy of *Tinicum* to Italy's RAI-TV and to meet with Aurelio Peccei, Manager of Fiat and Olivetti, who was interested in Earth Day and gave me a report by the Club of Rome on the global environmental and economic problems faced by mankind. It turned out that Denis had once met Peccei while doing translation work for Fiat and spoke highly of him because of his enlightened work as a philanthropist and because he had been an anti-fascist.

Throughout our visit, Denis went on about the once-promising film career he had before becoming an expat. I realized that the basis for our emerging father-son relationship would hinge on our common interest in film. After sharing with me the vagaries of his artistic ventures, he suggested that after leaving Rome I go to the British Film Institute in London before returning to America to see the showpiece that should have jump-started his career in films.

At a special screening of *Together* at the British Film Institute, the curator told me that he found the film about two deaf-mutes "much too depressing" and that he preferred more upbeat films about a the working-class, such as Karl Reisz's *Saturday Nights and Sunday Mornings* and Lindsay Anderson's *This Sporting Life*. I didn't bother telling him that I liked the downbeat approach of *Together* because it was free from the clichés of class consciousness. It didn't romanticize the poor and featured stellar acting performances by Michael Andrews and Eduardo Paolozzi, who played the deaf-mutes and later became well-known visual artists.

My visits to Rome and London prompted my mother to train the spotlight back on her past life with Denis. She repeatedly told me that he never had the wherewithal for marriage and fatherhood and that his promises never added up to action. She made disparaging excuses for him, in the belief that he couldn't have done for her what he did not do for anyone else. In her mind, he was as lost as she was. No one was to blame. I didn't have the heart to describe Denis's devoted relationship with Fausta.

As for Denis, he seemed vaguely optimistic that someday his ship could come in so long as he had "an iron in the fire." One such iron was his manuscript about Rome, "Centenary Story of a Capital," which he had shown me during our latest visit. I offered to shop his manuscript in New York and readily found an editor at Houghton Mifflin in New York who expressed initial interest. My father's work coincided with the 100th anniversary in 1970 of the conquest of Rome by the troops of unified Italy, which ended the temporal power of the papacy. According to the editor, this work needed a rewrite to make it publishable because it mixed "... anecdote, gossip, and rather opinionated, if interesting, narrative in a very strange way which I don't think would work out well between covers." I had similar reservations about this elliptical work, and since my father wasn't interested in doing a major rewrite, I let the matter drop.

20

TAKING STOCK

When I told Mutti about my father's writing projects, she said it was time to take stock of her life by delving into her personal history. She took college courses to improve her writing skills and began to expand the scope of her daybook entries by writing and later typing her thoughts for eventual inclusion in an autobiography. She also wrote poems dedicated to her parents and made pencil-and-ink drawings that drew inspiration from the artists she loved, such as Paul Klee, Marc Chagall, and others whose work was featured in her collection of *Petite Encylopédie de l'Art* books.

Mother's sideboard was a repository of her history where she enshrined photos and Judaica, including a menorah and Shabbos candlesticks that belonged to her parents. There were pictures of her mother and of her father in religious garb, as well as candid shots of her as a teenager with friends. Two cherished professional portraits had a special spot, a pretty one of her taken before she became Nurse Mary and another one of her as a young mother with two children. She wanted people to know what she looked like as an attractive, innocent young person. Rounding out the display were photos of Monika, me, and her beloved grandchildren. Current and deceased cats, including her favorites, "Kietzka" and "Tigerina," were part of the family gallery.

The cats became more of an emotional center of gravity for Mutti when Monika and I were grown and gone, but cats had always been an important part of our household, as were the sand fleas they harbored. Allergic to insect bites since early childhood, I went on a barbaric seek-and-destroy mission whenever I was around, catching these tiny pests on her cats as well as on my own skin. I picked them up between my thumb and index finger, and deftly crushed them with my nails to present the bloody evidence. To assuage my military tendencies, Mother tried to convert me into a fellow cat lover: "Peterle, Kietzka really loves you," she would say as she freshened up the litterbox in the kitchen corner. Sure enough, Kietzka would cozy up to me, which proved to her that a connection to the cat world was part of my destiny. That part of her cat world I didn't mind.

It would be farfetched to say that Mother was enmeshed in domesticity as she became middle aged, but she did enjoy preparing food and occasionally would venture to make some of her signature German dishes, including *Rolladen* [stuffed cabbage] and *Rotkohl* [red cabbage] that she knew how to flavor with the perfect mix of vinegar, raisins, and cloves. She also made genuine *Kartoffelpuffer* [potato pancakes] as well as her traditional full English breakfast that included bacon and a pot of Yuban coffee.

While letting you in on her latest efforts to diet or quit smoking, she would drag on a cigarette. Her Marlboros provided a bond of comfort in conversation and conveyed a sense of wartime abandon and sophistication like that portrayed by stars in Hollywood black-and-white films of the 40s. "Mother really wants to be a kid," Monika observed, fully understanding her mother's modus operandi.

Mutti subscribed to the "You are only as old as you feel" philosophy but was keenly aware of the aging process. Her fuller, more expressive face brought a warmth and wistful irony to the beauty of her youth. "Pleasantly plump, that is what I am," she would often say, looking in a mirror out of the corner of one eye. I teased her that the brightly colored red caftans she wore to camouflage her girth just made her look like the gypsies her mother warned her about. Her chin became rounded with age, more like her mother's. "I earned my double chin," she said, but her dark expressive eyes failed to dissemble. What she really meant was: "After all these years, all I have left is my cat!" Mutti's perennial diary included this entry of March 1970:

> It's about time to write again something. My childhood companions – a book with empty pages and a pen. Welcome, my companions from my lonely childhood! During those days, everything I wrote was very secret and I used to carry my book with me all the time in the secret breast pocket in my vest, which I sewed in myself. Today, in my so-called womanhood, things have not changed much. I am just as lonely. I just don't have to hide my secrets anymore. I blabber them out to anyone who comes across me first. God (or Nature) has created a world which is oriented towards killing and cruelty. Animals are driven to kill by the need to survive, but man kills not only for survival, but out of greed. Some shout about God and love and peace, but still kill for the sake of God. The average human child, mainly the male, is aggressive in a distinctively cruel way, even when his parents say, no! He will torture small animals and throw stones at windows, and finally gets trained by civilized adults around him. After he becomes a nice little peace-loving, civilized boy, he gets drafted into the army to learn how to kill, and all the training he has received as a little boy, not to kill and not to be cruel, goes to the winds. Oh, boy, what a mess!

Mother's easy targets were the rich old men who sublimated violence into power, the craven "old farts" who profited from war and exploitation. She targeted her ire at politicians, industry executives, and, of course, the "greedy" doctors who subjugated nurses and were insensitive to the emotional needs of their patients. She also took on the builders who put up ugly high-rise condos and malls in Santa Monica. They were the "filthy rich," Scrooge-like beasts who would steal candies from children. "All I want is a little house and garden somewhere in the country, Peter. Can you buy me one?"

As much as Mother was the mistress of hyperbole when it came to the selfishness of the rich, she also recognized the vice of rampant consumerism in ordinary people.

> Today I saw a lady lawyer on TV pleading with the public to help children who have fallen to drug addiction and are at risk of dying. The public is unsympathetic, even though their own children are

addicts. They preach, cry and disown, in short, they do nothing. Meanwhile, they live their meaningless lives concerned about perspiration, household odors, endless makeup, hair color, constantly new cars, bad breath, diets to lose weight, etc. etc. Being concerned with these important issues in life, they become afflicted with stomach upsets, headaches and visits to the psychiatrist. They, the adult parents, spend endless money for consumer items to either color, or rather dull their meaningless lives. These adults consume great amounts of alcohol which is a slow killer (heroin is a fast killer). They condemn the children for their escape methods but indulge in their own, alcohol and endless pills. *Oy veh!*

Perhaps Mother denigrated the rich so that she could feel better about being poor, but it was more complicated than that. I knew that her class anger was shear bravado because in the next breath she would admire the trappings of "classy" wealth.

Even though easy street was out of reach, she liked to patronize some establishments that catered to better-off clients. At the venerable Caruso's Menswear, she bought me high-end clothes and a carved wooden duck decoy. She spoke fondly of Bob Burns, a Scottish-themed restaurant on Wilshire Boulevard near Ocean Avenue where she dined with her friend, Bill Wintersole. This place was a sanctuary for expats that reminded her of the proper conviviality of "good old England."

Mother did what she could to seek a better life through upward mobility. She opted to build on whatever training and experience she had. In 1967, she enrolled in a Licensed Practical Nurse (LPN) certification program that enabled her to document her skills. Later, she also became a qualified medical technician which opened opportunities for better paying work. All along, her goal was to live "like a mensch." Some jobs lasted a while, such as one with Dr. Gudauskas in 1968 that she kept for about two years, and another in 1970 with Dr. Kaplan, who also employed Monika. This was a halcyon period during which she easily made friends and enjoyed interacting with patients. For a while, she managed her life, stayed on budget, and kept up with her medications, but her hard-won stability didn't last. A series of "run ins" with employers led to her quitting or getting fired, and finally joining the ranks of the unemployed.

As the recipient of unemployment benefits, she joked that she had joined the "leisure class," arguing that she had something in common with the rich who don't *necessarily* have to work for their money. Setting aside for a moment her innate work ethic, Mother made the case for unemployment compensation, even if not fully justified, as a form of reparation. She made another diary entry that boasted of her ability to make do with very little.

> Unemployment collection today, $47 per week. Long live Unemployment! Like a vacation – beach, bicycle rides, meeting people. No hassle with co-workers, bosses, and busses. It is like freedom. $47 is enough because I live on cottage cheese, carrots, and eggs.

Being out of a job afforded her free time to meet others living on the edge.

> I met Helena from Konigsberg today. A blonde Lea-like woman with a young (Black) lover, Chris. Also met Walter at the beach, a snow-white haired black man. He claims to have a PhD in some psychology field, also has had nine wives. Also claims to be some undercover man for the government. Later, I held a kitten in my arm for an hour. It was cozy and slept. Beautiful day.

Mother expressed mock ambivalence when opportunity finally knocked with a job offer. She kept a record of what happened.

> April 18. Tragedy struck. The Lawton School called me for three job interviews. I had to get put together with makeup and clothes, and I spent an hour putting my hair plus wiglet together. Am scared. Oy veh! Soon for the interview for EKG tech. I got the job! Shit! Only took it because it looked like an easy $500. Goodbye freedom! I wonder if it is worth it. April 20. I've been on this job now for a whole week, and still no feeling of achievement or satisfaction. I just take EKGs and mount them, ride the elevator umpteen times, up and down, for coffee, cigs. Met two amiable girls – X-ray Joanie and Medrec Yvonne.

Chewed the fat with R.N., L.V.N. bitches. Granted, I get off at four, home by five. So my vital energy is used up between eight and four, winding rubber bands around people's legs and wrists. I drag home feeling the workman's blues. Got to organize good activities like folk dancing, swimming, and cycling. stand up for their rights. The checks were two days late and some of the girls took it out on their patients by showing indifference and probably went home with stomach aches.

April 21. We didn't get paid today. You should have heard the bitching. So I organized all the complainers to leave their floor, all of them, and invade the business office to demand their two-week checks. You should have seen how they all backed out, all of them. There is nothing one can do to get the support of working people to stand up for their rights.

While empowered by respectable employment, Mutti embraced respectability by voicing typical "old world" immigrant complaints about people in America lacking character and standards. She said that Americans tend to put money, rather than people first.

Staunchly anti-war, she mocked phony patriotism during the Vietnam era when she commented about the public reaction to the tragic fate of the three Apollo 1 American astronauts – Edward H. White II, Virgil I. Grissom, and Roger B. Chaffee – who died in a horrific cabin fire on the launch pad at Cape Kennedy in 1967.

The world is crying. Granted, three men's lives lost. Anyway, they volunteered to go on the ship. Why doesn't the whole world cry when thousands of men die in the war in Vietnam and elsewhere? Half of these kids didn't even volunteer to be put there. Bloody politics. The stock market gets all shook up over this space crap but apparently booms when the war and its killing go well. Hello, Sodom and Gomorrah!

Mother allied herself with young people hellbent on saving the planet. She spent Earth Day 1970 with one of her elderly patients in a nursing home.

Today, I contacted an 89-year-old woman to watch Channel 4, Earth Day, together tomorrow, 7-9 a.m. That will be more enjoyable than watching it hiding away in an empty room by myself. Jewell Dillon is bright and "with it" – just a little too thin to look at, and she is about to lose interest in life. Anyway, tomorrow I'll be her company for two hours. Peter would approve. Happy Earth Day, kids! Thank you for trying. Happy Earth Day, motherfuckers, your "progress" is killing us. April 22. Lenin's birthday falls on Earth Day Teach-in. Our screwy democratic congressmen are saying that Earth Day shouldn't look like a birthday for old Lenin. The reactionaries didn't know about Lenin's birthday, but now they know.

Her modest proposal for improving the environment focused on reducing consumption.

1. Cars. Unless something is invented to cut out fumes, etc. cars only for doctors who make calls, nurses on call, fire department, police department. Let all the others ride busses unless they invent a smog killer. 2. Airplanes. Travel by train and bus. Cut down on speed. Forget having to be in Paris in eight hours, etc. This calls for rearranging our present economic system. Unemployed people, who used to work for General Motors and oil companies, will have to find other work. This sounds so drastic when I talk to a capitalist. Maybe his balls are held together by General Motors or Standard Oil. But the majority are not involved. Surely not everything runs on gas and oil. I am not talking about the Edison and Gas Company, but about unnecessary luxuries such as electric can openers and knives. Wouldn't it be beautiful if we go back to the basic things and work on improving our relationship with everything around us, even feed the birds every morning? You must always share your bread with others.

Mother liked to sing the German lyrics of "The Internationale" she learned at the communist rallies in the Berlin of her youth. The lines, *"Hört die Signale! Auf zum letzten Gefecht!"* were about the call to final battle. She conjured images of Zionists dancing the Hora in a kibbutz during the Six-Day War. The clenched fist salute reminded her of the last gasp of the Left before Hitler took over.

Yet, when it came right down to joining organizations, Mother was apolitical. She abhorred the political perversion and physical violence she experienced directly as a girl in Berlin. Although she was drawn to the romance of grass roots organizing for justice, she had no interest in the organizational necessities or the realities and betrayals that inevitably drain ideals from political movements. In East Berlin after the war, she smelled a rat when an attempt was made to recruit her for the Communist Party. She realized that the idealistic political enthusiasm for communism in her youth bore little resemblance to the authoritarian mindset of the East German DDR. Her instincts were to lay low and avoid being on the wrong side and that is exactly what she advised me to do when it came to the Vietnam War draft. "Become a conscientious objector or go to Canada!" she advised, not wanting me to go to jail as my father did as a conscientious objector during World War II.

For Mutti, everything came down to personal survival under duress. Human institutions were to be distrusted and avoided. "Life is too short," she said to undercut the ideological killjoys in her midst. Although she distrusted politics, she did not want to succumb to complete cynicism.

> I am leading such a useless life. I am doing nothing worthwhile. I don't mean to say that going to school or being a RN isn't rewarding. I want to do more, maybe fight for something worthwhile in life, give my time, not just through work to stuff my savings account.

Mutti became friendly with my classmate Robert's mother. Harriet was a kind and generous person who often invited Robert's friends for dinner and informal discussions afterwards. Her home was a salon where we discussed politics, current affairs and whatever we were reading. I took interest in the publications on Harriet's coffee table, including *The Progressive* and *The New Republic*. She believed it was a healthy thing to question conventional wisdom. Harriet's enlightened conversation was sprinkled with ideas informed by *Psychology Today* about the challenges of modern life. She used words such as "reasonable" and "sensible" intended to encourage wisdom and tolerance, particularly in matters related to racial injustice and religious tolerance. She often mentioned the Unitarian Church where the minister's "sermons" touched on politics, social problems, and economics, such as Keynesian theories as espoused by John Kenneth Galbraith who served as an advisor to four Democratic presidents.

Harriet told Mother about her Unitarian congregation and the wisdom of Reverend Pipes. When Mutti decided to go to church to find out for herself, things didn't go quite as well as expected. Although she agreed with Pipes's focus on contemporary issues and ideas about personal freedom, his sermon brought out the contrarian in her when he offered his views on homosexuality.

> I went to the Unitarian Church today. I was told that it is very informal, so I went in my favorite outfit – pants, sandals, poncho. All the people were dressed up, with flowers in buttonholes. I felt like an outsider although the sermon on homosexuality was interesting. "Let them do their thing," Rev. Pipes said. He said it was the fault of their parents who made them into homosexuals, particularly protective, seductive mothers, rejecting overpowering fathers, and vice versa.

Although Mutti agreed with Reverend Pipes that homosexuality should be accepted, she disagreed with his idea that homosexual is an affliction caused by parents.

> We could even say it is a natural thing – look at the animals, they have sex with whom they please and who is available. What about heterosexual relationships? Here the man and woman become perverts if they engage in sodomy, but it's okay because in "marriage" everything goes. But if two men or two women do it, it's criminal. Thanks to religious preaching of sin, those poor people have become outcasts of society. After the sermon came the anti-social hour. People cluster together and do not welcome newcomers. I couldn't even get a ride, even when I asked for one. Fuck all these social groups. Same goes for "Parents without Partners." People are so dead and unfriendly and discouraged.

Unable to fit in with the well-meaning Unitarians, Mother had better luck playing the Jewish card with UCLA's Hillel, the campus Jewish organization. At Hillel, she found a positive spirit that reminded her of an upbeat Zionism seeking to overturn the tradition of suffering and wailing that her father represented. She contributed money to Plant a Tree in Israel while making fun of her need to latch on to things Jewish, even trees. She wanted to embrace the muscular Zionism of her youth that had eluded her and, at the same time, make peace with the "pathetic" Judaism of guilt and anguish that she associated with acquiescence during the Holocaust. For a brief period, she flirted perversely with the group called Jews for Jesus. She said they were truly kind to her, even forgave her for not seeing the Christian light. Most of all, they put up with her incessant story telling. The inevitable falling out with these "Jesus Jews" came when they asked, "Would you settle for half a bagel?" They suggested that Judaism was a lonely half-bagel without Jesus. This didn't resonate with Mutti since she didn't like bagels.

After I came from Philadelphia to visit Mother, she wrote wistfully about my visit and her future.

> May 21, 1970. Peterle is home. Warm smile. Without wanting to, he is confirming and arousing new and old values. He makes me feel that I am not ready to go into complete withdrawal from people. He evokes in me the suppressed feeling that I still need a human male around. This is a sad issue, because such a man does not exist. People don't want to get involved unless they are young and foolish. I believe I am neither, no more. I would like to be with a professional man, politically left-oriented, to have basic agreements. It doesn't matter how old he is or what color eyes he has. If he is put together right, we could still have a sex exchange at the age (his age) of 90. Separate income into a mutual fund. All this is not easy.

> June 11. It really would be desirable to live with a man, a very desirable man, compatible, responsible (employed), passionate, and honest. It is beautiful to be loved. It does not happen too often that someone loves you, and then only too often we like to do the loving ourselves and only too seldom do we choose our love object wisely. And just as often do we smother and have feelings of possessiveness focused on the one we love. We must love the other person with open hands and open heart, allowing our loved one the feeling of freedom and growth.

As someone who offered frank sex education to her kids long before it was taught in the public schools, Mutti knew how to launch into a disquisition on what makes men and women tick. For her, there was always the clinical solution. She drew her elucidative diagrams and declared sex to be beautiful, so long as it was consensual and motivated by good intentions. But her ideas about sex still reflected her formative Victorian upbringing and she wrestled with ambiguity. The carnality of spontaneous sexuality was pitted against what she saw as the hypocrisy of conventional courtship that put men in the driver's seat to exploit female submissiveness. As she put it, people completely ignore each other. When animals meet, strangers or not, they will always sniff each other. After that, they decide whether they like each other or not.

When my mother expounded on sex, it was her way to offer roundabout advice. She often spoke about the propensity of males to resort to violence with women with the warning that I don't know my own strength. I took her advice to refrain from violence. There was one clear piece of advice that I found odd. She said that if my girlfriend were to threaten suicide, let her jump. I was taken aback until I inferred that suicide was not on the menu for her when it came to her own problems with men. As far as I know, my mother never attempted or threatened to commit suicide. It was against her religion.

Her overall message to me was that life wasn't all that simple and that true faith resides in the love for life. Mutti never really embraced the play-it-cool veneer from the beatniks who did all they could to eradicate conventional sentimentality from their lives the more they embraced drugs, recreational sex, and jazz. Alienation didn't work for her. Those who knew her well realized that she was still sentimental in her hopes and dreams, as reflected in her short poem that expressed her sense of loss with the passing of time:

Where are you going?
The mirror image is hazy.
Tears are blurring the vision of a fading dream.

Trying to account for her failure in finding and holding on to one man, she focused on her own shortcomings and said that for her there were no compatible men. Then she would admit that true love is possible, given the right conditions. Again, she used clinical language to describe the dynamics of sexual attraction when advising her lovelorn self.

Sex has little to do with intellectual compatibility. One can be attracted to one's own sex on this basis. So intellect has not much to do with sex attraction. Personality in sex attraction can be of help. Then again, a person can have a distorted or puny personality, yet might appear sexually attractive. Women, including myself, have difficulty accepting a man for purely sex reasons. There always must be a romantic giving of personality, character, and intellect. If this is not present, either the man will be rejected, or if the desire is strong, a little "inventing" takes place. The plain person will and must be seen with all these good qualities. The sex relation usually does not last, and the dear lady will be nursing a broken heart, quite unnecessarily. Had she taken this man for what he was, a sex attraction, no heart would be broken. The "ideal" man with all three attractions happens very seldom. So why not recognize a man for what he is and for what he presents? Men are much smarter. They want sex without deception and are therefore called "dirty dogs" by dishonest Victorian ladies.

21

MUTTI BECOMES OMI

While our mother struggled to sort out the issues of sex and marriage, her children had taken the plunge. In 1970, Linda and I eloped to Atlantic City, and in 1972, Monika and John went to Las Vegas for their civil ceremony. The similarities of these nuptial gambles didn't escape us. There was no family member present at either of our secular marriages.

"Pity the girl who marries Peter," Mother joked, citing as evidence my obliviousness, nonchalance, and untidiness. Now it was time to hope for the best. Our son, Ezra, made Mother a grandmother. "Just call me Omi," she said, reserving for herself a place with all the grannies of the Old World. For her, this was a mixed blessing. She may have lost a son but gained a grandson.

Mother wasn't in the position to disapprove of our out-of-faith marriages since both my sister and I had non-Jewish fathers. The idea of being Jewish was important to her, but fraught with conflict, since all her life she had bridled at its control over her. She would have to wait for another three years for the birth of Monika's son, who theoretically would be eligible for a bar mitzvah since tribal affiliation is conferred maternally. But that point was moot since the practice of any religion was absent in both our new families. Although I was fully aware of the Holocaust and its impact on my mother and her family, I saw no path forward through Judaism to work out its impact on me. The confusing practice of Jewish ritual à la Mutti failed to take hold during my childhood. The obligatory aspects of my Orthodox bar mitzvah didn't help matters. My disconnection from the nurturing communal aspects of Jewish life explains why I became predisposed to secularism based on agnosticism and respect for other people's faiths. Still, for all that, I considered myself a Jew and made no effort to hide behind my acquired German name that could be taken for Jewish anyhow.

Since Mother did not earn her kosher stripes herself, she lampooned her role as a Jewish mother with relish. She "forgave" us for not doing what she didn't do, and she then promptly forgave our spouses for not being Jewish so long they showed interest in her stories, which they did. Mutti felt duty bound to remind herself, and me occasionally, that our marrying non-Jews would have given her poor father still another reason for turning in his grave. She would have liked us to embrace our inherited membership in the tribe without becoming enmeshed in its grip.

Mother mocked the self-serving trappings of religion by citing the childhood prayer well known to German children, "*Lieber Got, mach mich fromm, dass ich in den Himmel komm*" [Dear God, make me religious so that I can go to heaven]. While she quoted Marx's view of religion as "the opiate of the people," she had an unabashed soft spot for rituals, such as the lighting of the sabbath candles and downing Manischewitz during Passover after saying kiddush. Although she did not want to emulate the earnest prayer and devotion of her father, she respected those whose participation in Jewish life solidified family ties and moral resolve because what mattered to our mother was family. In 1971, several months after Ezra was born, Mutti flew east to meet Linda and see her grandson for the first time. She also set aside several days to visit Ted and Elly in New Hampshire.

It didn't take long to see how her grandmother role would play out. At the airport, we easily spotted her outfit, red shirt over black pants, as she clutched her boxy 1930s vintage carry-on at Arrivals. She walked deliberately, then stopped to get her bearing. Shifting from uncertainty to outstretched arms, ready for the battery of hugs and kisses, she greeted her grandson, Ezra, and made a wonderful fuss. This scene was to be reenacted many times on her visits east.

Mutti stayed with us at the Graduate Towers at the University of Pennsylvania where we had a small one-bedroom unit, full of baby equipment and decorated with posters, including one of D.H. Lawrence. We put her in the bedroom where Ezra also slept in a crib, reserving the living room for us so we could catch a late-night movie on TV, assuming Linda was successful in rocking Ezra to sleep. Mother gave advice on how to approach babies, especially when they cried, recalling her days as a first-time mother who quieted her baby (me) by tightly swaddling him. I cited *Dr. Spock's Baby and Child Care*, in which he wrote that it would be okay to let sleep-resistant Ezra cry himself to sleep. Both mothers vehemently dismissed this self-serving, tough-love solution.

Sometimes Mother called me "Herr Professor" hoping that I would be accorded this lofty status. She struck a nerve. At that time, close to finishing my master's degree in communications, I was sending out résumés and proposals while doing odd jobs – substitute teaching, cab driving, working in the state liquor store in Philadelphia. This was a far cry from "my son, the doctor." She had no real concept of where I was going career-wise, nor did I. She didn't ask the kind of probing questions peppered with advice one would expect from a parent regarding their child's career plans, except for a few left-handed remarks that reflected the uncertainty of my enterprise. She had an odd way of expressing a faith that her children would find their way while zeroing in on their insecurities.

For Mother, the university symbolized a sanctuary freed from the drumbeat of modern life. Ah, what fun to chat with the "Herr Professors" and to drink coffee with students with dreams of an idealized future full of accolades! This is what she recalled from her days living on the fringes of Oxford and The Free University in Berlin, and later, dishing out hamburgers "on the house" to needy students at UCLA.

Having been denied the possibility of a university education, Mother relished the trappings of academia. She admired the university lifestyle, including its accommodation of uncertainty, without recognizing the dedicated attentiveness to minutiae that academic pursuits entail. She had only been on the periphery of university life in Oxford where my father was unable or unwilling to include her in his life the way she wanted. When she said he was "too smart for his own good," she was "knocking" his lack of practicality. There was also hurt and anger in her nostalgia for the Oxford days when she said that Denis made her feel "ever so little." Even so, there were instances when she expressed regret for not "having made it with Old Man Denis."

Mother had a sly way of linking me and my father that evoked faint praise and a certain scorn whenever I tuned her out. She always underscored the allowances she made for me to keep our mother-son relationship largely intact, a feather in her cap. The emotional distance between her and me decreased after she embraced her Omi role. In some respects, I was off the hook. She entertained Ezra with light-hearted buffoonery and mild horseplay. Ezra liked the attention, and Linda joined in the fun while I watched, not always amused.

After spending a week with us, Mother took off for New Hampshire to visit Ted and Elly, who would always think of her as *die kleine Mariechen* the youngest of the Silberstein cousins. This would be one of the few times she had seen them in this country; the first was at David Wellner's bar mitzvah. She had visited them in New Hampshire 1967 and often spoke of their continuous generosity and interest in her well-being.

After returning from New Hampshire, we noticed that her mood had darkened. She alluded to Elly's lack of understanding and insensitivity. We suspected that seeing her cousins stirred memories of her childhood days in Germany and her troubles after the war. It is highly likely that she resented being regarded as the family's charity case and grew angry hearing Elly lecture on how to achieve mental health. She told us that Ted made a game of flirting with her. So much for family togetherness.

During the remaining days of her visit with us, Mother's mood didn't change for the better. She was depressive, defensive, antagonistic. She talked a lot about the past, and we feared that she would have one of her manic episodes right there in Philadelphia where the pathways to psychiatric help were uncharted. We worried how she would fare on her flight home, but with a sigh of guilty relief, waved her off when she boarded her plane to Los Angeles. It would be a year until our next visit with Mother.

In June 1972, my little family left for California for a month to celebrate Monika's wedding to John Huntley. We stayed with Mutti in her apartment on 421 Marine Street, located in the Ocean Park neighborhood of Santa Monica. Ezra took his first independent steps on his first birthday in the living room of Mother's apartment and graduated quickly to explorer of the outside walkways.

Monika worried that the marriage hubbub would put Mother's mania in motion. Already there were signs that her mood was starting to build in anticipation of the wedding celebration, hosted by Freddie and Resi Silberstein in their home where Monika had also had her Sweet 16 party. Among the wedding guests were Fred Wellner, Omi and Opa Schulman, and other family friends. Things worked out surprisingly well. Once Mutti was in the social whirl, she put on her charm and bragged about her wonderful children and grandchild and hopes for more. The next day Monika and John were off to Las Vegas for the actual wedding ceremony.

For Linda, this visit was an eye-opener. Mother made sure that we were regaled by the constant flow of visitors, many of them her off-beat friends from Recovery, Inc. She said with glee that they were just dying to meet us. There was "Fat Kathy," a sweet, morbidly obese woman who lived in a trailer and who had been in and out of mental hospitals. At that time, she barely survived on welfare and on what her relatives gave her. Also, there was beautiful, but psychotic Carolyn, recently divorced from a movie director. Mother was her "soul mate," the only one in the world, according to Carolyn, who truly understood her. Another Recovery friend was Anna, who occasionally babysat Mother's cat. Although intelligent, Anna lacked affect. In her unmodulated voice, she complimented people to the point of embarrassment. This friendship ended when Mother turned on her troubled friend during one of her manic fits. Anna wouldn't forgive her and never saw her again. Mother often said that only her outgoing "crazy" friends understood her, but during tough times even they couldn't help her, and so she relied on her well-grounded friends who were stable enough to be able to lend her support. Among them were

Bertha and Bill who invited us over to their apartment for a dinner when we visited in 1972 as did Gene and Monti who had developed a genuine fondness for Mother in a friendship that lasted several years.

Even when her entourage left her apartment, there was barely enough room for the three of us to camp out. On top of that, psychological space was at a premium. With customary enthusiasm, Mutti regaled us with the details of her life, her friends, and her opinions about life and the state of the world. There was no place to hide from her incessant talk. While I escaped to the Santa Monica Public Library to work on my master's thesis, Linda remained in the apartment to contend with my mother's increasingly manic moods. My self-serving rationale was that my absence would provide Linda and Mother with an opportunity to know each other better.

One hot night, Mother chattered on while Linda completed preparations for Ezra's birthday. After she put Ezra down to sleep, she was desperate for fresh air and climbed out of the bedroom window without our knowing. Linda went for a brief walk to regain her peace of mind and magically reappeared at the front door without explanation, much to our surprise. Without further ado, she resumed her place in the ménage and did her best to manage in a situation that was quite foreign to her.

Linda and I went to the Kensington along with Monika, John and Omi to pay a visit to Albert and Estelle Stanley who took us out for breakfast at a pancake house. Later that week, Cousin Estelle took Monika and Linda out for a ladies' lunch at the Hotel Bel-Air. She was regal like Queen Elizbeth behind the steering wheel as her Oldsmobile slowly snaked its way through traffic. Luckily, the rambunctious LA drivers gave way that day to the prerogatives of an elderly driver. After their safe arrival, Monika and Linda had a wonderful time with Estelle, a gracious, intelligent person with a lovely talent for putting people at ease.

For an extended sanity break, Monika drove us to Santa Barbara to see Mother's UCLA friends, Linda and Al. Linda showed us her oil landscapes of the splendid coastal countryside.

Monika's fears that our visit and the wedding with all its excitement would send Omi into orbit were soon realized. We could no longer turn a blind eye to the familiar signs: incessant talking, grandiosity, and sleeplessness. After she stopped taking lithium to liberate her "true" self, the manic phase of her bipolar disorder was in full swing. She didn't care what happened as long as she was still "on top of the world."

We urged Mother to check in again with Dr. Lunsky. We were careful to soft-pedal our concerns by appealing to her rational side while trying to avoid obvious condescension. No dice! She knew we were pandering and said that going along with our game was "against her better judgement." She finally relented and allowed us to take her to see Dr. Lunsky who admitted her to Culver City Memorial to stabilize her. She was not afraid to go because she knew the "good doctor" would release her from the hospital as soon as she was stabilized with her meds.

Dr. Lunsky met with us alone in his office. He reiterated in a patronizing tone that the nature of "your mother's illness" would mean it would get worse with age. The good doctor summarily squelched whatever hope we had for our mother's chances for a merciful recovery in her dotage.

After Mother's release from Culver Memorial, Linda and I returned to Philadelphia. Monika and John began their year as newlyweds in Santa Monica, living close enough to keep an eye on Mother. There was also Mrs. Forrestal who championed her recovery and steered her into another training program that would enable her to enter the workforce once more. Soon enough, she was well enough to visit us again in Philadelphia.

The most memorable part of Mother's visits was her arrival. She would always drop her suitcase and fling her arms wide as she greeted us with hugs and chatter about how she spent the long flight from Los Angeles fortified with a good glass of wine, and always, some nice man sitting next to her listening to her stories. From her shoulder bag she pulled out trinkets for all of us and the *pièce de résistance* would be Cadbury milk chocolate bars with hazelnuts or a box of See's chocolates. Unwrapping presents was part of the ritual. "Look what I have for you," she said in her resonant voice to charm the child in us.

The regular visits continued after we moved from university housing at Penn. She visited us in Chestnut Hill, Pennsylvania, and later on in Carneys Point and Princeton Junction, New Jersey, and finally in Newtown, Pennsylvania where we bought a house.

The length of Mutti's visits eventually shortened to a manageable ten days that allowed us to concentrate attention on her without having our lives upended. She no longer detoured to see Elly and Ted in New Hampshire, although they continued to help her out. To ensure the success of Mother's visits, we planned things she liked to do, such as feeding ducks at the lake in the park. We also introduced her to some of our close friends who took to her lively personality. She was not particularly interested in sightseeing related to our local historical landmarks, but was up for nature outings, and the best way to keep her happy was to find a place to sit down and listen to her stories about her parents, her early life, her days in England, and, inevitably, her views on marriage, politics, religion, and mental health. Linda listened patiently to these stories even though she had heard them before while I became fidgety and tried to change the topic.

One of Mother's favorite topics was her love of animals. She lectured us on the differences between humans and animals, proving that not only four-footed furry creatures, but even "lesser" non-mammalian species, birds and even insects, were better at what they were meant to do than people. When the patience of her listener wore thin, Mother sat by herself, sipping her coffee while writing postcards, posing as the outsider who may have outstayed her welcome.

This silence didn't last long. Like a fighter going the distance, she took a deep breath and launched another set of stories. The more she told them, the more I found it difficult to remember the details, such as the number of sisters in my grandmother's family, or why so-and-so was an idiot. Planning her visit was like charting camp activities. We tried to intersperse the sitting and listening sessions with short outings to her favorite spots. Our friends invited us to parties when she came East to visit. We took her to the Princeton campus to see the black squirrels "who are probably better educated than all these people with PhDs." We scoured the countryside for goose and duck sighting opportunities, and often ended up gazing at farm animals at a petting zoo in Pennington where, much to her delight, a goat once tried to eat Mother's dress.

She welcomed any opportunity to feed geese, ducks and pigeons from her bag of breadcrumbs prompting these feathered friends to engulf us. When she mentioned "pidgeons" in her letters, we knew that this deliberate use of the archaic spelling was a preemptive disapproval of our failure to appreciate these plentiful creatures. On one visit when Linda was pregnant with our second son, Nick, we went to the Philadelphia Zoo where Mutti fed what became a flock of pigeons landing all around and on us. Linda forcefully shooed pigeons from herself and Ezra citing the risk of catching Psittacosis.

According to Monika, Mother was arrested, booked, and released for feeding pigeons in upscale Pacific Palisades, nestled in the foothills of the Santa Monica Mountains. At the court hearing, the judged asked her to cease and desist illegal bird feeding, but Mother replied that they would have to put her in jail to stop her from feeding her beloved birds. She paid the fine and went home thinking about the shortcomings of human justice.

Our mother had many fans, especially her grandchildren, who loved it when she lampooned stuffiness and pretension. In retrospect, I should have taken more genuine pleasure in her harmless absurdities, but I didn't have it in me. Linda had more fun with Mother. She tried to enjoy Mother's playful side and appreciated the warmth our kids felt for her. While Linda was inclined to grin and bear it, my patience timed out repeatedly.

Although Mother was the vociferous defender of creatures large and small, she was not a vegetarian. Munching a hamburger and on occasion a bite of steak tartare, she voiced the opinion that all meat eaters should slaughter what they eat, at least once in their lives. She described how her mother used to wring the neck of the chicken destined for the oven. "Just like that," she demonstrated how it was done in Mecklenburg. She reminded us that her gentle father also killed rabbits. He wasn't like "those stupid hunters" who killed just for the fun of it.

Mother enlisted Ezra as an early co-conspirator in her war against "mindless" authority, including the kind imposed by hapless parents.

She was the fun-loving Omi who saved him from boring chores. She volunteered to help clean which consisted of showing our son how to sweep crumbs under the rug. Linda and I would wait for nightfall to retreat to our bed sanctuary where we performed a postmortem of the past day. Linda advised me not to be so grumpy with my mother since it only made her behavior worse.

I looked forward to Mother's visits with mixed feelings. I knew these meant a lot to her and I wanted her to be part of our lives. Besides, the kids loved to see her. But I also regarded her prolonged presence as a threat to my respite from her *Sturm und Drang*.

There was one memorable visit in 1975 when we lived in Princeton Junction in a rented bungalow-style house on a busy road. We were within a long walking distance to Princeton University and a 15-minute car ride away from my job at Mercer County Community College. Our first week with Mother was filled with outings to the places we knew she would like, including the Princeton campus, nearby Lake Carnegie, and the charming Marquand Park, located on Lovers Lane which was always good for a laugh. As usual, the initial enthusiasm gave way to quiet periods interspersed with restlessness. Mother expressed hints of resentment through sarcastic jabs at our wonderful "little situation" as if to imply that I shouldn't be satisfied with our modest status quo. She teased me by pretending she thought I worked at Princeton University, which she knew I didn't, slyly intimating that the Ivy League would be more suitable for me than working for a community college. She continued her subversion through sugarcoated but pointed remarks about our parenting and lifestyle. I knew her code words all too well to miss them, since she consistently applied them to belittle her friends and relatives when they annoyed her.

Her keen sense of language and flare for the artful gesture were skillfully aimed at our weak spots. Billing herself as a "free spirit" above the fray of human pettiness, she would continue her jabs until she decided it was time for the obligatory rest cure in one of our bedrooms. For a brief period, she stuck us in "outer environment" so that she could regain her composure. At a later point, she would make up by being super nice and generous with more compliments. Mother was a game player, but she tried to keep her uncontrollable feelings in some bounds.

On one particularly challenging day of antagonistic banter, I knew I should have looked the other way and countered the onslaught with a defense of feigned indifference. Instead, I invited Mother to go for a walk to have things out while Linda remained behind to prepare dinner.

We walked along the canal near Lake Carnegie within sight of gothic Princeton buildings that loomed like Christminster in Hardy's *Jude the Obscure* whose working-class protagonist dreamt of becoming a scholar at a prestigious university. Mother pointed out the Canada geese flying in formation above us. The cool winds of fall rustled through the trees, scattering additional leaves on the ground. There was a frost lick on the grass. Winter was a month away. At first, I said little. She knew from my silences that something was up but still counted on my never really talking things over. For the first time, as far as I could remember, I finally summoned the chutzpah to say in plain language what I felt, not what I should feel. I wanted to confront her.

I foolishly thought that "honesty" might be liberating for both of us, and against my better judgment, I let her have it. I said something like, "Why can't you stop being so perverse? Why do you deliberately try to annoy us? I think your mental illness is being used as an excuse! I really think you can do more to help yourself!" I got on my high horse, as Mother called it, and rode it across the point of no return. I was naive to think that things would be better if she understood how I really felt growing up. Confronting her only made her feel worse. It forced her to confront, at least for the moment, what she knew all too well, that her mental illness had created a permanent barrier between us. I should have understood that weaponized truth doesn't make anybody free. By rejecting the little white lies in our relationship, I was in effect rejecting her by creating a bigger lie. By implication, I didn't love her enough because I wouldn't go along with what I despairingly and condescendingly called her tyrannical game.

I had really hurt her feelings. I had broken our implicit trust by bringing up "the truth" as I felt it then, the sum of my hurts excluding hers. The minute sense of victory that comes with pulling off the veil was quickly followed by the vast emptiness of defeat. What was this battle about? What was I trying to prove? Why couldn't I be more generous? Wasn't I the lucky one – healthy, no discernible mental problems, a beautiful family? Why confront her merely to satisfy my urge to let her know how I felt? Doesn't she really know that already? Hasn't she suffered enough?

For once, I didn't give her any wiggle room. I forgot my mitzvah. I didn't consider the intransigent nature of the mental health issues that accounted for her behavior, let alone the trauma of losing her parents and any semblance of a normal youth due to the Holocaust. I wanted from her an admission on my terms, not hers. I wanted her to be "normal" even though I knew better. My quest was absurd when measured against the uncompromising requirements of filial piety. I should have understood that our unique circumstances demanded that I understand her, not for me to be understood. I knew better, but this time I didn't want to know better. I wanted to be freed from a tyranny honed through her long suffering.

What made things worse was that she didn't try to argue with me. She cried. "Yes, you're right," she said quietly, but had no way of offering me what she thought I wanted, which was for her to be someone she couldn't be. It wasn't so much what I said that made her cry. It was not the anger but the coldness and hopelessness of my voice that shut her out. Instead of guilt, I felt at a loss. This was the moment when I forgot the Fifth Commandment. In a fit of disregard, I ignored how much I owed her. Mother gave me precious life and a chance to live a normal life. This time I couldn't bring myself to comfort her. We went back to the house saying nothing. There were no words to undo what I expressed because I didn't feel the regret of credible remorse. I internalized futility, never to confront her again, and it was only a matter of time before Mother was up to her old tricks again. As she had done before, she called me her prodigal son with a smile and knowing look. I simply accepted that. Things went back to "normal" as if nothing had happened. But she had a way of letting me know about our emotional fault line when she said, "I want you to meet so-and-so who is taking great care of me," rubbing in the fact that I had chosen to be remote both physically and psychologically, not to mention geographically. There was always the familiar left-handed compliment when she talked about my unwillingness to sit on her lap, or anyone else's lap for that matter when I was a child, with the motherly, "I have always understood you." Perhaps she believed that my personality, which I must have inherited from my father, enabled me to make the most of a freedom she never had. She continued to call me out if I didn't write or call her soon enough. When I did call, she said, "You must be a mind reader, I just thought of you."

The dynamics of our growing family changed with the birth of Mutti's grandchildren. After our older son, Ezra, was born in 1971, Mutti came East to visit our family on a regular basis. We didn't see Monika and John after their wedding until the birth of their older son, Ian, in 1975. The birth of Monika's second son in 1979 came two years after the birth of our second son, Nicky, in 1977. Mutti never saw her four grandchildren at the same time until the mid 1980s.

Monika and John bought a house in Sherman Oaks in 1973, which could be reached from Santa Monica in about a half hour's drive. On her weekly visit there, Mutti headed north on Sepulveda Boulevard that cut a straight swath through the dry brush of the Santa Monica Mountains, zigzagging under the San Diego Freeway to reappear on the other side hemmed in by boarded-up restaurants and defunct businesses of a bygone era. "I just don't like it," was Mother's explanation for avoiding the freeway that would have cut her trip down from 45 to a mere 20 minutes on a good day.

Mother drove an old Plymouth that her cousin Freddie had given her. As she approached her destination, Mother would always wave hello at the house of Monika's neighbor, who had starred in the TV series, *Car 54, Where are You?*

Her visit began with a happy fuss over little Ian. Shrieks of joy erupted with the unveiling of the presents Mutti brought. Soon there were splashes in the swimming pool. Monika appeared with a tray of sandwiches. "Just what the doctor ordered," Mother wrote to me, bragging about the Sherman Oaks happy days.

With grandchildren on both coasts, Mother settled into being Omi, looking forward to her weekly visits to Sherman Oaks. When she came East to visit us, she brought poolside photos of Monika's family in a house that we did not have the opportunity to visit because of distance and circumstances. Gainfully employed, Mutti seemed settled in her apartment in West Los Angeles, with nothing but praise for her amiable Jewish landlady.

Then out of the blue, this happy period came to an end. Monika received a phone call from the landlady, urging her to put an end to Mother's all-night ruckus. Mother had been blasting her record player out of her window, cursing "I won't let these Gestapo bastards near me," and calling the police to complain about her neighbors. After days of this, the landlady had enough and began eviction proceedings. "You want me to move," Mother yelled at her, "I'll move!" and so she tossed her belongings and furniture out of the windows. She tried pushing her living room couch through and left it dangling in full view.

Monika and John arrived at the scene, giving the futile path of reason another try. They gathered up her belongings and talked Mother into going to Brotman Medical Center in Culver City to be admitted. John called a cab and coaxed her into going with him while Monika stayed behind to sort things out. That same day, the Brotman staff was holding an open house and Mother managed to get away into the crowd while John was trying to get her signed in. After mixing with the guests, she left the hospital grounds and took a bus back to her apartment where she continued to carry on. John and Monika followed her, and when they arrived, Mother called the police to complain that her daughter and son-in-law were stealing from her. At one point, John wrestled her to the ground. The police showed up and took her into custody, kicking and screaming, straight to the same psych ward.

While Mother was in the hospital, her landlady evicted her. Monika moved her belongings, including her cat, to Sherman Oaks where Mother stayed after her discharge until she found another place that she could afford. The more Mother relied on Monika to help her get out of messes, the more Monika was apt to worry and try to convince her to do what had to be done to lead a stable life.

As Mother was settling into her next new apartment in Santa Monica, Monika and her family moved in 1981 to Santa Maria, 150 miles north, where John took a new job as manager of an optical store. Monika and

John made frequent trips to LA to visit her or arranged for her to visit them to make sure that she was all right. For a year, Monika and John lived in a rented house in Santa Maria. Then they bought a spacious well-decorated home with a tidy front lawn and large back yard that Monika landscaped with beautiful trees and plantings. There was a modern kitchen and wall-to-wall carpeting, a far cry from the life on a kibbutz exalted by Mutti.

When Monika and John could not come to get Mutti for her weekly visits, she took the Greyhound bus and described her four-hour trip to Santa Maria as quite a slog with all the poor Mexicans who had to travel that way. This was a hint that she should be chauffeured both ways. She spent happy hours playing with Ian and Peter and went out for excursions with the family to parks in the area. But at times when everyone was asleep, she stayed up and paced. She was ready to go home, back to her cat in familiar surroundings, her comfort zone. Monika and John usually drove her back. "Well, you know Mutti," Monika would say to me when I telephoned guiltily to ask how the visit went.

Mother formed mocking alliances with her grandchildren to kickstart the fun. Up to her tricks, she said, "Your mother doesn't approve of your naughty Omi." Monika looked on, not sure whether to be amused or annoyed with Mutti's use of taboo words or touching on bathroom topics. When younger, Ian enjoyed the silliness of naughtiness, Omi-style. When Ian was older, he tried to get her to buy him Playboy magazine, having caught on to Omi's penchant for rebellious fun.

Ian enjoyed Omi's conspiracies and tricks. Our "poor defenseless" mother accused Monika of being an insensitive meddler, using her mocking voice to echo what Monika said, "Mother, I don't think you should wear that! Mother, why don't you get your shit together."

For all the mischievous pranks Mutti pulled with her grandsons, Monika was still glad that she had a warm relationship with them, unlike John's mother, whom they rarely saw. Monika did worry that the kids would one day witness one of Mutti's inevitable breakdowns. She managed to shield them until Ian saw her in a depressed state during a visit to a sanitarium where she had been brought down from a manic episode. Ezra and Nick were told about Mutti's problems but never came into direct contact with one of Mutti's manic rants or deep depressions.

While Monika was attentive to her mother, she focused on providing her own children with all the stability, educational advantages, and social activities that would help them thrive. Both her sons did well in school, went on to college, and pursued rewarding careers. Monika followed John's career path by obtaining an optician's license and opened her own optical shop. After selling the business, she went into real estate and then returned to optical work.

In 1982, a year after Monika and John moved to Santa Maria, Mutti turned 60. Monika and her family kept in touch on a regular basis, and there were periodic visits with my family on the east coast. By the mid-80s, her social life outside of family slowed down, and she compensated for her out-of-town family connections by joining the local Chabad House, located on 17th Street between Wilshire and Santa Monica Boulevard, a short bus ride from where she lived. The head of this Lubavitcher congregation was Rabbi Levitansky who had a full beard and *peyot* [side locks]. His 12 children included ten-year-old Sholom Dovber Levitansky, whom she befriended and called "Sholom Bear."

The turnabout in her social life which became centered around Chabad reflected her yearnings for a Jewish way of life, one fashioned by her own imaginings. It seemed to me that she wanted to make a statement about the absence of Judaism in her two children's families without being hypocritical. For me, there was the message that I had yet to fulfill my mitzvah as a Jew who, at the very least, could say kaddish for her parents. Mental images of the photos of Stephan and Gertrud Krotoczynski in Mutt's apartment stayed in my mind as a constant reminder of what I should do, if only I could bring myself to do it.

When I visited her during a business trip to California, Mutti just wanted me to see Chabad for myself, inviting me to meet the rabbi and his family without expecting me to experience an epiphany. This house of worship was an unpretentious single-story building. Its entrance corridor, flanked by two offices, led to a large common area with folding chairs, a place used for both for religious and community activities. I noticed prayer books stacked on a long table and someone's coat slung over a worn armchair. The odors of vigorously cooking meals emanated from the kitchen in the back.

Mother had warned me about the dowdiness of the "Chabadniks," as she called them. She used vivid language to describe the observant women with their hair covered. While they tended numerous young children, she said they catered to the "rebbe" who watched on with amusement while taking well-timed swigs from a bottle of Manischewitz. She made fun of the Jewish dietary laws against *tref* ("unclean" things like bacon) that she enjoyed on the sly.

Despite her discomfort with Orthodox Judaism, Mutti was amenable to the openness of these folks to admit her to their community, even when they purged her Christian given name by calling her Miriam. She didn't complain about the traditional roles of women at Chabad. Apparently, it didn't bother her that women were not allowed to become rabbis, even though this had become possible in 1973 in Reform Judaism and ten years later in Conservative Judaism.

It didn't take much to figure out what attracted her to the Chabad House. "They don't give a damn what anybody outside their group thinks," she said approvingly with a wink. She liked that they wore clothing that set them apart and had lots of kids on purpose to make their community grow. She praised the rebbe's lifestyle that bucked the sterile middle-class conventions. She wanted us to accept these fulfilled people or at least give them their due. "I don't care what you kids think, but these people are completely sincere," she told us, handing me their pamphlet describing the various charitable programs they ran for Jews and non-Jews alike. Their commitment to good works and outreach appealed to her.

The Chabadniks accepted her on the strength of her being the daughter of a cantor. They knew she was a child of the Holocaust and for a long time put up with her eccentric approach to Judaism. She gave money to the Chabad House in honor of her parents and commissioned prayers to be said for them in Chabad services. "These are the real Jews, not the fake ones you find on Wilshire Boulevard." They provided her with a place to express the spirit of her Jewish identity, unlike the "respectable" upscale German Jews whom she accused of worshipping at the altar of money and expediency.

What the good rebbe didn't know was that our mother was a committed pantheist who revered the medical missionary, Albert Schweitzer. She said he avoided doing harm to creatures large and small and would have admired the industrious ants who were at home in her kitchen.

Chabad House became part of her routine. She brought the rebbe's children little presents and then enticed them to rebel against their parents by encouraging them to violate the rules. Monika and I regarded her involvement in Chabad as a mild embarrassment intended to show us up. According to Monika, "Mother is just doing her thing" to remind us of our shortcomings when it came to filial obligations. We had long become used to taking her antics in stride, something she did for amusement out of the need to be obstreperous. However, even the Chabadniks' tolerance had limits. When Mother, in one of her mood swings, told Rabbi Levitansky to go straight to hell, he banned her from seeing his family. Her relationship with Chabad, which had endured for five years, finally came to an end, much to my relief. Monika and I regarded her interloper status as inappropriate and intrusive, especially her friendship with Sholom Bear.

Mutti would have been terribly upset to know that Sholom Bear, who later became a rabbi, would be accused of child molesting in 2015, decades after she had known him. His conviction involved no prison time, just one year of counseling. We still have several photos of him as a cute little boy that Mutti sent to let us know that she was a beloved part of the Chabad family.

As time went on, Monika and I were no longer central players in Mother's recovery loop. Mother didn't want Monika to talk sense to her. She didn't want me to use her favorite phrase, *die goldene Mittestraße,* to voice my hapless vote for moderation in all things when it came to her mental health. Mother explained, "Your mother is by nature excessive. Your mother is, after all a Leo." We were the killjoys who would wring the last drop of exuberance out of her life. There were times when Monika and I did appreciate the Leo in her, especially during the early years when her self-centeredness was attractive and fun. With advancing age, her medications had taken their toll. She became more self-deprecating, referring constantly to her age, hardly fulfilling the desired expectation of growing old gracefully that she herself considered an important virtue.

Our conversations with her became delusionary when Mutti described the silver lining of our lives. "Kids, you turned out fine because you didn't do what I did." She never mentioned the absence of Judaism in our families, except in jest. More than once she told us that our fractured childhoods were "character building" and that "you kids turned out better than some cousins who were handed things on a platter," as if virtue comes from the crucible of hardship.

Mutti had her version of the fickle finger of fate: even if you work hard and do right by your spouse and kids, they may still treat you poorly. So maybe you are better off being a pain-in-the-ass because that will test the goodwill in others who are forced to cope with you. Hardship is good because it makes you appreciate what you have. God works in strange ways. "Even that is for the best," she would repeat in Hebrew in a monotone, bringing to our deaf ears the wisdom of ancient rabbis that her parents had packed in her suitcase before she boarded the Kindertransport train. Whether we liked it or not, we were in league with her, particularly when she handed us heartfelt sentiments as she recovered from her bipolar episodes. Tamping down second thoughts about how well she fulfilled the obligations of motherhood, she found the conviction to express, "I really love you kids" without strings ostensibly attached. There were times when we also said the same to her without quite enough oomph to make her feel good. It seemed to me that there was an empty space in our relationship that always needed to be filled. Monika found ways to enjoy the "good times" with her while I went on my own way. Monika's expression of tolerance was expressed in the phrase that she often used, "Well, if that makes Mutti happy."

Mutti forgave Monika and me for not embracing all the tempests of her personality because she knew we loved her, but not as unconditionally as she wanted. Our feelings from childhood preserved the person we wanted her to be, the person we knew she could be, the person she sometimes was. This was a fragile "love" that was in large part rooted in hope. "Mother isn't being herself," Monika said, as if she had a clear idea of who Mother really was. "We are fooling ourselves into thinking that she will ever be well, or that she is now well at all," I said to Monika, observing the extent to which borderline "craziness" lingered during her ephemeral recoveries. It was hard at first to tell whether she was really going to flip out or whether she was faking it for attention. Monika and I compared notes to determine whether she was really on the brink, or whether it was just "Mutti being Mutti." But one unfailing warning sign persisted, her insistence on telling her stories in an angry voice, regardless of whether anyone wanted to listen.

The frequency of her telephone calls was also an accurate warning sign. Each time the phone rang, there was a long silence on the other end. Then her voice emerged with a special message. "Peter," she said deliberately, as if I should already know what she had to say. "Your mother is a ... rich woman." Now was the time to agree with her, not to argue. "Your mother is just ... fine," she would reassure me aggressively. Accepted phone calls would stretch into an hour. She would be more argumentative than usual. We dared not mention the likelihood that she was heading for a fall. Whenever we told her that she was getting high, she accused us of trying to foment a breakdown.

She would call in the middle of the night. "Peter, this is your mother. Do you know who I am? I want to tell you about your sister. She is a real bitch. I can't forgive her." Mutti inveighed against her daughter for trying to talk sense to her. I was also on her shit list, and she said I wasn't worthy of her father's little finger. "You're just like your fucking father," enunciating the four-letter part in her best British.

Whenever she went manic, Mother called, not just us but everyone she ever knew, drawing from the reservoir of names in her address book. She ran up phone bills. "Mother, this is costing you a fortune." She would have none of this, ignoring all cues for bringing phone conversations to an amicable close.

When she called us at three o'clock in the morning, I let the phone ring. In those days, there was no caller ID and phones didn't go automatically into voicemail. She knew I was there and that I didn't want to answer. Eventually, I would talk to her and made some last-ditch effort to calm her down. When that didn't work, I would hang up and not answer the phone again.

I always felt guilty for not jumping right in, flying out to Los Angeles to handle everything. During the earlier years with a young family, not having the money to do this on a dime put me out of the running as a dutiful son ready for real-time heroics. "Peter, don't worry, there really isn't much we can do," Monika said when I called her about Mutti's latest episode. She assured me. "It's only a matter of time; we have to wait." And when the phone no longer rang, I realized that something had happened to put Mother out of circulation. Monika would call and let me know the particulars, what Mutti did to be arrested, where she was hospitalized, and whom to call. Monika did what could to be done and never complained about it. I felt a day late and a dollar short.

22

JUST A LITTLE GARDEN, PLEASE

Mutti adhered to the tried-and-true real estate rule, "location, location, location." In Berlin, she managed to find a place in Charlottenburg and in California she found us a place just outside of Beverly Hills, and finally ended up living in Santa Monica's preferred location north of Wilshire Boulevard. But, in the end, her toney aspirations were out of reach as were her wishes for a bucolic refuge.

"All I want is my own little place in the country, just a little garden," Mutti often said wistfully after recovering from a breakdown. Like so many people in Southern California who had been drawn there by the promise of a balmy climate and easy living, Mutti wished for halcyon living elsewhere while people continued to pour in seeking year-round sunshine but ended up inhaling smog.

"Most of the people here are asleep," Mother commented on the anesthetized state of her fellow Angelinos. In a superior voice she offered a running commentary on its lost souls, but never included herself as one of them. No matter how crazy even she thought she was, Mother professed to know what the good life included. She expressed her standards for surviving in this world in a slow and precise voice, revving-up her latent Oxford accent to accentuate her condescending mood with a smile and knowing nod.

She prided herself on being a cultured European who longed for an old-world life that was denied to her. She entertained a myth that good old England was an antidote to modern living, but apparently so was sun-drenched, tree-hungry Israel where she might have gone if she had dared to flee Europe in 1939. "Kids, someday I am going to live in Israel on a kibbutz," she once said emphatically, rejecting the elusive charms of Europe and the American Dream in one fell swoop.

But when dreams of a life somewhere else faded into the reality of being stuck in greater Los Angeles, she would make her state visit to the vast Pacific Ocean in queenly fashion before putting "the entire stinking city" into Dr. Low's outer environment. When she returned home, the roar of the ocean segued to the purr of her cat. Then, she revisited reality and knew that she was lucky to have landed in her beloved Santa Monica.

Mother went to the beach regularly in Santa Monica and also biked to Venice Beach where she felt at home with all those retired Jews, beatniks, and bums. She hated the new Santa Monica Mall and cursed the money-grubbing boom that drained the old-fashioned American charms from downtown Santa Monica. She said that she didn't care about money with the certainty of someone who did. She quoted the standard money-related maxims, "Money is the root of all evil" and "Money makes the world go around." To show her true colors, she took an anti-materialistic stand by not buying real shoes, and instead wore cheap, rubber flip-flops everywhere in any weather. Monika bought her some substantial Birkenstock sandals that she consented to wear since they were standard equipment for the hippies who "let their freak flags fly" against the establishment in dress and deeds.

She was fond of the German maxim, *"Du musst dich den Sechser dreimal umdrehen."* This sage advice urged one to turn a six-pfennig coin over three times, meaning that turning it over in your pocket would prevent you from taking it out too fast. Mother was a great saver, accumulating what she said were huge sums. "Peter, you will never guess how much I have in my bank account," and I would wait, spellbound, for the answer which usually ran in the hundreds, and sometimes even exceeded a thousand. "You have a millionaire mother. We're rich!" This rolling in riches narrative was standard fare during Mother's bipolar highs, but also crept into the conversation when she was ostensibly stable. The chronic lack of resources she faced would have been hard for anyone to keep at bay, so why not dream? Living the simple life of honest-to-God poverty was Mother's defiant credo. Yet, she was keenly aware of the social humiliation that comes with poverty. When I was a child, she would give me some change and say in German, "This is so that the dogs don't pee on you."

Perhaps her financial situation would have been better had she received equitable Holocaust reparations from the German government. Her applications to the Entschädigungsamt Berlin [Compensation Office Berlin] date back to 1952 in Germany with no evidence that she received compensation at that time. The application process continued after she arrived in the United States. In 1956, on the advice of her cousin Freddie Silberstein, Mutti filled out paperwork and submitted it through Dr. Erich Meyer, a lawyer in Berlin, who may have represented her per bono. The filings detailed the hardships she suffered and finally resulted in a settlement of 400 Deutschmarks, amounting to about $100 at the exchange rate then. Freddie believed she was entitled to more, so she submitted another claim sometime after 1967 which meant going through another long application process documenting her history of mental illness. She eventually received a letter denying her claim. Dated October 10, 1979, this letter stated the reasons in dense German legalese that I translated into idiomatic English as best I could:

In 1975, we informed you that you were awarded 400 Deutschmarks in compensation on April 1, 1959, for health damages. This award was made to your foreign Deutschmark account through Handelsgesellschaft, Berlin W. 15 Uhlandstrasse 165/166 [the government's bursar]. This decision recognized the persecution-related suffering due to delimited aggravation: Depression. The persecution-related reduction in employability for this was 100 percent from May 1941 until December 31, 1941. Your appeal of this decision was dismissed by judgment of the Berlin Regional Court. This judgment is final. In response to the notification sent on September 10, 1975, we refer again to the legal remedy provided by that judgement. We hope that this letter resolves this matter.

Her lawyer in Berlin argued that Mary's mental illness resulted from the traumatic loss of her parents and family during the Holocaust. According to the testimony of a doctor hired by the West German government to review her case, her diagnosed condition, manic depressive psychosis, was "endogenic." He asserted that the root cause of her mental illness was genetic and had nothing to do with the trauma of forced separation from her parents and the extermination of her mother and relatives. Since her damages didn't involve property and valuables, Mother was not eligible for the kind of reparation payments that put some of her cousins on what she called "easy street." One might have thought it was just sour grapes in reaction to not receiving reparations when Mother said that German blood money could in no way compensate for the loss of her parents and family, but her deeply felt bitterness persisted. In 1989, two years before she died, she refused an official invitation from the *Regierende Bürgermeister von Berlin Senatskanzlei* [Berlin Mayor's Office] to go back to Germany for an all-expense-paid visit to the city for a reunion of Berlin Jews who had been forced to flee Nazi Germany. Fresh in her mind was the humiliation of the reparations process; always haunting her was the devastating loss of her parents. Unlike in 1947, there was nothing to go back for, no reason at all to go back to Berlin. Mutti drew swastikas on the airmailed invitation from the mayor.

Before she turned 60, Mutti still seemed physically healthy, at least healthy enough to live on her own. "Healthy as a horse," she often said. Although her unrelenting mental breakdowns made it increasingly difficult for her to hold on to any job, she still worked part-time as a babysitter to supplement her disability allowance. No longer able to afford a car, she traveled by bus instead. Whenever she could, she rode her bike to the beach, to the store, and even to Venice, until she fell off the bike in 1982, sustaining a head injury which caused her to lose her sense of smell.

The bike accident was a turning point in her life. No longer in good physical shape, she ceased to ride her beloved bike and gave it away. She had gained a lot of weight as a side effect of her medications which didn't help her body or her mental state. After another mental breakdown, which caused her to lose her apartment, Monika and I thought she might be better off in an affordable group living situation for people her age. We assumed that once she was taken in, there would be no way of evicting her. The unlikely option of her living with one of our families was never discussed except in jest. When Monika first moved to Santa Maria, she had offered Mutti the opportunity to move in with her family, or to live in an apartment nearby. Mother wanted nothing of this. For her, all roads led to independence in Santa Monica where she felt at home. Realizing this, Monika located a potential group living arrangement in Santa Monica close to the beach, but Mother rejected this option, even when this facility agreed to let her bring her cat.

Mother wanted to be free to live the way she wanted. With the help of her contacts at the Santa Monica Housing Authority, she found a tiny rent-controlled efficiency in a good neighborhood only four blocks from the beach. "You really have to hand it to her," Monika said, commenting on Mutti's grit and resourcefulness. Nevertheless, we still believed she would be better off in a group situation and worried about what would happen if she left a gas burner on, given her lack of smell.

"I don't need any interference from my children," our mother said emphatically when the topic of her living situation came up. We eased up once it appeared that she was managing well enough on her own. Mother had all day to figure out how she should live, now that she no longer held any job.

The new apartment was tiny but affordable. There were two small rooms, one serving as the living room with kitchenette and the other a bedroom barely large enough for the double bed. The important thing was its location in what Mother considered a ritzy area north of Wilshire, a few blocks from the beach. However, the inside of the apartment was dark because of another building in front, surrounding bushes, and a tall fence that blocked the sunlight. Mutti said that this tiny dark apartment suited her just right. She felt at home with her plants clustered inside and outside of her apartment where nearly a dozen large and small cactuses guarded the entrance way. She had an avocado tree outside that bore fruit for sandwiches.

Her landlady, an elderly Syrian woman, lived in a bungalow just off the street. A pathway from her flower garden led to the two-unit building where Mother lived. Their mutual interest in gardening and cats gave Mutti a vehicle for befriending the old lady.

Monika said that our mother lived in a world of her own. Sure enough, her shrine-like gallery of family photos, Judaica and memorabilia, artfully arranged in her antique wooden sideboard, were still the focal point of her latest apartment where she received visitors with open arms and made sure that they were properly introduced to her cat, Tigerina, lounging on the table in the kitchenette. She had managed to keep and bring her world with her again.

Chagall, Matisse, Rembrandt, Van Gogh, and Klee had, of course, come along to grace the walls along with Rubens whose full-figured nudes appealed to her. Her books included Jewish prayer books and the Communist Manifesto, in addition to her collection of classic paperbacks – Shakespeare, Goethe, and Heine – some which were carefully bookmarked with dried flowers. There were also the remains of the Jahrzeit candle she had burned for her father.

Mutti made a point of making friends with her neighbors, but not with the "would-be" writer upstairs, who complained if she played *The Three Penny Opera* too loud. Next door was a young couple, a homosexual man living platonically with a heterosexual woman. They had lots of plants and an emu that strutted in their backyard. Mother became friendly with them exchanging lots of short visits back and forth. She often mentioned them in letters and phone calls and formally introduced them to me during one of my stays. The friendship with these neighbors came to an end when, during one of her breakdowns, she called the authorities regarding their "illegal" possession of an exotic bird (actually, emus are legal as pets in in California). The couple wouldn't talk to Mother even after she recovered and then apologized for what she did.

Subsequently, Mother finally had a falling out with the Syrian landlady and decided to move to another rent control apartment nearby that was more to her liking. This apartment, located on 6th Street near Montana Avenue, was on the second floor of a four-unit building in a small apartment complex with a landscaped open space below. The door opened to a porch lined with her cactuses. The kitchen window was positioned to let the light come in and to let her cat out. She didn't want a vacuum cleaner to scare her cat, nor was she interested in a color TV to pass the time. For her, it was enough to have space to recreate her familiar environment with her past and current loved ones represented among the things that she cherished .

Mutti lived in this apartment for the remaining few years of her life in the 1980s until her death. Immersed in the prophylaxis of her daily routine, she audited classes at Santa Monica College where she had once been enrolled as a regular student. She sat in on drama and literature classes, plus went twice a week for a swim in the college pool. She was proud of being a student and sent me numerous school-assigned papers for comments. The college was a perfect place to improve her writing skills and spend time with young people. "What I am really interested in," she confided to me, "is the swimming pool." She loved the rhythm and stability of making her usual rounds in Santa Monica as much as she had loved exploring the woods at Savernake during nursing school. Her retail pantheon on Wilshire Boulevard still included Mike Caruso's men's clothing store, where she bought me birthday presents ."Nothing is too good for my Peter." She could reach her branch of Citizens National Bank by crossing Wilshire. Her "personal" banker, a young woman, took care of her spiritual as well as banking needs. As for her coffee hang-out, she abandoned Zucky's when it ceased to be a "real delicatessen" that no longer welcomed her because of the ruckus she caused. Her loyalties shifted to Polly's bakery across the street renowned for its pies.

There were plenty of needy people in Santa Monica's popular shopping district – old-fashioned bums, homeless people, winos, plus an assortment of "poor, crazy people" with supermarket carts full of their worldly belongings. She befriended them and assured Monika and me that this posed no danger because she knew how to talk to them.

"It's good to have a routine," Mother counseled me as always. I finally realized that this bromide meant that if one has no explicit purpose or destination in life, it is better for one's health to invent a circle of tasks that brings you peace. "Peter, you are always running around as if you were a chicken with your head cut off," she would tease me because there were no visible life-affirming routines in my life. She had a point. I ate too fast, and I was always rushing off to some place helter-skelter.

"Ah, but you're a genius," she gave me a gratuitous free pass that I didn't deserve but liked to hear anyway.

Mother's circuitous routines drove her daughter to distraction. Monika was all about finding the shortest distance between two points. She liked to get things done efficiently with no muss or fuss. Walking into Mutti's impromptu life, she would say with a laugh, "Oy veh, Mother, you sure can be goofy!" We knew Mother's haphazard routines kept her going, not merely the physical ones that took her to the streets of Santa Monica, but also the verbal ones like the ritualized stories about her father and mother, childhood events, the Nazis, the good old British, poor Heinz, and old man Denis – those perennial characters who were responsible, in one way or another, for our being here.

On her regular walk to Santa Monica Beach for an ocean swim one day, Mutti ran into trouble. After jumping a few waves and diving underneath to avoid being pummeled, she ventured beyond the breakers to put her breaststroke into action. She had done that for years, but this time could have been fatal. She was caught in a rip tide that took her out to sea. Unable to swim back to shore, she was swept south towards Venice. She stayed afloat and swam slowly with her steady breaststroke to conserve energy. Two lifeguards came by boat to pull her out of the water. From that point on, she eliminated the ocean swim from her routine. When her swims and bike riding finally ended, she counted herself lucky that she was fit enough to still swim in a pool and to walk or hop on a bus to her favorite places within walking distance of the Santa Monica Pier.

Mutti said she did her best to stay healthy. Her diet consisted of the ordinary four food groups, and her vitamin regimen was the brand, One A Day. When her doctor urged her to stop smoking because of an Emphysema diagnosis, she pretty much stopped with a modicum of fanfare. She was at heart a nurse who respected but selectively obeyed doctor's orders. Fully aware of the perils of over-medication, she perversely kept her bathroom well stocked with over-the-counter remedies.

Her nursing acumen came into play when Cousin Albert needed care. He had been ill for a few years and Mother took care of him for several months during a period between her manic spells. "I made peace with the old man," she said, never quite giving him his full due in her mixed bag of gratitude and resentment. Albert, five years older than Estelle, died at the age of 93 in 1973. According to Mother, Albert's son stuck his mother in a nursing home. What I didn't know at the time and later found out from her grandson, Steven, was that Albert Junior took meticulous care of his mother while she lived in the Kensington. After she had to move to an assistant living facility, he visited her daily. When I visited Estelle a year before she died, I was saddened to see the impact of age. She was frail, barely able to walk and very unhappy about being incapacitated. Estelle died on May 3, 1982, at the age of 97.

With the $500 Estelle left for me in her will, I bought a suit to honor her for buying me my first suit for my high school graduation at Henshey's. A decade after Estelle died, this venerable department store went out of business because it could not compete with the Santa Monica Mall. For us, the passing of Albert and Estelle symbolized the end of a golden era in the history of Santa Monica. The real estate boom in Santa Monica began in earnest after our cousins died. The iconic Kensington was sold and then razed to make room for the five-star Loews Santa Monica Beach Hotel.

23

HELL HATH NO FURY

As my years in Santa Monica became fixed memories, I thought more about my tenuous connection to my father in Rome. I knew all too well Denis was not a family man, but still felt obligated to give him the opportunity to forge some ties with his most recent descendent, Ezra. Having been told that a picture is worth a thousand words, even more if moving, I mailed him a 16mm film clip of his first grandson that he could view on his 16mm projector. It featured Ezra's initial solo walk on his first birthday in Santa Monica in 1972. While he expressed appreciation for this gesture that must have piqued his curiosity, there was no uptick in his family involvement.

Correspondence with my father dwindled after the late 1970s. I gave up writing him after my letters remained unanswered, recalling my disappointment as a teenager when he dropped the ball after being miraculously reconnected to our lives. My mother, meanwhile, never ceased her dogged outreach to her ex as a reminder of their bond that he had sporadically acknowledged. This time there was an explanation for his silence that I did not anticipate.

In 1982, Denis finally sent me a letter. He asked me to keep his current new address from my mother. He wrote that she been on a campaign to track him down since she hadn't heard from him, and telephoned the Italian authorities in Rome and Florence through the British consulate, claiming she was dying and wanted to contact her long-lost husband. Unaware of her mental condition, the Italian authorities believed her story that Denis was a bigamist who married an Italian woman without obtaining a divorce. Mother's letters and phone calls prompted the Carabinieri to investigate her allegations. They sent out a team to find her rightful "husband" at his address in Terni, Umbria located in a rural area north of Rome. Denis described this unfortunate comedy of errors.

> The Carabinieri were out for my blood after that mad dash in a jeep during which one of their men got hurt when they were coming down the bed of a torrent leading to my shack down here, and only to be told that my wife in America was not dying and that she was not even my wife.

Denis's explanation to the Italian police didn't go over well. They thought that this foreigner had made fools of them, and so they let Mother's false accusation of bigamy stand and proceeded with an investigation that sullied his reputation and set off a damaging series of events. His work dried up and the authorities blocked him from obtaining the papers needed to do freelance work. His in-laws were appalled by the scent of scandal. He ran out of money. At the age of 67, he had no pension or savings. His wife moved in with her sister, while he was homeless for several months, sleeping in his car until he was able to borrow money from a friend to become reestablished.

When I last saw my father, he lambasted the corruption, xenophobia, gullibility, and inconsistency of Italian culture that made his dour England seem quite merry in comparison. He talked incessantly about his precarious existence in Italy because of its bias against foreigners, explaining to me as a foreigner he was not eligible to participate in the country's public pension system.

This time, the bias against foreigners was fomented as the result of my mother's actions. To my dismay, he rubbed my nose into the mess caused by my mother in an angry letter, as if I were her legal representative.

To sum up, Mrs. Mary Wiesner, or Miss Mary Krotoczynski, or whatever other name she chooses to call herself by has been the direct and deliberate cause of serious damage to me, my life, and to Fausta. Whether she knew she would do this or not doesn't interest me. She has done it. So long as she was harmless, I could put up with mentally deficient letters, her 40-year-old saga as a student nurse, her suffocating maternalism, etc. sheerly from pity. I regarded her as a genuine war victim. After studying all she has written about herself and all she has written to and about her strings of lovers (she sent me the lot twice over) my feelings have shrunk to the size of a surgeon's electric needle puncturing those fat, presumptuous, self-indulgent, ignorant Krotoczynski frontal lobes to get at the real source of megalomania. But now that's all the interest I have left. I don't want any more information from her or about her.

To help set the record straight, I wrote a letter on his behalf to the Italian authorities explaining that my mother was mentally ill and that there was no factual basis for her allegation. My father thanked me for helping to clear his name and thereby expediting the paperwork needed for him to work in Italy. But all this came at a personal cost. Although I deplored my mother's actions, I was also put off by my father's over-the-top venting that overshadowed any consideration that he might have had for me, if not for my mother. Although he didn't exactly blame me for the things my mother did, he wouldn't accept my view that they were the direct result of her mental illness. His thankyou was unadulterated gall.

I have also reread your covering letter, which says almost the last word on the subject of the K. phenomenon. I only wish I could still take such a clinically fair view of the facts. But at present I'm in a very weak position depending as I do for any sort of civil status on bureaucracy. In England, we could both erroneously think of your mother as her own victim alone (I image it's true of America, too). Here, it would be zany to do so. Any action of the type she took can have explosive consequences. All the same, your letter would seem to be almost the last word by a very civilized American about a mother that passeth all comprehension. Maybe, however, if you read all her diary, comments, analyses and poems you might be inclined to join me in thinking she can be held to account for her actions. I am convinced she knows what's she's doing and of the possible consequences, and that she also acts in the conviction that whatever they are, nothing can happen to her which she has not already woven into an acceptable pattern of living. But, if she doesn't want to experience the present horrors of an Italian *goal* [jail], she must keep a very low profile. Every letter that she now writes will surely be opened.

He cut off correspondence with Mother and didn't write me much either. The virulence of his anger only widened the distance between us. I had no choice but to stay loyal to my mother who, despite her sporadic recklessness, never abandoned me emotionally.

My father could have softened his anger for my benefit, but he was too pig-headed and self-centered to bother. He was caught up in the conceits of a rational world that tended to underestimate the insidious nature of mental illness. I had no desire to tell him that I, too, was angry at my mother, even though I understood that mental illness was at the root of her transgressions. I expected him to acknowledge this after I explained the situation. As for writing him from that point on, I was at a loss for words.

To make matters worse, Mother's telephone spree to all the people she knew in Europe caused another crisis, her loss of telephone service. She was unable to pay off the huge telephone bill she piled up vilifying Denis. Cousin Fred Wellner stepped in as her chief advocate, not knowing the backstory. He approached the entire family to take up a collection to pay the phone bill and to supplement her income with regular contributions, adding this postscript in the letter he sent out.

> Please remember, Marie's actions and behavior are an illness over which she has no control, like ANY illness and we all get a share of it. Luckily with most of us it settles in the body and not in the brain. We do not have any choice when or where it will hit either of us next. So please, do not criticize or judge her. She didn't ask for it and she had so many *Backpfeifen* in her life.

Cousin Fred's admonitions were in line with what he said when we were kids. I couldn't help flashing back to hearing him say "Now don't do anything to upset your mother" after her mental breakdowns Instead of being grateful, I resented Fred's tacit assumption that my sister and I were somehow part of our mother's difficulties and that I had to be bought off. I thought he didn't acknowledge the trauma we suffered from witnessing her nervous breakdowns and having to adjust to being in foster homes with strangers. In retrospect, I know he gave us invaluable assistance and meant well when he took me aside to give advice, never realizing the humiliation I was feeling. He had the shadow of his lost parents hanging over him, too, something I couldn't take in fully as a kid. My emotional reservoirs were drained from dealing with our own situation.

Monika and I were in our thirties and married with school-age children when Fred's letter arrived. We were dumbfounded that he had sent it without any prior discussion. Our reaction was swift. We declined to participate and explained that we preferred to help her in our own way. I wrote him a terse letter to explain that money sent by relatives to her directly at that point would very likely be spent on more irresponsible phone calls to Italy. I did not try to suggest that Mutti could sort out her own problems once her mania subsided, but to some extent, that's what happened.

After the letter incident, Monika and I were not predisposed to appreciate Fred's help which seemed intrusive and judgmental, no matter how well meant. Things might have been different if we had been able to forge a warmer emotional relationship over the years to give us the opportunity to appreciate his generosity and sincerity. That never happened. He discontinued social ties with our family while continuing to help our mother and most likely fielding the cost of her telephone calls. This was in stark contrast to other relatives who forged individual relationships with my sister and me during our adolescence and kept up social ties with our family afterwards.

A few weeks passed and, as usual, Mutti recovered and was back on her meds. She pulled herself together and called the phone company to arrange to pay her bill over time. I don't know if Fred helped her pay the bill, but I suspect he did. At any rate, there was a lot of wishful thinking on my part that things would stay calm, at least for a while. This was reflected in my somewhat sanctimonious letter which didn't allude to my interaction with Fred or convey my sad feeling that nothing ahead looked good.

Liebe Mutti,

I'm glad that you are finally home and that you have achieved some equilibrium. We have spent a busy and happy Christmas, although it would have been much happier had you been well. We had Linda's family over for Christmas day and that took a lot of preparation on Linda's part. The kids enjoyed getting presents and, to a lesser extent, dressing up for the occasion. It's nice to see kids enjoy things. We went to a raucous New Year's party at Bob and Lynn's, and to Linda's parents for New Year's Day. I hope that things will work out for you concerning the apartment. Obviously, things could be much easier if you had millionaires for children. You said something about your phone being cut off. If that should happen, don't hesitate to call us collect, preferably on the weekend when I am sure to be home. I hope that the clothing we sent is okay and that it fits. Is there anything else you need? I'm glad that you were able to spend a nice New Year's with your neighbors. I hope you could stay well this time for a long period and work out an arrangement with Dr. Weinstock to become quickly hospitalized should the manic phase reappear (hopefully not too soon). I wish you were able to "nip the problem in the bud" before doing the sort of things to wreck your life to be regretted later. Please understand the emotional exhaustion of both Monika and me resulting from your illnesses, but hopefully with a little time, we can get things back to "normal" again. Both Ezra and Nicolas, and Linda, give you their love.

In the coming years, we were able to increase the frequency of our visits to California to see Mutti and Monika and her family. For periods of time, there was a semblance of stability. We pretended that things were okay, waiting for the other shoe to drop. And sure enough, it did.

24

DOWNWARD SPIRAL

Late in 1990, Mother was up all night with her stereo blaring out her window. In the early morning hours, she locked herself out of her apartment and broke the window to get in but was not able to climb through. She created a commotion that woke the neighbors who called the police. Half-naked, she screamed until the police arrived to take her to a mental health clinic that took Medi-Cal, California's Medicaid program for low-income families.

The police contacted Monika to inform her that Mother had been arrested and that she had been placed in a clinic in downtown Los Angeles. When Monika called, the clinic's receptionist would not confirm that she was their patient. When I followed up by phone, she told me, "We are not at liberty to divulge whether anyone has been hospitalized." I explained that I was more interested in giving the clinic information about Mother's medical history, which could potentially help determine proper care, than finding out whether she was there. After I threatened to sue if anything went wrong, the clinic became more cooperative.

The attending physician was not aware that Mother was being treated with lithium for bipolar disorder when he prescribed anti-psychotic drugs to make her more manageable. As a result, her speech became slurred and she trembled, barely able to keep her balance. Monika arranged a transfer to Culver Memorial where the staff knew her. It took weeks for her to recover physically as well as medically from her bout at the clinic.

After Mother's medications were under control, the hospital transferred her to a nursing home in Santa Monica that took psychiatric patients. However, the staff felt she was too disruptive, and sent her back to Culver Memorial, which kept her another week until she was fully stabilized. She was then placed in a Jewish elder care facility in Culver City to recover. The staff there liked her but felt that she was not capable of living on her own and wanted her to stay permanently.

Making things more complicated was the fact that Mother was soon to reach the maximum number of hospital days covered by Medicare over a lifetime. Once she exceeded her limit, Culver Memorial could no longer admit her on an emergency basis, and her only alternative would be LA County and the State mental health system which were known for warehousing mental patients. This meant that we had to find a safe place for her – ideally one run by Jews for crazy Jews.

Mother liked the idea of being taken care of. Still, she resisted being institutionalized, even in a benign Jewish place like the one in Culver City. She feared that all or most of her Social Security benefits would go to the home and that she would be left penniless. She wanted to live in her own place with her cat, which had been put in a cat hotel while she was in the hospital.

Mother discharged herself and returned home on a trial basis. If she could manage on her own, then all would be well and good. If she wanted to return to the nursing home, she would be welcomed there, on the assumption that we could meet her expenses. The choice was hers. At first, she had trouble adjusting to being on her own and went back to Culver City for another week, but then she gained confidence and returned to her apartment, determined not to be institutionalized anywhere. Her apartment became her Alamo where she would defy the authorities, including Tim, her solicitous social worker at the time, who reluctantly became convinced that she was unfit to live by herself. Time was running out because her landlord had begun eviction procedures because of the ruckus she caused.

Linda and I flew from Pennsylvania to help Monika sort out the crisis. We told Mother that we were coming to celebrate her 69th birthday. We didn't let on that we came to visit for other reasons as well. When we arrived at her apartment, we were shocked to see how much Mutti had failed. Minutes after we arrived, she began lighting candles without candle holders right on her living room rug. She had sorted letters and bills into piles on the floor and placed them next to her armchair so that she could reach them while soaking her swollen feet in a wash tub. Although she was in poor health, she declared herself well. She wanted to make the point that she was determined to live on her own without interference from her children.

We looked around and noticed that the refrigerator wasn't stocked. She refused to have her laundry done and insisted on washing clothes in her bathtub, an impossible task for someone who had trouble walking and getting up. It was obvious that she couldn't take care of herself, so we arranged with Tim for a caregiver to help her out, cook her meals, and straighten up. This worked for a month until Mutti didn't want the caregiver to come anymore. She was cool to the idea of having anyone come in to help, and her condition continued to decline. There was evidence of incontinence. Tim said that she would be better off in a supervised facility and that it would be best to persuade her to go immediately while she was well enough to be accepted by a place where she would have the freedom to come and go. He hoped she might be a lot happier in a place where she would have plenty of company, but there were obstacles to the plan. The places that would admit her didn't allow pets, and Mother was adamant that she wouldn't part with her cat. There were, of course, additional complications. What would happen if Mother had one of her violent manic outbursts in a supervised care facility? Tim told us that that the "good" places were not staffed to handle troubled people who need to be subdued physically and sedated. He described the hierarchy of medical facilities which were classified in terms of the level of security imposed on patients, an inferno-like downward spiral from the most livable ones on the top to maximum security "lock-up" facilities at the bottom.

We learned that once someone is declared to be legally incompetent, the state assumes the guardianship over the individual and has the power to place them in a lock-up facility. To avoid the involvement of the state, Tim and his colleagues suggested that Monika and I become Mutti's conservators. That would give us control over her finances and the power to place her in any affordable facility of our choosing that would accept her. Even if there were no option other than to place her in a lock-up facility, we still would have the opportunity to choose the best one available and to look out for her welfare. Should she recover, we could get her released, which would be difficult to do if the state had full control.

Neither Monika nor I had the resources to pay for private care. Monika consulted her lawyer to find out what obligations and liabilities we faced in becoming her conservators. Would we be liable for medical bills not paid by the state? Would we have to pay her debts should she decide to run up thousands in telephone bills? Worst of all, would she turn completely against us? Others had warned us about becoming too involved because we risked losing support from the state which was forever on the lookout for anyone to assume responsibility. Monika's lawyer warned her against being a conservator, suggesting instead that we talk her into giving us power of attorney, which is easier to obtain. However, the drawback was that Mutti could take back the power of attorney whenever she wanted. We had little time to waste with eviction looming. We met with the staff at the Senior Center in Santa Monica, who convinced us that it was in Mother's best interest for us to sue for conservatorship. We were referred to a lawyer specializing in these matters. He would obtain a temporary conservatorship that would give us the power to have her committed against her will, if necessary, and still retain some influence over her well-being. We acted quickly, talked to the lawyer by phone, got together the information needed to draw up the petition. We talked to him again on his car phone as he made his way from Westwood to meet with us at Mother's apartment, giving him some background information in preparation for his encounter with Mother.

The lawyer, Ralph, was in his fifties, a handsome Italian American from the East Coast, who had studied law at Georgetown. We met him as he drove up in a Lincoln convertible. After shaking hands with us, he wanted me to confirm the terms of his service and asked for an upfront payment which we had been told to expect. He had already explained on the phone that the most preferable way to proceed was to get Mutti to agree to our becoming her conservators. He would talk to her about her options and at the same time gather evidence to force the issue in court if appropriate. Our lawyer climbed the outside stairs of Mother's apartment, introduced himself, and acted as if she were his client. Mother first tried to impress him with her bundle of official-looking documents, including her US citizenship papers. He gently chided her for not keeping these in a safe place. After some chitchat, she said that she trusted her son even though she didn't quite approve of what I was up to. She asked him a lot of questions about being a lawyer, whether he made a lot of money, realizing that he must be costing somebody something. "I need a lawyer, too," she said jokingly. "Maybe you can represent me," subtly conveying to us that she was really "in on the joke." I accompanied Ralph to his car and talked to him a bit about the close relationship Mutti had with Tim, her social worker who sympathized with her struggle to maintain her independence. "It's not necessarily good for professionals to become too emotionally involved," he said, trying to get me on his professional wavelength. While I saw Ralph out, Linda stayed upstairs with Mutti who told her, "I don't trust that guy. I only trust Peter and Monika." She paused and added, "Don't know why I didn't include you. I trust you, too." This last statement made my wife very happy, since she hadn't always been sure which of Mutti's lists she was on.

Meanwhile, Mother, sensing a threat to her freedom, took steps to clean up her act. She decided to fight this "conservatorship thing." Much to our surprise, she acted friendly towards us. I told her that we wanted to do it for her sake, because in our judgment things had gone too far. We said there was no choice since she was about to be evicted with no place to go. I also told her that if she proved that she could live alone, we would back off and not use the power of the conservatorship to have her institutionalized, the last thing we wanted. We wanted nothing more than for her to win, to prove us all wrong. Mutti didn't say anything else. She didn't want to leave her apartment. She didn't want to give up her cat. She wanted her freedom. She was prepared to fight us quietly, without anger. She would "forgive" her children for what they were about to do. Little did we know she held the trump card.

The next day was her birthday. We were all ready for a pleasant occasion. Mother invited Bill Wintersole, Resi and Freddie Silberstein, and a few surprise guests. Mutti's latest compadres came, ready to entertain us – Edie, in her seventies, dressed in a flowered dress and high-platform shoes, and Edie's boyfriend, Frank, a Mexican man about the same age, who had lived in California all his life and made his living playing violin. He played "My Yiddishe Mama" for Mutti and other sentimental favorites. Although older than Mother, Edie was in much better physical shape. She danced a sort of flamenco dance to Frank's tunes with surprising agility and grace. She spoke a little French and wanted us to know that she was cultured and had studied at the Sorbonne. Edie told me what a special person Mother was and how much she loved her. For Mother, this was a special treat to see "her people" on stage in front of the family. I recorded all this on video. Monika's son, young Peter, who would eventually become a casting director and producer of reality shows, also recorded some reaction shots. Monika and I exchanged glances as if to say, "Mother is still doing her thing." We saw her smile, despite her physical pain, as she sat, a bit disheveled, with her ankles badly swollen. This was her party, the way she wanted it. I felt embarrassed, pained, and touched all at once. I thought about her as she had once been and wondered what she was thinking, and whether she had any idea that her life would come to this. Her old beau, Bill Wintersole, looked subdued. "Why are you smoking, Maria? It isn't good for your health." She just shook him off and said it didn't matter anymore. As cousin Resi left, she told us to get deli for dinner for Bill and Mother. She hoped Bill would stay and chat more with his old flame, but Bill had been saddened enough and left saying sweet goodbyes.

Earlier on the day of the party, Mother took my Berkeley Diploma off the wall and gave it to me. "I won't be needing this. Take it," she said ominously. I took it, not saying a word because I didn't want to acknowledge the truth. She was obviously not in good health because of emphysema and cardiovascular problems that she never discussed but which had become obvious. Before we left for the airport to fly back to Philadelphia, we got Mother a roast beef takeout dinner to eat that evening after we would be gone. Her only request was for double mashed potatoes. I started to protest and urge her to get some vegies instead, but Linda just looked at me and said, "Get the double mashed!" Mutti's recently placed trust in Linda was validated. I went back several times to say goodbye as we headed off to catch our plane. We intended to be back soon after the conservatorship was in place to get Mother situated in a safer environment. Little did I realize that we would be back sooner than planned.

25

KADDISH

On a hot August day in 1991, my sister left a phone message with my son while I was out getting a haircut. As I returned her call, I prepared myself for the news. Mutti was picked up by the police, brought to Culver Memorial, put under heavy sedation, try to call her tomorrow. However, this time there was a long silence, then the tearful news from Monika, "Peter, Mutti died." The sense of loss that we felt over a lifetime became searingly real with its finality. There was no more hope of her ever getting better. We took no comfort in the cliché, "It is all for the best. She is in a better place."

Mutti had sent us each a postcard the day before she died with a sweet greeting and expressions of love, as if nothing were wrong. Now Linda and I were flying back to LA to join Monika in making funeral arrangements. First, we wanted to know exactly what happened but couldn't find out much more than the basic facts. She collapsed in front of Mike Caruso's Menswear and was taken to the Santa Monica Medical Center in an ambulance. There were no details, no way to talk to anybody who might have witnessed how it happened. She was just another old person who vanished from the scene. At least she died freely out and about in Santa Monica with her sandals on.

The death certificate stated the immediate cause of death: cardiac arrest, due to myocardial infarction and atherosclerosis. The contributing cause of death was ten years of arterial sclerosis, which she had never mentioned to us although she had been under the care of the doctor who had diagnosed it.

We went to pick up her belongings, a small cloth purse instead of the designer bag I had bought her. Her watch was missing. There were only a few scraps of paper and a few pennies in her bag. I signed some papers to receive what had been brought with her to the hospital. The guard explained that things tend to disappear when a person dies on the street. In the end, Mutti had it her own way. She triumphed over the system because she died independent and free from institutionalization. We were spared having to become her conservators. She beat us to the punch. She took care of everything. There was enough money in her account to cover a burial plot, pay for the funeral, and take care of the small debts she left behind.

Grief gave way to practicalities as we arranged the funeral. Mutti had always said she preferred a no-frills Orthodox burial in a plain pine casket, so we decided on Glasband-Willen, an Orthodox mortuary in the familiar Fairfax district which I had known growing up. The neighborhood had become home to a lot of Russian Jews and looked much like it had years ago, only a bit run down. I felt ashamed and guilty, and rushed through the arrangements at the mortuary with Monika. I did not want to see my mother's body and learned that according to Jewish tradition this is okay. I hadn't known that it is considered disrespectful to look at the deceased because they can't look back. My reasons had little to do with respect. I just didn't want to take in the finality of Mutti's death.

The sympathetic funeral director recommended Rabbi Levin to conduct the service. I immediately called to fill him in about Mother's life, her years as a refugee, and struggle with manic depression. Just a few facts about her, he assured me, would help him sum things up on the burial day. The graveside ceremony was scheduled for August 25, eight days after her death. I assumed we had to hasten the burial date, not realizing that although Jewish tradition requires quick burial, the essential tradition is all about respecting the needs and feelings of the family and the dignity of those who died. There was so little I knew about Jewish tradition. I thought that there were all kinds of requirements that had to be met, no matter what. Instead, it was about

Kavod Hamet – honoring the dead and attending to the feelings of the mourners.

The funeral director of California's First Jewish Mortuary gave Monika and me each seven-day candles for sitting *shiva*, and we later paid the rabbi $300 dollars to say kaddish three times a day for 11 months minus a week. This came to 33 cents a prayer, a bargain for getting God's attention.

Linda helped me get through the aftermath of Mutti's death. We spent time at Mother's apartment and took stock of her belongings to be divided and given away. This was emotionally draining for both of us. Cleaning and emptying out her apartment evoked a mixture of sadness and weariness. I felt wistful seeing the lovingly placed Judaica, photos, and familiar knickknacks on her wooden sideboard for the last time. I felt like an intruder dismantling the remnants of her life. Linda's presence helped me to diffuse my guilty feelings as I sorted orphaned possessions and intrusive memories.

A lot of things were given away to the downstairs neighbors, who had just claim to some form of reparation because of the ruckus Mother caused. One neighbor took in her cat. We gave Mother's plants to her social worker, but told him that Mother's best furniture "was spoken for." We managed to give some things away to charity. Much was put out in the trash. Monika and I divided up photos and keepsakes. I wound up with a suitcase of diaries and writings. Whatever keepsake furniture remained went to Monika's household in Santa Maria.

To get rid of the fleas, I had set off a bug bomb so that Linda and I could stay in the apartment. We took walks in the world Mother had known. We headed west on Wilshire, then left along Ocean Avenue, up and down the Santa Monica Pier, then down to 1746 Ocean Avenue to where our cousins' hotel once stood. We slept in her bed as she had done, capturing the cool, gentle breezes from the Pacific as we lay talking about her. We ate at the restaurants she liked, including Café Casino on Ocean Avenue, and strolled by Mike Caruso's on Wilshire where she bought me the tie I would cut at the funeral, to follow the Jewish keriah tradition of tearing garments to represent the tear in the fabric of the family when a loved one dies.

On the day of the funeral, we took the Santa Monica Freeway from Lincoln Boulevard to East Los Angeles, then the Long Beach Freeway to exit 19, right onto Southeastern Ave until we reached the Home of Peace Memorial Park, located behind a wall in Whittier, California. Within sight of palm trees planted decades ago, this Jewish cemetery boasted large mausoleums that paid tribute to the once well-heeled deceased. In that respect, it was not so different from Weissensee, the cemetery in Berlin where Mother's father and grandparents were buried.

Monika and John, accompanied by their sons, Ian and Peter, arrived from Santa Maria. Resi and Fred Silberstein, the only representatives from the Berlin *mishpachah*, were there along with their very glamorous daughter, Marion, who alighted from the car in a skimpy miniskirt which Mutti would have loved. Marion seemed to have been genuinely fond of Mother who had been fond of her. Accompanying Marion was her husband, Steven, who sneezed a lot. Cousin Fred stayed away and did not acknowledge Mother's passing, but I think that was because of hard feelings toward Monika and me, not toward her. Ted and Elly sent their condolences.

Bill Wintersole was there, as was Mother's best friend, Evelyn, plus her son, Corky. Corky, dying of AIDS, sat off to the side, depressed. He and Evelyn loved Mutti with a genuine appreciation for her free spirit. With them, Mutti had always felt liberated from her history. Tim arrived late with Tom, an official from the Santa Monica Housing Authority who had known her and had helped her get one of her apartments. They had gotten lost exiting the Santa Monica Freeway on the way to the funeral. Rabbi Levin, whom I had only spoken to by phone, was there ready to conduct the service. Mother's plot was in the King David Section, Row S, Grave 76, a stone's throw from the row of upscale mausoleums. She would have liked the idea of being buried under the two small trees that sheltered her grave. We were sad when these trees were later cut down to make room for additional graves.

Our small group of funeral attendees made a semi-circle. We winced at the cliché condolences, "It's for the best," "Her suffering is over," "It's good she went quickly." I tried to be businesslike about the whole matter, wanting everything to come off well. Monika, who had expected to break down, managed to hold back most of the tears. Rabbi Levin reminded us that Judaism does an excellent job of making our memory of the dead eternal. He began by reiterating the facts about Mutti that I had provided him. He said that Mother would continue to live through the cherished memories of her friends and relatives, and that prayers for the dead support the collective memory of those who have passed, only he said it with memorable eloquence and grace for which we were grateful.

Then came a somewhat unexpected, but not wholly welcome diversion. Rabbi Avrohom Levitansky, who had kicked Mutti out of the Chabad House for overstepping the boundaries of propriety, showed up. I had informed him of Mutti's death as a courtesy, but he just chided me for not following Orthodox rules for burial such as ritual washing of the body, burial within 48 hours. I shared his reaction with Rabbi Levin, who was Orthodox but not Hassidic. He promised me that he would take care of Rabbi Levitansky if he came. Rabbi Levin called the shots as promised, acknowledging his younger colleague's presence but limiting his role to being the first to shovel dirt on the casket when the time came. Mother would have enjoyed the two-rabbi send off.

Mutti was buried among palm trees, about as far from the Holy Land as you can get. Often taken for being Mexican because of her dark complexion, it seems only fitting that her burial place is near a Mexican American neighborhood. She always liked her Chicano neighbors and made sure to learn a few sentences of Spanish so she could exchange pleasantries.

After the service, we met at Mutti's favorite restaurant, Bob Burns, on Wilshire Boulevard. The idea was to tell fond "Maria stories." Tim and Tom told how she took on the Santa Monica Redevelopment Authority, successfully fighting the impending eviction of tenants by railing against the "ugly, money-grubbing development" that engulfed Santa Monica. They marveled at her ability to work the system in getting a rent-controlled apartment, north of Wilshire only a few blocks from the beach, for only $240 a month. It all felt anticlimactic and inconsequential listening to these strangers talk about her as if they knew her, which of course they did, just not the way we knew her.

There was little we wanted to add. Her ordeal was finally over, and it was time to get her affairs in order. We closed her bank accounts, notified Social Security, and turned over her keys to the landlord who was relieved to have her out. While at her bank, Linda and I ran into the lovely woman who had played castanets to accompany her flamenco dancing at Mother's last birthday party. She was so sad to hear of Mother's death and insisted that we take advantage of the free coffee station offered by the bank so we could sit and talk about her friend.

In the months that followed, letters came from the few remaining significant people in her life – Rudi in England, Jenny in Belgium, Monika's father in Germany, and then my father in Italy. They all knew her when she was a young woman and had no real idea of the challenges she faced at the end of her life.

Monika's father sent a note and enclosed money for Monika to buy some flowers to put on her grave. Rudi and Jenny wrote sweet letters of condolence. When my wife, Linda, and I visited Rudi and Emmy Sabor in England not long after my mother died, Rudi described his fond memories of the Jewish Girls School and its sense of purpose and solidarity that harbored the students and teachers from the fear and despair outside its walls. He praised Mary's beautiful singing voice and regretted that she didn't have the opportunity to realize its potential. Rudi and the other teachers at school opened Mary's eyes to the world's possibilities, the finer things in art and music that she would value for the rest of her life.

Six months after Mother died, our son, Nick, was at home to take a condolence call from my father, who never mentioned that call in the letter he sent later to acknowledge Mother's passing.

> It was not altogether unexpected to hear of your mother's death. I sensed that something had happened to her when I failed to get her unfailing reminder of my birthday with the usual pleas to "let bygones be bygones." I went to the American Embassy in Rome with the intention of finding your phone number and calling you but then though better of it.

In a self-involved explanation, he revisited the trouble Mother caused him to explain why he hadn't written for a while and went on to reminisce.

I sometimes asked myself how I should feel when I received news that Mary had died. When I met her for the first time, she was a nurse in the Radcliffe Infirmary, and I was stoking the night fires at Cowley Hospital to pay college dues (later I was given a grant). I am down here trying to get the past into accurate focus from cuttings and letters which I have kept as well as from the story she wrote about her life. It was in 1985 I think she sent me this asking me to try and find her an editor. One of things I have always wanted to do and like many others have left undone was to come over and see you and discuss reorganizing all her writings which I still have. Lack of money was the chief reason for never doing this but there was also the problem of how to handle Mary without having further trouble. I feel very bad about all this waste of genuine effort on your mother's part to try and do something with her life when I think I might have been able to do something to help her. The thought revives my feelings for her at Oxford when she was desperately trying to be independent but couldn't stand the discipline of a hospital. When she came knocking at the door one day to tell me she had jumped over the wall, I shared rooms just opposite with Leonard Nicholson, a communist statistician lecturing at the university. I remember my surprise at Nicholson's willingness to let her share my room. But we were all extreme leftists, and a Polish girl refugee from Nazi persecution added the necessary touch of exotic realism to the intellectual marxism of Nicholson and the Stalinist dour socialism of a Scots lecturer in economics who lived in the flat above with his girlfriend. I had come up to the university from a military prison camp after being court-martialed for the second time, and Mary was my first feminine experience after two and a half years of jankers and jails. I still have McLaren's paperback, *The Nature of Society* which made more impression on me than anything I had read of Marx. With a group of fellow travelers, I had founded The October Society, anti-Stalin and broadly Trotskyist. It was tolerated by Nicholson but treated with contempt and hostility by the Scottish economist and his girlfriend. She had deserted a noble family to join the proletariat but had lost nothing of her haughty sense of superiority. This isn't the right moment for me to continue these reminiscences which help me to get back to my state of mind at the time, but I'll pick up the threads again in the future – the only way in which I can try and explain my feelings about your mother. News of her end was a big pang, and though I'm not in a state to want to know more details, I hope there will be time shortly when we can meet, and you can tell me more.

After wrapping up his feelings about her death as a "big pang," Denis wrote about his struggles to make a living doing translations, his health issues as a 75-year-old, and the success of Fausta in making a living restoring old masters for Rome's museums. He wrote, "She sends you and family all best wishes and joins me in the condolences for the sad passing of the dark woman in my (and of course your) life."

I was put off by his letter and didn't write him. I found his "honesty" disingenuous. He wrote again in 1993, two years after Mutti's death. His letter touched on the same repetitive themes of his life as an expat, his inability to find steady work as a foreigner in Italy and hopes for cashing in on a writing project. Again, he mentioned coming to the United States to help me with the biography about Mother, but like so many things he promised, I knew that would never happen.

There were no letters in the next few years. In 2000, I finally wrote to his old address in Umbria, with no reply. I wondered if he had died and contacted the British Consulate in Rome to get his address. They contacted him, and we resumed our pattern of occasional letters. By this time, he was in his eighties. In 2003, Linda and I went to Rome to visit him and Fausta. It was obvious that his health was failing, and we kept our visits to his apartment brief. Our conversation often shifted to his film, *Together*, and to his life as a semi-invalid. We never mentioned my mother, letting bygones be bygones, and we got to know Fausta who was warm and hospitable. As we conversed over a lovely dinner at their apartment one evening, I felt like this was something we might have done again and again had we lived nearer.

A year later in January, I received a distraught telephone call from Fausta informing me that my father had died at the age of 89. He was buried in Rome. His death notice was online in Italian: "*Nome*: Denis Faulkner *Nascita*: 10 Aprile 1915. *Morte*: 14 Gennaio 2004. *Luogo di sepoltura*: Roma (RM), Cimitero Flaminio." I was deeply saddened by his death and regretted the emotional and physical distance that defined our relationship. There would be no more amends. In 2015, we visited Fausta during a family trip. It did not occur to me to visit Denis's grave during this short stay. Fausta took a sincere interest in us and in our children and grandchildren, and she has become a good friend. We didn't talk about Denis much.

26

HOLOCAUST PILGRIMAGE

A decade after we came to America in 1954, Mutti began thinking of how to memorialize the death of her mother. Since there was no separate grave for her in Riga where she was buried in a mass grave, she decided to arrange to have her name added to her father's new headstone for his grave in Weissensee. Although Mutti knew by 1942 that her mother had been deported to Riga and killed there, she wasn't sure how she was killed or where she was buried. Several years after we arrived in America, she still thought that her mother may have been gassed in the train on the way to Riga. By 1975, she definitely knew that Gertrud Krotoczynski died in the Rumbula massacre, the second largest after Babi Yar. Knowing this compelled her to request that the phrase, "Gertrud Krotoczynski shot in Riga" be added to the inscription on her father's tombstone in Weissensee cemetery. She wanted people to know about the abhorrent circumstances of her death.

The location of Weissensee cemetery in East Berlin before the wall came down may explain why it took ten years to fulfill her request. Finally in 1986, just five years before her own death, she received a letter from the cemetery that her father's tombstone was erected and engraved as she envisioned.

There was another unresolved issued related to the death of her parents. Mother told me that her first failing was to have been born a girl because her father wanted a boy who would say kaddish for him after his death. That explains why she kickstarted my bar mitzvah and why I have always been prepared for that deed by keeping a yarmulke handy in case I had the opportunity to say kaddish for him. This mission also took a long while to complete.

In 1987, two years before the Berlin Wall fell, my son, Ezra, went to Berlin with his German class while he was a student at the Quaker-run George School near where we live in Newtown, Pa. He told his teacher that his great-grandfather was buried in the east sector which wasn't on the group's itinerary. On the spur of the moment, his teacher agreed to cross over to the communist sector with Ezra to visit his great-grandfather's grave. After wandering about asking directions for the Jewish cemetery, they finally ended up at the well-known Old Jewish Cemetery but didn't find anyone there to help find Stephan Krotoczynski's grave.

Linda and I traveled to Berlin on business in 1999, 12 years after Ezra's visit and eight years after German reunification. Then there was no Checkpoint Charlie, and it was easy to explore the eastern part of the city to look for my grandfather's grave. I wasn't sure of the name of the cemetery but remembered that it had seemed very old to me as a child. So we started out on our first day to the Old Jewish Cemetery, which our son had visited. It turned out that this venerable cemetery was mostly a resting place for notables, such as Moses Mendelssohn, who died more than a century before Stephan Krotoczynski's time. The next day, we had the good fortune to be overheard on the U-Bahn talking about our search for my grandfather's grave by someone who knew a great deal more than we did. Elisa Klapheck, then a journalist and now a prominent rabbi, asked us a few questions, then told us that it was more likely that Stephan Krotoczynski's grave would be in the Jewish Cemetery Weissensee, the second largest Jewish cemetery in Europe, established in 1880 and located in the former East Berlin. She was right.

I finally had the opportunity to say kaddish for my grandfather and grandmother at their "shared" grave site, but it wasn't that simple. I had brought the required kippah but needed to find my grandfather's grave as well as those of my great grandparents among the hundreds of graves at Weissensee. A reluctant staff member at the cemetery information office gave us a map and put an "x" to indicate where the graves were located. We wandered around and found my grandfather's grave near the perimeter of the cemetery. I stood by the headstone engraved with the names of both my grandparents and finally had the opportunity to fulfill my mitzvah. We then found the graves of my Silberstein great grandparents in a section of elaborate headstones that reflected the prosperity of the Jewish community in the Berlin that once was.

After our trip, I began the long process of going through the documents in Mutti's red suitcase, including her autobiography, with the intention of writing about her life and family. Sure enough, buried in her papers, I found correspondence that contained information about the location of my grandfather's grave. The Weissensee information was in the suitcase all along, intended for me to use when I got to Berlin as Mutti must have known I would! I realized how few details I had discussed with her about our family's roots and her efforts to memorialize her parents. But I had vividly remembered how she looked the night in 1952 when she took me and my sister to visit her father's grave at an old Jewish cemetery just before she was about to be hospitalized for depression. Now I know that the old Weissensee cemetery in my memory is not to be confused with Mendelssohn's Old Jewish Cemetery in Mitte.

In 2005, Linda and I traveled to Berlin for a conference. We explored the city, visited my grandfather's grave again, and spent a day wandering around Oranienburger Straße, which was once the hub of the Jewish community. We looked for the Jüdische Mädchenschule that Mutti fondly remembered and found the building on 11-13 Auguststraße vacant and shuttered. According to the plaque at the entrance, this building had once been a hospital and a school, but it did not mention specifically that it was the Jewish Girls School. Later we found out that the Nazis closed the school on June 30th, 1942, three years after Mutti left Berlin on the Kindertransport. By then, many of its pupils and teachers had been deported and presumably murdered in death camps. In 1950, it was reopened and named the Berthold Brecht Secondary School. This school closed due to lack of enrollment after German reunification in 1996. In 2009, the building was officially returned to the Jewish community through the Jewish Claims Conference.

After stopping at the Mädchenschule, we took a short walk to the Neue Synagogue that had been rebuilt after the War. We attended an exhibit of photos by Joseph Pisarek depicting Jewish life in Berlin Mitte during the 1930s. Linda had a hunch that we would see a picture of my mother there, and sure enough, after we passed through the security checkpoint, we entered the exhibit area where Linda flipped through a succession of photos in an old-fashioned rotary photograph viewer that was under glass. She thought she spotted Mother in a photo of a school play and kept repeating the sequence of photos several times to confirm her suspicions before calling me over to see it.

The school play pictured in the photo was about Rabbi Akiva, the great scholar and legendary teacher, one of the greatest folk heroes in Jewish culture. We talked to the director of the Neue Synagogue who arranged for us to obtain a copy of this photo from the Pisarek collection, and later we sent a copy to her former schoolmate, Jenny, who confirmed that it was Mother in the photo.

On a business trip to Berlin in 2006, I visited the Neue Synagogue again and met with its research director, Dr. Chana Schütz, to find out more about the Mädchenschule. She took me to the abandoned building on Auguststraße where, after entering its dark and empty shell, we came across the papier-mâché set of the school play about Rabbi Akiva. Dr. Schütz told me that there were plans in the works for the Jewish community to acquire the building and to develop it commercially.

In 2012, the Mädchenschule was reopened as a cultural center that included the Michael Fuchs Gallery, restaurants and a Kennedy Museum that has since closed. Visitors are informed about the architectural and historical significance of this building that was designed in the New Objectivity style by the Jewish architect, Alexander Beer, who later died in Theresienstadt with his family.

Mother had such fond memories of her school. It was up to me to be sure that our family knew about the history and survival of the building of her beloved Mädchenschule. I went on the web to learn more about how this sturdy and well-designed school building had been repurposed as a cultural center. In May 2016, I saw online that there was an exhibit in the Michael Fuchs Art Gallery by Tomi Ungerer, which featured *Cul-de-Sac,* a painting depicting the lower torso of a naked woman wearing high heels, sitting on the rear of a motorcycle with the California license plate, number 644552, heading down a highway into the sunset. Mother would have loved the brash irony of this triumph of what the Nazis would have called "Degenerate Art" hanging in her old school. I would continue my quest to delve further into the history of 11-13 Auguststraße, but many unknowns will remain. Teachers and students from school who perished during the Holocaust are among the millions of forgotten Holocaust victims. There are no alumni groups or reunions or class photos to remember them by. What was once an educational oasis in Nazi Berlin is now another kind of oasis to celebrate brave new Berlin with a nod to its Weimar past.

In 2018, Linda and I traveled again to Berlin before going on to Riga, Krakow and Warsaw. On top of our list was a visit to see for ourselves the repurposed school building. We met with Dr. Schütz at the Neue Synagogue Research Department whom I had met years before. Her colleague, Barbara Welker, joined in to help us learn more about my mother's school and to locate records pertaining to the local Jewish Community during the prewar years. I asked whether there was any chance of locating records of the students and teachers who attended the Jewish Girls School under the auspices of the Jewish Community. If so, I hoped these could be matched up with the Yad Vashem database in Israel to find out who survived and who didn't. Frau Welker explained that many records from that period were destroyed; however, she suggested that information might be gleaned about some former students who lived at Ahawah, a Jewish orphanage several doors down the street on Auguststraße.[1]

When we entered the repurposed building, we saw a small exhibit in the hallway that provided information about the former Mädchenschule. We were surprised to see the same photograph of the "Rabbi Akiva" players we had found earlier at the Neue Synagogue. There was my mother on the wall of her old school for all to see among a group of girls in costumes. They all looked so innocent. Later that day, we met with Frau Ulrike Gardeler at the firm, 40 Grüntuch-Ernst Architects, who explained how she and her colleagues sought to preserve the original character and look of the school as it was designed by Alexander Beer. They wanted to honor its history while supporting the building's current uses as a cultural and dining destination.

Between visits to Berlin, I had made progress at home with historical and genealogical research. I retrieved more detailed information from the Yad Vashem database about the deportation and deaths of my grandmother and other relatives in Berlin. Genealogy services like Ancestry.com provided additional personal information about my family and the places where they lived.

I read about the German artist, Gunter Demnig, who had the idea to commemorate victims of Nazi persecution on a personal level by placing stones called "*Stolpersteine*" in the sidewalks at the last address where they lived by choice before fleeing or being deported. Each of the Stolpersteine is the size of a cobblestone and has a brass cap engraved with the name and life dates of the victim. The first one was laid by Demnig in Cologne in 1992. As part of an art project in 1996, he placed Stolpersteine at the last known addresses of 50 Jews who had lived in the East Berlin district of Kreuzberg before being deported. His project spread widely, and on May 26, 2023, the number of Stolpersteine placed across Europe reached one hundred thousand.

I emailed the Stolpersteine Project in Berlin to inquire about the possibility of Stolpersteine for my mother and her parents. In response, I was invited to submit a full application and to meet with project volunteers in Berlin to identify the site of my family's address in an area that had been completely redeveloped after the war.

While in Berlin in 2018, we met Mary, an English volunteer who lived in Berlin. She helped us locate where my grandparents' last address, Walnertheaterstrasse 3, had been. The street is now called Holzmarktstrasse and is adjacent to public housing and a school in East Berlin. Mary showed us several Stolpersteine in this neighborhood. She asked us whether we would be interested in working with teachers and students at the Max Planck Gymnasium, a high school in the neighborhood that was interested in sponsoring our

Stolpersteine project. We were delighted to cooperate and completed the application process. Though delayed because of Covid, the ceremony plans were delayed to 2023.

In 2018, we also visited various historic sites related to the Holocaust, starting with the memorial at Gleis 17 [Track 17] of Grunewald train station where my grandmother, Gertrud, and more than 50,000 Berlin Jews boarded trains headed for ghettos and concentration camps in Theresienstadt, Minsk, Riga, Kaunas and Lodz. Several transports went directly to Auschwitz-Birkenau and other death camps. My grandmother boarded one of the first trains, Da 31, in late November 1941 with 942 other Berlin Jews. This train passed through Frankfurt an der Oder, Posen, Warsaw, Bialystok, Kowno, and the Riga Ghetto. The Riga Skirotova Railway Station was the final stop.

All along the tracks at Gleis 17 are grates that serve as memorial plaques, each engraved with the date, destination, and number of passengers for each of the fateful trains. Linda and I placed flowers on the one for Gertrud's train. Nearby, a family with two children were down on the tracks, lighting a candle. Many mourners had left stones to honor loved ones. What struck me was the total absence of the names of those who boarded the trains.

Afterwards, we took a train to another memorial site, the Wannsee Conference, located at a major lakeside tourist destination. Nazis met there on January 20, 1942, to plan the deportation and murder of European Jews, about a month after my grandmother was deported. One of the participants in the Wannsee Conference was SS-Sturmbannführer Rudolf Lang who was the coordinator of Einsatzgruppe A, a mobile squad of killers, who had already enlisted Latvian collaborators to help carry out the massacre of Jews in Rumbula Forest, seven miles from Riga, Latvia.

About 25,000 Jews were buried in six mass graves at Rumbula, including Gertrud Krotoczynski and my great aunt Anna Baumgardt who arrived there later. The gruesome details were provided by perpetrators who described the mass killings as a planned military operation. There were accounts by survivors, one of them, Frida Michelson, wrote about what she saw in her book, *I Survived Rumbula*, originally published in 1979: "As we came to the forest, we heard shooting again. This was the horrible portent of our future. If I had any doubts about the intentions of our tormenters, they were all gone now ... We were all numb with terror and followed orders mechanically. We were incapable of thinking and were submitting to everything like a docile herd of cattle."

The massacres in Latvia were kept out of public view until 1964 when the Soviet-era authorities allowed the placement of a memorial stone at Rumbula with the inscription, "To the victims of fascism" in Yiddish as well as Latvian and Russian. This stone replaced a previous plaque in Yiddish that was placed in 1963. Finally, in 2002, the Rumbula Memorial was completed, 11 years after Latvia's independence from the Soviet Union. It was funded by individuals and organizations from the United States, Germany, Israel, and Latvia.

When we got to Latvia to see where Gertrud died and to honor her memory, we were lucky to find a wonderful guide, Yelena, a Latvian of Russian descent. We asked her to take us to the memorial burial grounds in Rumbula Forest on the outskirts of Riga. Before heading out, she drove us through the streets of the former Riga Ghetto to visit the Latvian Holocaust Museum. On the ground outside the museum were cobblestones from the Riga Ghetto that led to steps where visitors could see and step inside a railroad car, the kind used to transport Jews to Riga. On a wall were photographs of Jews in the process of being deported. One was of an older woman, alone in a crowd of people, who resembled my grandmother. Perhaps she was.

Rabbi Barkahan, who helped found the museum, greeted us in the gift shop and explained his work to honor those murdered in Latvia. He said that all victims of genocide, Jewish and non-Jewish, should be remembered, a belief he put into practice by mounting an exhibit on the Armenian genocide at his museum. Linda took a picture of us, two old men of about the same age. Rabbi Barkahan had a wonderful beard and a smile that reflected his loving, positive attitude.

We bought his book, *Extermination of the Jews in Latvia 1941-1945*. I asked him about current attitudes about the Holocaust in Latvia, he shook his head and laughed. He said that the fate of the Jewish people in Latvia is not a primary concern. Latvians prefer to focus on their own victimization by the Russians as well as by the Germans. Many deny Latvian complicity in the murder of Jews and place most of the blame squarely on the Nazis. Local involvement also facilitated the killings of Jews in neighboring Lithuania, where more than 200,000 Jews were killed over a three-year period by the Nazis and local militias. In Estonia, 1,000 Jews were murdered in addition to many ethnic Estonians and Russians, for the most part Soviet prisoners, and also Jews deported from other parts of Europe.

Rabbi Barkahan gave us a Jahrzeit candle and led us to a wall covered with a list of the names of the thousands of victims murdered in Riga. I found where Gertrud Krotoczynski was listed, then lit and placed the candle at the foot of the memorial. After we told him that we were going to Rumbula to say kaddish for my grandmother, he said that her spirit would always have a true home at his memorial museum despite the violence perpetrated on her in Riga.

Afterwards, Jelena drove us several miles out of town down a wide highway until we came across a sculpture of tangled branches and leaves that form an arch at the entrance of the Rumbula Forest Memorial. There were outdoor sculptures and installations, including the demarcation of six burial pits among the trees of the forest. The names of a few of the victims were etched on stones placed around the central memorial installation.

The extent of Latvian complicity in the Rumbula Massacre is acknowledged today in the terse inscription at the site: "Here, on November 30 and December 8 of 1941, the Nazis and their Latvian collaborators shot to death more than 25,000 Jews who were prisoners of the Riga Ghetto – children, women, elderly men, and approximately 1,000 Jews who had been deported from Germany. In the summer of 1944, hundreds of Jewish men from the Riga-Kaiserwald concentration camp were also killed here."

With all the heavy history in mind, I struggled to be composed so that I could finally say kaddish for my grandmother after years of anticipation. Jelena said it was likely that my grandmother's remains were in the pit closest to the railroad tracks since she arrived on the first train. We found the likely location. I put on my yarmulke and placed a stone among the ones left by other mourners. Linda and Jelena waited for me as I wandered off to say kaddish within sight of the tracks from where my grandmother and others were forced to march to a clearing in the forest. There was silence other than the surrounding natural sounds as I began to recite the prayer. I spent a brief period in meditation before I rejoined Linda and Jelena. There was still more to know about this atrocity that I didn't want to take in.

It's hard to believe there would have been anything in their experience that would have prepared my grandmother and the other victims for what would come. The SS clustered people into groups and ordered them to relinquish their belongings, strip off their clothing, and descend into the pit. According to first-hand accounts the SS and their Latvian accomplices forced them to line up to be shot, or to lay face down to be killed by gunshots to the head.

After visiting the Rumbula Memorial, Linda and I flew to Krakow for an unsettling visit to Auschwitz where more than a million people perished, including Mother's aunt, Paula Schlamm, and her best friend, Thea. Today, Auschwitz is a world heritage site visited by millions of tourists every year. For some, Auschwitz-Birkenau is primarily a crime scene and for others it is a place for mourning relatives at the consecrated area near the location of the Birkenau crematoria that no longer exist today. But this is not anything like a regular cemetery that would visibly document the names as well as the dates of birth and death of the individuals interred.

Our Polish guide at Auschwitz discussed the unimaginable scale of extermination at Auschwitz-Birkenau where over a million of those who died were Jewish men, women, and children. She mentioned that thousands of Polish victims also died, along with Roma, Sinti, and prisoners from several European countries. Up to early 1942, Auschwitz functioned as a typical concentration camp where many inmates died of deliberate starvation, illness, and maltreatment. Afterwards, Auschwitz became the main destination for Jews transported for work or extermination. As soon as their trains arrived, the new Auschwitz inmates were divided quickly into two groups, those who were fit for work and those who were not. Those judged to be unsuitable for forced labor went to the gas chambers.

We walked to the memorial site marking the former location of the Birkenau death chambers that the Nazis reduced to rubble after abandoning Auschwitz. I thought about Thea's husband, Edgar, who participated in the development of the death chambers. In his account after the war, he mentions that the chambers were designed with phony signs to deceive arrivals about the nature of what went on within.

In 1959, seven years after his meeting with my mother, Edgar testified about his work as a camp electrician at a hearing, which was documented by Bruno Baum in his work about resistance activities in Auschwitz.[2] Edgar and Bruno may have known each other in Berlin at Siemens before they were inmates in Auschwitz where they provided support for developing the mass extermination facilities that involved Siemens personnel and technology. While there is documentation of Baum as an active communist during the prewar years, there is no evidence that Steinmetz was active politically.

Baum included the text of Steinmetz's testimony in his book because it gave credence to corporate culpability in Auschwitz. Since the Nazis destroyed the crematoria to hide evidence of their crimes, Steinmetz's testimony was useful in contradicting Holocaust deniers. He testified at a hearing:

> I was the foreman of an inmate electrician column. In this capacity I got to know the crematoria. These were four crematoria listed separately from each other; a fifth was decommissioned because it was too small. Each crematorium had five incineration ovens, each with three fires. The gas chambers were located under the combustion furnaces. These were accessible from the outside by stairs, and there was a slide for the sick. At the entrance there was the inscription "Bathroom" [for washing up] in all the languages in question. Below were, besides the dressing room, the actual gas chambers...usually a large gas chamber and several small ones. The gasification plants were sufficient to gas up to 20,000 people in a 24-hour period. In some cases, the crematoria were not sufficient, and the type of cremation incineration in open pits, which was common until the crematoria were built, had to be used. This often happened in the early summer of 1944.

Edgar Steinmetz's testimony was essential in describing the technical aspects of the mass killings at Auschwitz and implicating Siemens employees in the process. He had full knowledge of the operations, and was aware that certain components, such as the exhausters for the technical extractors of the gasification plants, were made by Siemens. He knew some Siemens employees who came to Auschwitz, including one named "Ernst" from the cable plant in Berlin with whom he supervised the laying of a 30,000-volt cable to supply the Weischel Union Metallwerke factory. This was a munitions factory known as the "Union" set up at Auschwitz to utilize forced labor. The Union employed about 2,000 prisoners, mostly young Jewish women, many of whom lost fingers operating metal stamping machines. In late summer 1944, Edgar also met with people from Siemens - TB Katowice who built the transformers as well as the disinfection system for the camp, all made from Siemens components.[3]

I wondered what I would have done if I were in Edgar's shoes. Would I have tried to survive at any cost? Would I have committed suicide out of despair, or participated in risky resistance activities? If given the chance, would I have opted for survival as a privileged worker or even a Kapo? Like many of my fellow visitors, I was never forced to make such choices under horrific circumstances.

After taking a whiff of spring air at the Birkenau memorial site, I saw mourners honor their loved ones by lighting candles and saying kaddish. Some had placed papers with names on them under small rocks to commemorate their identities, if only fleetingly. Near the platform where the death trains once arrived, I spotted a patch of yellow chrysanthemums on a meadow that might have been seen by prisoners before they entered the gas chambers.

27

KAVOD HAMET

Kavod Hamet is Hebrew for honoring and showing respect for the dead. It is the precept that guides the Jewish approach to death and mourning. Saying the Mourner's kaddish is done to glorify God at a time when one would be most likely to cave into despair. The dead are honored, and the living affirm their faith. Whatever guidelines Judaism offers in resolving the conundrum of mourning with respect to the deceased, the focus clearly extends to the mitigation of grief for those left behind.

Jewish sons and daughters say kaddish for their parents and quietly light a Jahrzeit candle on the anniversary of their deaths. Although Mother did that for her parents, I have not followed this Jewish tradition because I am not one for such religious practices. Instead, I took her at her word that she wanted to be remembered by having her story told. I went through the autobiographical writings, letters, photos and documents that she preserved for posterity so that there would be an explanation, a way of lighting another kind of candle for her that would do her justice. She wanted the unvarnished truth, to hide nothing. Most of all, she did not want to be forgotten and would have been happy to have Jahrzeit candles lit for her, too.

In this memoir, I have revisited scenes from her life and our times together as a family, scattered snapshots that evoke memories from assorted time periods in three countries. I can hear her voice threading through the images with reverberating snippets of things she said about her life. I can almost hear her say, "Remember, I am a Leo. I am the life of the party!" How well she learned the perils of being the center of attention. Her sense of irony did not necessarily serve her well, especially in later life when everything seemed too late. There was a price to pay for being too young at heart. "Always listen to your mother," she'd enjoin, knowing that she never really listened to her own advice, or ours.

When she was up against the expectations of others who didn't understand the clarity of existential pleasure, she could be thick skinned. "I am a fighter," she often said sardonically, confident that she would get back up on her feet before the final count. Mutti would talk about her secrets for muddling through. She had her recipes for living life large when she could, and living small while the bipolar roller coaster nemesis held sway.

Everything was okay for the moment, so long as she kept moving. She papered over recurring depression, easily made friends, was keen in her ability to know when she "hit it off." Her sonorous British-flavored English, with a faint hint of German, could be beguiling. But the pain of losing her parents and family never went away and could often be seen in her eyes. It defined her legacy and our painful inheritance.

For a lifetime, Mutti depended on her circle of friends and acquaintances, but with age and limited mobility, her circle shrank. Alone with her cat and surrounded by art posters, she mounted a collage of photos of her family and friends on the wall that she rearranged and "edited" by cropping their edges mercilessly. "Animals are better than people," she quipped. "They never disappoint me." She wasn't always joking when she told us that her cat was her only true friend. We were too far away and "too busy" to give her back the time she needed. Underneath her declaration of personal independence was the realization that her mental illness created a barrier between her and her children.

There were reasons for that. Mutti's needs led to the exhaustion of those close to her. It has not been easy to squelch my resentment of the impact my mother's mental illness has had on my life, yet I feel an unfailing love for her. Over time, I came to recognize the depth of my sadness for being unable to rescue her from the heinous legacy of Nazi crimes and the demons of mental illness. My inner voice tells me I should be grateful for having had the opportunity to lead the normal life she had always wanted – a career, a wonderful marriage, and children. Perhaps I could have done more for her while she was alive. Now that she is gone, my calling is to honor her memory by writing and thinking about her, and to work with others to resist the politics of injustice that pave the way to persecution and genocide.

Mutti spent many hours of her life alone, often in silence. She looked forward to hearing from Monika and me, and said she was overjoyed to see us when we came. She told people she had "such wonderful children," as if to prompt us to prove ourselves worthy. With faint praise, she acknowledged the success of our separate lives and told us how much she valued her freedom whenever we lectured her on what would be best for her.

Mutti produced an extensive set of fanciful pencil drawings in a unique style about humble members of the animal kingdom. She portrayed tiny "innocent" creatures, usually ants, caterpillars, and snails that called out for her protection. She wanted us to take pleasure in observing the visible lives of these humble beings and believed that we could benefit from their "wisdom." Humans also appeared in her drawings, often in whimsical poses. Mutti's flirtation with pantheism removed her from the enigma of her troubled life and expectations. Her wild kingdom kept the persistent call of Judaism at bay.

Mutti preserved her sense of joy despite hardships and disappointments by compartmentalizing her anger. She was besieged by the stigma associated with her bipolar condition and fought valiantly for the independence of her spirit. Once a captivating presence, she was, towards the end, vulnerable and alone.

So often she had wished for a better future through the continuity of the generations in the circle of life envisioned in Judaism, but she knew the die was cast. She declared herself a fatalist to ward off the demons that would define her. She was determined to nourish the hopes she had for us that her parents had for her, a better life in

America. Her last written words were on a postcard and expressed her love for us all.

Despite her struggles with mental illness and diminishing prospects as the years went by, Mutti lived her life with optimism, passion, determination, and resilience. That is what we always wanted to believe. She loved my sister and me mightily, and for that alone she deserved our love and gratefulness. With sadness and unresolvable regret about missed opportunities, we will never forget her voice and wish we could hear it again.

SELECTED BIBLIOGRAPHY

Angrick, Andrei and Peter Klein. *The "Final Solution" in Riga*. New York and Oxford: Berghan Books, 2009.

Bargur, Ayelet. *Ahawah Heisst Liebe; Die Geschichte des Judischen Kinderheims in der Berliner Augustrasse.* Munich: Deutscher Taschenbuch Verlag, 2004.

Barkahan, Menachem (Ed.). *Extermination of the Jews in Latvia 1941-1945.* Riga, Latvia: Society "Shamir", 2008.

Birnbaum, Shira. *Trauma and Resilience in Holocaust Memoir: Strategies of Self-Preservation and Inter-Generational Encounter with Narrative.* Lanham, Maryland: Lexington Books, 2021.

Brass, Karen Zauder. *Trauma Filters Through: A Second-Generation Personal Account by the Daughter of Holocaust Survivor. David Zauder.* Pine, Colorado: Chazak Publishing, 2018.

Baumel-Schwarz, Judith Tydor. *Never Look Back: The Jewish Refugee Children in Great Britain, 1938-1945.* West Lafayette, Indiana: Purdue University Press, 2012.

Brenner, Michael. *After the Holocaust: Rebuilding Jewish Lives in Postwar Germany.* Princeton: Princeton University Press, 1999.

Brenner, Michael and Derek J. Penslar. *In Search of Jewish Community: Jewish Identities in Germany and Austria, 1918-1933*. Bloomington and Indianapolis: University of Indiana Press,1998.

Elon, Elon. *The Pity of It All: A Portrait if the German-Jewish Epoch 1743-1933*. New York, New York: Metropolitan Books, Henry Holt and Company, 2002.

Fehrs, Jorge H. *Von der Heidereutergasse zum Roseneck: Judische Schulen in Berlin 1712-1942*. Berlin: Edition Hentrich, 1993.

Frankel, Adam. *The Survivors: A Story of War, Inheritance, and Healing*. New York: Harper Collins, 2019.

Hammel, Andrea. "The Kinder's Children: Second Generation and the Kindertransport" in Gigliotti, Simone and Monica Tempian, eds. *The Young Victims of the Nazi Regime: Migration, the Holocaust, and Postwar Displacement*. London: Bloomsbury Academic, 2016.

Kluger, Ruth and Lore Segal. *Still Alive: A Holocaust Girlhood Remembered*. New York: The Feminist Press at the City University of New York, 2001.

Luner, Gerda Nothmann. *Gerda's Story: Memoir of a Holocaust Survivor*. Elmhurst: Elmhurst College, 2002.

MacDonogh, Giles. *Berlin: A Portrait of its History, Politics, architecture and Society*. New York: St. Martin's Press, 1997.

Meyer, Beate, Hermann Simon, and Chana Schutz. *Jews in Nazi Berlin from Kristallnacht to Liberation. Chicago and London:* The University of Chicago Press, 2009.

Michelson, Frida and Wolf Goodman, eds. *I Survived Rumbuli. Washington DC: Holocaust Library, 1979.*

Nachama, Andreas, Julius H. Schoeps, and Hermann Simon, eds. *Jews in Berlin*, Berlin: Henschel Verlag, 2002.

Rapaport, Lynn. *Jews in Germany after the Holocaust: Memory, Identity, and Jewish-German Relations.* Cambridge: Cambridge University Press, 1997.

Sabor, Rudolph. *The Real Wagner*. London: Andre Deutsch, 1987.

Silber, Daniel B. *Refuge in Hell: How Berlin's Jewish Hospital Outlasted the Nazis*. Boston and New York: Houghton Mifflin Company, 2003.

Trotten, Samuel and William S. Parsons, Israel W. Charney. *Century of Genocide: Eyewitness Accounts and Critical Views*. New York and London: Garland Publishing, 1997.

Whiteman, Dorit Bader. *The Uprooted: A Hitler Legacy, Voices of Those Who Escaped before the Final Solution*. New York: Plenum Press, 1993.

Williams, Amy and William Niven. *National and Transnational Memories of the Kindertransport*. Suffolk, United Kingdom: Camden House, 2023.

NOTES

2. Mecklenburg

1. Uta Hinz. *Gefangen im Großen Krieg: Kriegsgefangenschaft in Deutschland, 1914-1921.* Essen: Klartext Verlag, 2006.

3. Nazi Berlin

1. Jörg H. Fehrs. *Von der Heitereutergasse zum Rosenneck: Judische Schulen in Berlin* 1712-1942. Berlin: Hentrich, 1993.
2. Rudolph Sabor. Interviewer: Bea Lewkowitz. *Refugee Voices.* Interview 144, 14 January 2007. London: The AJR Audio-Visual History Collection. The Wiener Holocaust Library. https://wiener.soutron.net/Portal/Default/en-GB/RecordView/Index/65851.
3. Siegfried Silberstein's business, Morgenrocke, is listed in *Jewish Businesses in Berlin 1930-1945,* Humboldt University: www2.huberlin.de/djgb/www/find?language=en_US.
4. Ernst is quoted by Uwe Werner in his book, *Anthroposophen in der Zeit des Nationalsozialismus (1933-1945).* Berlin: Oldenbourg Wissenschaftsverlag, 1999, which documents the fate of the Anthroposophical Society in Nazi Germany, including the banning of Rudolph Steiner's writings, the closure of Waldorf schools and mass arrests of those associated with the Society.

4. Kindertransport

1. Henry L. Feingold. *The Politics of Rescue,* p.150. New Brunswick: Rutgers University Press, 1970.
2. Gertrud referred to her daughter affectionately by using the north German word for cat.

5. Nurse Mary

1. Martin Salomonski was a rabbi who served as chaplain in the Kaiser's army, noted for championing Jewish veterans who served during World War I. Stephan Krotoczynski knew Rabbi Salomonski through their association with synagogues, including the New Synagogue in Berlin, which espoused Liberal Judaism that reconciled Jewish traditions and values in the context of secular society.
2. *Pfingsten* is the German word for Pentecost, and most likely refers to Shavuot, the Jewish harvest holiday that is celebrated seven weeks after Passover when God gave the Torah to the nation of Israel assembled on Mount Sinai.
3. Dr. Van der Zyl was a rabbi at the Neue Synagogue in Berlin before he left for London in 1939 as a refugee. After internment as an enemy alien, he served as a rabbi and became the first director of the Jewish Theological College of London that was later renamed Leo Baeck College.

6. Oxford Days

1. Denis Horne, "The Free Cinema Hoax" Melbourne: *Film Journal*, April 1961. https://archive.org/details/horne-cinema-hoax.
2. www.olympedia.org/athletes/79616.
3. Monica married John McLaren Dewar, who was born in Oban, Scotland, and served in the British Bomber Command.

7. Repatriation

1. The Nazi authorities allowed this hospital to function on a limited basis, under the corrupt but resourceful leadership of Dr. Walter Lustig, a Jew, who collaborated with the deportations while also sheltering Jews from deportation and certain death. At the end of the war, Dr. Lustig was executed by the Russians as a Nazi collaborator.
2. www.ajrrefugeevoices.org.uk/RefugeeVoices/Ernst-Mitchell.

8. Fleeing Berlin

1. When I visited the Kinderheim site many decades later, I became aware of its dark history. Close to where one of the buildings once stood, a plaque documented that in 1942, the Nazis deported 150 of its children, including 70 infants, who were subsequently murdered at Auschwitz. Later, the SS used the orphanage building as a transit point for 55,000 Jews sent to Theresienstadt where many died or were subsequently deported to Auschwitz for extermination.

9. Mutti's Quest for her Lost Past

1. According to the Yad Vashem Shoah Names Database, Minna Abrahamsohn was deported to Theresienstadt, Czechoslovakia on August 14, 1942, and presumably killed there. Anna Baumgardt was deported to Riga on January 25 in 1942, Rosa Elias was sent to Theresienstadt on August 5, 1942, and perished on September 26, 1942, in Treblinka. Paula Silberstein was murdered in Auschwitz in 1943. Regina Wellner and her husband, Salo, were deported to Piaski, Poland and presumably killed in Trawniki during Aktion Erntefest [Operation Harvest Festival] in November 1943. Rosa Heibel Krotoschinski was murdered in the Warsaw Ghetto. No record was found concerning the deportation and death of Malka Lowenthal Krotoschinski.
2. Bruno Baum, *Resistance in Auschwitz*. Berlin: Kongress Verlag, 1962. See chapter 26 for more information about Edgar's work at Auschwitz and his association with individuals involved in resistance activities.
3. www.ajrrefugeevoices.org.uk/RefugeeVoices/Rudolph-Sabor, 2007.
4. "Not every flowering dream bloomed" is originally a line from Goethe's poem, "Prometheus."
5. Rudolph Sabor, *The Real Wagner*, André Deutsch, London, 1987.

11. Transplanted Mishpachah

1. Information about the musical careers of both brothers is available from the University of Hamburg's searchable database: <www.lexm.uni-hamburg.de/content/index.xml> and at the Archives at the Leo Baeck Institute in New York.

12. Under the Roller Coaster

1. www.latimes.com/archives/la-xpm-1986-04-21-me-932-story.html.

15. Mutti's Beatnik Refuge

1. Numerous Beat luminaries passed through to give readings, including Allen Ginsberg, Maurice Lacey, Charles Bukowski, and Clare Horner. One performer, Taylor Mead, who billed himself as "the faggot from New York" later appeared in a film by the underground filmmaker, Jonas Mekas. The place was a hangout for those known locally and beyond including Jim Morrison and Ray Manzarek of The Doors. Closed in 1966, The Venice West Café site was designated a Los Angeles City landmark in 2010 in recognition of the café's role in the development of mid-20th-century Bohemian counterculture. See Ray Manzarek's video about Venice Beach scene during the 960s: www.youtube.com/watch?v=eSkllKaA8dE.

16. Notes from the Loony Bin

1. www.nimh.nih.gov/health/topics/bipolar-disorder.
2. Manfred Guttmacher, MD testified before the Senate Subcommittee on Constitutional Rights of the Mentally Ill, 1961, "I think one should go to the extreme of always explaining to a patient if he is going to get electroshock why he is going to get it and what it is going to be like and so forth and so on. But as far as getting permission from the patient is concerned, this is not necessary."

17. Picking up the Pieces

1. "Three Months of Crisis: Chronology of Events," *California Monthly*, February 1965. Bancroft Library. https://bancroft.berkeley.edu/FSM/chron.html.
2. Abraham Low, *Mental Health Through Will-Training*, Glencoe, Illinois: Willet Publishing, 1950.
3. Ned Glass was born in Poland in 1906. After a start in Vaudeville and then on Broadway, he appeared numerous times in movies and television, including *West Side Story* and *Charade*. His career was interrupted after he was blacklisted during the McCarthy era, but with help from friends in the industry he found film work. His last role was as a small-time thief in a 1981 episode of *Cagney and Lacey*. He died two years later in Encino, California.
4. I didn't know then of Mutti's friend, Ernst Champanier, and his connection to Theosophy.

18. The Nostalgia of Displacement

1. Ronald Reagan's inauguration as governor in January 1967 led to the immediate dismissal of Clark Kerr as President of the University of California. Reagan appointees on the Board of Regents voted him out because of his tolerant approach to student demonstrations that were incorrectly described as "riots" by conservative politicians.
2. https://en.wikipedia.org/wiki/James_Pike.

26. Holocaust Pilgrimage

1. Regina Scheer, *Ahawah: The Forgotten House: Searching for Traces in Jewish Berlin*, Berlin: Aufbau Taschenbuch Verlag, 2020. There was also the documentary, *The Children of Auguststraße*, produced in 2014. Many of the Ahawah children were rescued and resettled in Israel. Several others, not old enough to emigrate to Israel, were deported and killed.
2. Bruno Baum, *Resistance in Auschwitz*, Berlin: Kongress Verlag, 1962.
3. After the war, Bruno Baum wrote about his resistance activities with the Sonderkommandos, a squad of Auschwitz prisoners conscripted to remove and dispose of the remains of death chamber victims. Brave women working in the Union smuggled gunpowder out of the factory to supply the Sonderkommandos who blew up one of the crematoria. It is not known whether Steinmetz participated in the resistance.

ACKNOWLEDGMENTS

I have my mother, Mary Krotoczynski Wiesner, to thank for entrusting me with the writings, correspondence, and documents that she safeguarded over a 50-year period covering her journey from Berlin on the Kindertransport through her years in Germany, England, and the United States. I am grateful to have been able to gain from these a deeper understanding of her challenges and her courage

My sister, Monika Huntley, contributed her unique perspective on the struggle our mother faced raising us, the impact of her mental illness on our family, and the exuberance of her spirit in spite of it all. I am grateful to mother's cousins, some refugees themselves, who faithfully helped her through mental and financial struggles while they were alive and to their children who shared family history with me for this book. My cousin, David Wellner, shared stories about his parents' flight from Germany and their early years in America. Cousins Marion Gordon and Steven Stanley also provided me with information about their families.

I benefited from the input, support, and encouragement of my wife, Linda, my sons, Ezra and Nicolas, and my nephews, Noel, Ian and Peter, who all took an interest in this story of a colorful but difficult life. My sister-in-law, Marcia, and my daughters-in-law, Christina and Amanda, brought fresh insights. Thanks to my five grandchildren – Olivia, Alexander, Aiden, Ella, and Beatrice – for giving me faith that telling even the painful stories of our past can inform the future.

I am lucky to have friends like Lynn Waterhouse, Mike Gregg, Karyn Traut, and Art Levy who read drafts of the manuscript and provided valuable comments and suggestions.

To provide a broader context for my mother's own account and the memories of those who knew her well, I reached out to the Jewish organizations that helped her during her refugee years in England and Germany. World Jewish Relief, established as the Central British Fund for German Jewry (CBF) in 1933, supplied me with information from the case files of the Jewish Refugee Committee. Dr. Chana Schütz and Barbara Welker at the Centrum Judaicum of the Neue Synagogue provided documents about my mother's interaction with the Jewish Community of Berlin, including copies of documents from its case files and records from the Berlin Jewish Hospital from the post-war years. They also introduced me to Ulrike Gardeler of Grüntuch-Ernst Architects, an architect who provided information about the firm's faithful restoration of the Jewish Girls School attended by my mother.

Yad Vashem and the U.S. Holocaust Museum made online resources available for background research. The Central Database of Shoah Victims' Names yielded information about the deportation and fate of family members on both sides of my mother's family. Dr. Frank Mecklenburg and other staff members at Leo Baeck Institute facilitated my research on the Jewish community in Berlin. Dr. Jude Richter at the U.S. Holocaust Museum answered questions related to the resources available online.

Numerous other museums and memorials in the United States provided resources, including the USC Shoah Foundation, the American Jewish Historical Society, the Museum of Jewish Heritage, the American Sephardi Federation, YIVO Institute for Jewish Research, and the Yeshiva University Museum.

I gained a deeper understanding of the Holocaust legacy in Europe by visiting the Jewish Museum Berlin, the Weissensee Cemetery, the Memorial to the Murdered Jews of Europe, and the German Resistance Memorial Center in Berlin, as well as the Wannsee Conference, Museum Friedland in Mecklenburg, the Jewish Museum of Riga, the Riga Ghetto and Latvian Holocaust Museum and the Rumbula Forest Memorial, the POLIN Museum of the History of Polish Jews in Warsaw, Galicia Jewish Museum in Krakow, and the Memorial and Museum Auschwitz-Birkenau.

While working on the memoir, I attended conferences and meetings organized by the World Federation of Jewish Child Survivors of the Holocaust and Descendants and the Kindertransport Association and also benefited from the resources of the Association of Jewish Refugees. These organizations put me in touch with survivors and refugees whose diverse stories helped me to envision a use for my research in Holocaust awareness education. I am also pleased and grateful to be collaborating with historian Sophia Shmitz of Stolpersteine Berlin and the teachers and students at Max-Planck Gymnasium to commemorate my mother and grandparents with Stolpersteine as part of the memorial project started by artist Gunter Demnig.

Lastly, I want to acknowledge Amsterdam Publishers for taking on this project as part of its important effort to publish books that commemorate victims and survivors of the Holocaust. Special thanks to Liesbeth Heenk, the founder of Amsterdam Publishers, and her team, who advised and counseled me in bringing this project to fruition.

ABOUT THE AUTHOR

Peter Wiesner was born in South Croydon, England, spent his childhood in both East and West Berlin, and immigrated to the US in 1954, settling in Santa Monica, California. In 1967, he received a degree in History from the University of California at Berkeley and earned a master's in communication from the University of Pennsylvania. After earning a doctorate in education from Rutgers University, with a focus on distance education and instructional design, he worked for several educational institutions from 1974 to 1984, and then spent five years at Rutgers University as a television producer. From 1989 to 2013, he was an educator at IEEE, an international professional association for electrical and computer engineers, where he directed publications and educational programs for member outreach and continuing education, including software, educational standards, courseware and video programs for engineers and the general public. His lifetime interest in films led him to produce numerous television documentaries on social, technological as well as environmental issues pertaining to green engineering and sustainability on a global scale.

After retirement, he wrote his debut novel, *Xtremus* (Montag Press, 2015), a dystopian sci-fi satire about the demise of high technology resulting from technological overreach, and subsequently focused on writing about his mother's struggles as a Holocaust refugee and other topics related to the Holocaust. In addition to his lifetime pursuits in literature and the visual arts, he is involved in educational activities and outreach that promote racial tolerance and social equity. Since 1980, he and his wife, Linda, have lived in Bucks County, Pennsylvania. They have two married sons and five grandchildren.

PHOTOS

Silberstein Family Berlin, circa 1880

Silberstein Family Berlin, circa 1910

327

Abraham Silberstein, Berlin, circa 1895

Marie Silberstein née Rosenbaum, Berlin, circa 1895

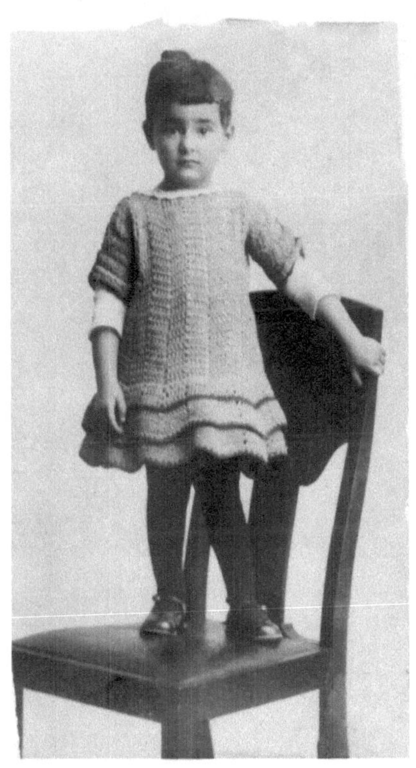

Mary Krotoczynski, age two, Friedland, Mecklenburg, 1924

Stephan Krotoczynski, Berlin, circa 1935

Gertrud Krotoczynski née Silberstein, Berlin, circa 1935

Mary (center right, back), Jewish Girl School Play, Bildarchiv, aka-images, Berlin, 1935

Mary and best school friend, Jenny Stanesco, Berlin, 1937

Mary and Dorothea Schindler, Berlin, 1939

Nurse Mary, Savernake Hospital, Marlborough, 1941

Denis Horne, England, circa 1940

Wiesner family outing, Berlin, 1947

Mary and Heinz Wiesner, wedding day Berlin, 1948

Mary and her children, Berlin Lichterfelde, 1953

Monika, Santa Monica, 1956

Mary and her children, Santa Monica, 1959

Mary and Monika, Big Sur camping trip, 1960

Mary, Santa Monica, 1960

Denis and Peter, Rome, 1967

Mary, Santa Monica, 1970

Peter and Monika, ages 40 and 37, Central California, 1985

Mary, age 67, at home in Santa Monica, 1989

Headstone for Mary's parents, Weissensee Cemetery Berlin

Remetz. Resistance Fighter and Survivor of the Warsaw Ghetto,
by Jan Yohay Remetz

My March Through Hell. A Young Girl's Terrifying Journey to Survival, by
Halina Kleiner with Edwin Stepp

Roman's Journey, by Roman Halter

Beyond Borders. Escaping the Holocaust and Fighting the Nazis. 1938-1948, by
Rudi Haymann

The Engineers. A memoir of survival through World War II in Poland and
Hungary, by Henry Reiss

A Spark of Hope. An Autobiography, by Luba Wrobel Goldberg

The series **Holocaust Survivor True Stories**
consists of the following biographies:

Among the Reeds. The true story of how a family survived the Holocaust,
by Tammy Bottner

A Holocaust Memoir of Love & Resilience. Mama's Survival from Lithuania to
America, by Ettie Zilber

Living among the Dead. My Grandmother's Holocaust Survival Story of Love
and Strength, by Adena Bernstein Astrowsky

Heart Songs. A Holocaust Memoir, by Barbara Gilford

Shoes of the Shoah. The Tomorrow of Yesterday, by Dorothy Pierce

Hidden in Berlin. A Holocaust Memoir, by Evelyn Joseph Grossman

Separated Together. The Incredible True WWII Story of Soulmates Stranded
an Ocean Apart, by Kenneth P. Price, Ph.D.

The Man Across the River. The incredible story of one man's will to survive the
Holocaust, by Zvi Wiesenfeld

If Anyone Calls, Tell Them I Died. A Memoir, by Emanuel (Manu) Rosen

The House on Thrömerstrasse. A Story of Rebirth and Renewal in the Wake of
the Holocaust, by Ron Vincent

Dancing with my Father. His hidden past. Her quest for truth. How Nazi
Vienna shaped a family's identity, by Jo Sorochinsky

The Story Keeper. Weaving the Threads of Time and Memory - A Memoir, by
Fred Feldman

Krisia's Silence. The Girl who was not on Schindler's List, by Ronny Hein

Defying Death on the Danube. A Holocaust Survival Story,
by Debbie J. Callahan with Henry Stern

A Doorway to Heroism. A decorated German-Jewish Soldier who became an
American Hero, by Rabbi W. Jack Romberg

The Shoemaker's Son. The Life of a Holocaust Resister, by Laura Beth Bakst

The Redhead of Auschwitz. A True Story, by Nechama Birnbaum

Land of Many Bridges. My Father's Story, by Bela Ruth Samuel Tenenholtz

Creating Beauty from the Abyss. The Amazing Story of Sam Herciger,
Auschwitz Survivor and Artist, by Lesley Ann Richardson

On Sunny Days We Sang. A Holocaust Story of Survival and Resilience,
by Jeannette Grunhaus de Gelman

Painful Joy. A Holocaust Family Memoir, by Max J. Friedman

I Give You My Heart. A True Story of Courage and Survival, by Wendy Holden

In the Time of Madmen, by Mark A. Prelas

Monsters and Miracles. Horror, Heroes and the Holocaust,
by Ira Wesley Kitmacher

Flower of Vlora. Growing up Jewish in Communist Albania, by Anna Kohen

Aftermath: Coming of Age on Three Continents. A Memoir,
by Annette Libeskind Berkovits

Not a real Enemy. The True Story of a Hungarian Jewish Man's Fight for
Freedom, by Robert Wolf

Zaidy's War. Four Armies, Three Continents, Two Brothers. One Man's
Impossible Story of Endurance, by Martin Bodek

The Glassmaker's Son. Looking for the World my Father left behind in Nazi
Germany, by Peter Kupfer

The Apprentice of Buchenwald. The True Story of the Teenage Boy Who
Sabotaged Hitler's War Machine, by Oren Schneider

Good for a Single Journey, by Helen Joyce

Burying the Ghosts. She escaped Nazi Germany only to have her life torn
apart by the woman she saved from the camps: her mother, by Sonia Case

American Wolf. From Nazi Refugee to American Spy. A True Story, by Audrey Birnbaum

Bipolar Refugee. A Saga of Survival and Resilience, by Peter Wiesner

In the Wake of Madness. My Family's Escape from the Nazis, by Bettie Lennett Denny

Before the Beginning and After the End, by Hymie Anisman

I Will Give Them an Everlasting Name. Jacksonville's Stories of the Holocaust, by Samuel Cox

Hiding in Holland. A Resistance Memoir, by Shulamit Reinharz

The series **Jewish Children in the Holocaust** consists of the following
autobiographies of Jewish children hidden during WWII in the Netherlands:

Searching for Home. The Impact of WWII on a Hidden Child,
by Joseph Gosler

Sounds from Silence. Reflections of a Child Holocaust Survivor, Psychiatrist
and Teacher, by Robert Krell

Sabine's Odyssey. A Hidden Child and her Dutch Rescuers, by Agnes Schipper

The Journey of a Hidden Child, by Harry Pila and Robin Black

The series **New Jewish Fiction** consists of the following novels, written by Jewish authors. All novels are set in the time during or after the Holocaust.

The Corset Maker. A Novel, by Annette Libeskind Berkovits

Escaping the Whale. The Holocaust is over. But is it ever over for the next generation? by Ruth Rotkowitz

When the Music Stopped. Willy Rosen's Holocaust, by Casey Hayes

Hands of Gold. One Man's Quest to Find the Silver Lining in Misfortune, by Roni Robbins

The Girl Who Counted Numbers. A Novel, by Roslyn Bernstein

There was a garden in Nuremberg. A Novel, by Navina Michal Clemerson

The Butterfly and the Axe, by Omer Bartov

To Live Another Day. A Novel, by Elizabeth Rosenberg

A Worthy Life. Based on a True Story, by Dahlia Moore

The Right to Happiness. After all they went through. Stories, by Helen Schary Motro

The series **Holocaust Heritage** consists of the following memoirs by 2G:

The Cello Still Sings. A Generational Story of the Holocaust and of the Transformative Power of Music, by Janet Horvath

The Fire and the Bonfire. A Journey into Memory, by Ardyn Halter

The Silk Factory: Finding Threads of My Family's True Holocaust Story, by Michael Hickins

Winter Light. The Memoir of a Child of Holocaust Survivors, by Grace Feuerverger

Stumbling Stones, by Joanna Rosenthall

The Unspeakable. Breaking decades of family silence surrounding the Holocaust, by Nicola Hanefeld

Hidden in Plain Sight. A Journey into Memory and Place, by Julie Brill

The series **Holocaust Books for Young Adults** consists of the following novels, based on true stories:

The Boy behind the Door. How Salomon Kool Escaped the Nazis. Inspired by a True Story, by David Tabatsky

Running for Shelter. A True Story, by Suzette Sheft

The Precious Few. An Inspirational Saga of Courage based on True Stories, by David Twain with Art Twain

The Sun will Shine on You again one Day, by Cynthia Monsour

The series **WWII Historical Fiction** consists of the following novels, some of which are based on true stories:

Mendelevski's Box. A Heartwarming and Heartbreaking Jewish Survivor's Story, by Roger Swindells

A Quiet Genocide. The Untold Holocaust of Disabled Children in WWII Germany, by Glenn Bryant

The Knife-Edge Path, by Patrick T. Leahy

Brave Face. The Inspiring WWII Memoir of a Dutch/German Child, by I. Caroline Crocker and Meta A. Evenbly

When We Had Wings. The Gripping Story of an Orphan in Janusz Korczak's Orphanage. A Historical Novel, by Tami Shem-Tov

Jacob's Courage. Romance and Survival amidst the Horrors of War, by Charles S. Weinblatt

A Semblance of Justice. Based on true Holocaust experiences, by Wolf Holles

Dark Shadows Hover, by Jordan Steven Sher

Katie O'Connor, This Grey Place

Amsterdam Publishers Newsletter

Subscribe to our Newsletter by selecting the menu at the top (right) of
amsterdampublishers.com or scan the QR-code below.

Receive a variety of content such as:

- A welcome message by the founder
- Free Holocaust memoirs
- Book recommendations
- News about upcoming releases
- Chance to become an AP Reviewer.